On This Day

March

On This Day

Յայսմաւուրք

The Armenian Church Synaxarion
(*Yaysmawurkʿ*)

March

A parallel Armenian-English text
translated and edited by

Edward G. Mathews Jr.

Brigham Young University Press • Provo, Utah

This publication was made possible by a generous grant from the Dolores Zohrab Liebmann Fund.

The paper used in this publication meets the minimum requirements of the American National Standard for Information Sciences—Permanence of Paper for Printed Library Materials. ANSI Z39.48-1984.

Library of Congress Cataloging-in-Publication data

Armenian Church.
[Haysmawurk']
On this day : the Armenian Church Synaxarion (Yaysmawurk'); a parallel Armenian-English text / translated and edited by Edward G. Mathews Jr.
pages cm.—(Eastern Christian texts ; 1)
Armenian original and English translation in parallel texts; notes and introduction in English.
Includes bibliographical references and index.
ISBN 978-0-8425-2864-1; ISBN 978-0-8425-2998-3 (March)
1. Armenian Church—Liturgy—Texts. 2. Saints—Armenia—Biography. 3. Christian saints—Biography. I. Mathews, Edward G., Jr., 1954- II. Armenian Church. Haysmawurk'. III. Armenian Church. Haysmawurk'. English. IV. Title. V. Title: Armenian Church Synaxarion.
BX129.A1A672 2014
264'.0162034-dc23

2014024336

Printed in the United States of America

http://meti.byu.edu

Contents

Introduction

This text and translation of the month of March is the third volume of our projected twelve-volume text and English translation of the Armenian liturgical book known as the *Yaysmawurkʿ*, or *Synaxarion*. The reader can consult the introduction in the first volume, that of January, for a brief discussion of the history and versions of the *Yaysmawurkʿ* and its historical place in the worship of the Armenian Church.[1]

For this March volume I have made the following editorial decisions vis-à-vis the text as found in Bayan's eclectic edition. Bayan included two nearly identical entries for Smbat and the two hundred fifty martyrs killed by Bugha, one on March 2 and the other on March 4. I have retained the former and deleted the latter. I have also omitted an entry for Vanakan Vardapet, the famous thirteenth-century monk, found on March 18, as a slightly fuller account was already included on January 29.[2]

Further Acknowledgments

As with the previous volumes, thanks are due to many people who helped bring this third volume into print. I offer my very profound thanks to my dear friend and colleague Anoushavan Srpazan Tanielian, whose busy schedule gives him no free time at all, but who nonetheless found the time to go through the entire manuscript. His selflessness and industry have been a constant source of admiration and encouragement. I again thank Brigham Young University Press and the Middle Eastern Texts Initiative for accepting this volume for publication. Special thanks

1. Mathews, *On This Day: The Armenian Church Synaxarion—January*, xvii-xx.
2. Mathews, *On This Day: The Armenian Church Synaxarion—January*, 240-43.

are due to Shirley Ricks, who took over editorial duties from Mrs. Angela Barrionuevo (who, along with her team, so competently saw the previous volumes through all the various stages of editing, typesetting, and print). Mrs. Ricks and her team have demonstrated equally remarkable skill and attention to every detail throughout the entire production of this volume. Without the help of these and others, this volume would be far more replete with my errors and omissions. A very special thanks also goes to my friend Dr. Christina Maranci, who suggested the cover art for this volume.

Any and all errors and omissions that remain despite the best efforts of all these people are to be laid at my feet alone.

On This Day

MARCH

ՄԵՀԵԿԻ ԻԳ

Մարտի Ա

Վարք եւ վկայութիւն սրբուհւոյն Եւդոկիայ

1. *Կինս այս՝ երանելին Եւդոկիա՝ պոռնիկ էր ի քաղաքէն Իլիուպօլեայ, ի սահմանս Փիւնիկեցւոց, յաւուրս Տրայանոսի կռապաշտ արքային: Եւ էր ի չար ախտ պոռնկութեան, եւ վասն գեղեցկութեան նորա բազումք մտանէին առ նա. եւ ժողովեաց բազում ինչս եւ ստացուածս, եւ եղեւ մեծատուն յոյժ:*

2. *Եւ էր մերձակայ դրացի Գերմանոս ոմն ճգնաւոր կրօնաւոր, եւ ընթեռնոյր գիրս վասն ահեղ դատաստանին Քրիստոսի, եւ հատուցման ըստ գործոց: Եւ մինչդեռ նա յանկողնին իւրում անկեալ կայր եւ լսէր մտադիւրութեամբ գրոցն, գիտացեալ Գերմանոսի գնաց առ նա եւ ուսոյց նմա զբանս փրկութեան: Եւ նորա փակեալ զսենեակն իւր՝ արգելաւ զեօթն օր, եւ ելաց դառնապէս զմեղս իւր: Եւ յետ եօթն աւուր տեսանէ յանուրջս որ լոյս մեծ ծագեաց զանձամբն, եւ այր մի սպիտակազգեստ կալեալ զձեռանէն եհան յերկինս: Տեսանէ եւ այր մի երկայն սեւադէմ՝ եւ կրճտէր զատամունս իւր եւ ասէր. Անիրաւիս յիս ով հրեշտակապետ եթէ կամիս զդա կեցուցանել առ զամենայն զոսկի զարդարանս եւ զհանդերձս իւր եւ պահեա առ քեզ: Եւ ձայն եղեւ ի լուսոյն եւ ասէ. Այսպէս հաճեցաւ Աստուած յորդիս մարդկան, եւ ընդունի զորս ապաշխարեն զմեղս իւրեանց:*

March 1

Meheki 23

The life and martyrdom of the holy Eudocia

1. This blessed woman, Eudocia, was a prostitute from the city of Heliopolis,[1] within the borders of Phoenicia, in the days of the impious emperor Trajan.[2] She was engaged in the evil vice of prostitution, and because of her beauty many men would come to her. She amassed a great amount of goods and possessions, and she became extremely wealthy.

2. There was in a nearby village a certain Germanos who was a very austere ascetic. He was accustomed to reading the scriptures on the subject of the dreadful judgment of Christ and of the recompense for one's deeds. One day while he was reclining on his bed intently reading such passages, Germanos came to understand them, and so he went to her and taught her the words of salvation. Then locking herself up in her room, she confined herself there for seven days and wept bitterly over her sins. After these seven days she saw in a dream a great light shining around her and a man clothed in white who took her by the hand and led her up to heaven. She also saw another man with a long swarthy face. He was gnashing his teeth and said, "You are being unjust to me, O Archangel. If you wish to save this one, take away all her gold, her jewelry, and her garments, and keep them for yourself." But a voice came from the light and said, "Thus is God pleased with His children, and He receives those who repent of their sins."

---

1. Modern-day Baalbek, in Lebanon.
2. Trajan was Roman emperor from 98 to 117.

3. *Եւ ընդ առաւօտն երթեալ առ եպիսկոպոսն Թէոդիտոս՝ մկրտեցաւ, եւ գնացին ի միասին ի տուն իւր, եւ գրեաց զամենայն ինչս իւր, քանզի բազում ունէր ոսկի, արծաթ, դիպակ եւ մեծագին պատմուճանք, զամենայն բաշխեաց աղքատաց, եւ մտեալ ի կուսանաց վանս զգեցաւ մի մազեղէն, եւ մեծ ճգնութեամբ կեցեալ պաՀօք եւ աղօթիւք եւ յոտնկաց տքնութեամբ:*

4. *Եւ ոմն մի պոռնիկ յառաջին տոփողացն իւրոց կամեցաւ զնա տեսանել, եւ զգեցեալ Հանդերձս կրօնաւորի՝ գնաց առ նա, եւ սկսաւ յիշեցուցանել նմա զառաջին մեղսասէր ուրախութիւնն, եւ խրատ տայր թողուլ զճգնութեան վարս եւ ամուսնանալ: Եւ սաստեաց նմա երանելին Եւդոկիա, եւ առժամայն անկաւ այրն եւ մեռաւ: Եւ ի գիշերին յայնմիկ երեւեցաւ նմա Հրեշտակն Տեառն եւ ասէ. Եւդոկիա յարո զմեռեալն եւ ծանիր զզօրութիւնն Աստուծոյ: Եւ յորժամ զարթեաւ եւ աղօթեաց առ Աստուած՝ կենդանացաւ մեռեալն:*

5. *Ընդ աւուրսն ընդ այնոսիկ թագաւորեաց Աւրելիանոս կռապաշտն, եւ երթեալ առաջին տոփողքն մատնեցին եթէ քրիստոնեայ եղեւ, եւ ունի զարքունի գանձ բազում յոյժ: Առաքեաց զօրականս առ նա, եւ նա զնոսա առժամայն մաՀացոյց: Գնաց եւ որդի թագաւորին, զի տարցէ զԵւդոկիա առ թագաւորն, եւ ի ճանապարՀին անկեալ բեկան ոտքն, եւ ի գիշերին յայնմիկ մեռաւ: Եւ յորժամ ծանրացաւ ի տրտմութենէն թագաւորն ապա յորժամ լուաւ եթէ այլ մեռեալ յարոյց՝ գրեաց առ նա թուղթ աղերսանաց թերեւս կենդանացուսցէ զորդի նորա: Եւ դարձեալ գրեաց առ նա. Եթէ ստուգութեամբ Հաւատաս ի Քրիստոս կատարին խնդրուածք քո: Եւ յորժամ դարձան թղթաբերքն՝ Հանդիպեցան մաՀճացն յոր բարձեալ էին զմեռեալն եւ տանէին, եդին ի վերայ մեռելոյն զգրեալ թուղթն Եւդոկիայ, եւ առժամայն կենդանացաւ:*

6. *Եւ թագաւորն Հաւատաց ի Քրիստոս եւ մկրտեցաւ ամենայն ընտանեօքն: Եւ որդին որ յարեաւ ի մեռելոց եղեւ եպիսկոպոս: Եւ քոյր նորա գնաց առ երանելին Եւդոկիա, եւ ճգնութեամբ եկաց առ նա մինչեւ ի վախճանն:*

7. *Եւ դատաւորն Իլիուպօլեաց Դիոգինէս կռապաշտն՝ առաքեաց զօրականս զի տարցեն առ նա զերանելին Եւդոկիա: Եւ երեւեցաւ նմա Տէր եւ ասէ. Հաստատուն կաց ի Հաւատս եւ քաջալերեաց Եւդոկիա, զի Հանդերձեալ եւ Հանդիպիլ մարտիրոսութեան:*

3. In the morning [Eudocia] went to the bishop Theodotos and was baptized. Then they both returned to her house, and she inventoried all her possessions, for she had much gold, silver, and very expensive brocaded garments. She distributed them all to the poor, went to a convent for women, put on a hair shirt, and lived there with great asceticism: in fasting, in prayer, and in standing vigils.

4. A certain licentious man, one of her former paramours, wanted to see her. So he dressed up in the garments of an ascetic and went to her, and he began to recount to her the joy they used to enjoy in their sinful behavior. He then counseled her to abandon her ascetic lifestyle and to marry him. The blessed Eudocia censured him, and immediately the man fell down and died. On that night an angel of the Lord appeared to her and said, "Eudocia, raise up that dead man and know the power of God." When she awoke, she prayed to God, and the dead man came back to life.

5. During that time, the impious Aurelian became governor. Some of her former paramours came to him and reported that [Eudocia] had become a Christian and that she had kept a vast royal fortune. He then sent soldiers to her, but she immediately caused them to fall down dead. The governor's son then went so that he might bring Eudocia back to the governor, but on the way he fell down and broke his ankle. On that very night he died. The governor was overcome with grief, but when he heard that she had raised up another man who had died, he wrote to her a letter of supplication that perhaps she might also bring his son back to life. She wrote back to him, "If you truly believe in Christ, your prayers will be fulfilled." When they returned, those messengers came upon the bier that was transporting the dead body. They placed that letter written by Eudocia on the dead son, and immediately he came back to life.

6. The governor then believed in Christ, and he was baptized along with his entire family. His son who had been raised from the dead became a bishop. His sister went to the blessed Eudocia and lived an ascetic life with her until her death.

7. Diogenes, the impious judge of Heliopolis, sent soldiers to bring the blessed Eudocia to him. The Lord appeared to her and said, "Stand firm in your faith, Eudocia, and have courage for you are about to undergo martyrdom."

8. *Եւ ելեալ ի վանացն առ ընդ իւր մասն ի կենարար մարմնոյ եւ յարենէ Տեառն, եւ կացեալ առաջի դատաւորին խոստովանեցաւ զՔրիստոս պայծառ երեսօք, եւ ոչ խրատու եւ ողոքանաց լուաւ, եւ ոչ ի սպառնալեացն երկեաւ: Եւ նա հրամայեաց մերկացուցանել զնա եւ ի կախաղանին տանջել: Եւ յորժամ կամեցան զօրականքն մերկացուցանել՝ գտին զմասն սուրբ օրինացն, եւ առեալ ի ձեռս իւրեանց ետուն ցդատաւորն. եւ առժամայն զօրականքն հրով կիզան եւ մեռան. եւ դատաւորն կիսայրեաց եղեալ՝ աղաղակէր դառնապէս: Եւ որք տեսին զսքանչելիսն հաւատացին ի Քրիստոս, եւ աղաչեցին զսրբուհին զի կենդանացուսցէ զհրով այրեցեալսն. եւ նորա աղօթեալ՝ յարեան ամենեքեան եւ հաւատացին ի Քրիստոս:*

9. *Եւ զկին մի մեռեալ որոյ անուն էր Ներփիրմինա աղօթիւք կենդանացոյց. եւ ինքն եւ այր իւր Դիոդորոս հաւատացին ի Քրիստոս:*

10. *Եւ ի չնչմանէ վիշապի մեռաւ երիտասարդ մի կնոջ այրւոյ միամօր որդի, եւ հրամայեաց երանելին Եւդոկիա Դիոդորոսի աղօթել առ Աստուած վասն մեռելոյն ի վիշապէն. եւ նա վստահացեալ ի սրբութիւնն Եւդոկիայ՝ աղաչեաց զԱստուած եւ յարեաւ մեռեալն, եւ վիշապն հերձեալ սատակեցաւ: Եւ բազումք ի հեթանոսաց հաւատացին ի Քրիստոս եւ մկրտեցան:*

11. *Եւ յետ Դիոգինեսի եղեւ դատաւոր Բիկենդիոս, եւ ազդեցին նմա վասն սրբուհւոյն Եւդոկիայ. առաքեաց զօրականս եւ հատին զգլուխ նորա ի Մարտի Ա եւ կատարեաց զընթացս իւր ապաշխարութեամբ եւ մարտիրոսութեամբ, եւ չնորհս տուան նշխարացն բժշկել զամենայն ցաւս եւ զհիւանդութիւն մարդկան:*

Վկայութիւն Սիմոնի Կիւրենացւոյ որ եբարձ զխաչն Քրիստոսի

12. *Սուրբն Սիմոն Կիւրենացի գոլով այր արդար, եւ արդարագործութեամբ վաստակէր յագարակի եւ ապրէր. զոր կալեալ հրէայքն մինչ գայր յագարակէ եւ եդին ի վերայ նորա զփայտ խաչին Քրիստոսի մինչեւ ի Գողգոթա բերել զկնի Քրիստոսի: Եւ անդ ապա տեսեալ Սիմոնի ի ժամ խաչելութեանն զսքանչելիսն որ եղեն՝ հաւատաց ի Քրիստոս գաղտ ի ժողովրդենէն:*

8. [Eudocia] then departed her dwelling, taking with her a portion of the life-giving body and blood of the Lord. She stood before the judge and professed Christ, her face luminous. She paid no heed to their warnings or to their persuasive tactics, and she showed no fear of their threats. So the judge ordered her to be disrobed and to be tortured on the gallows. But when the soldiers went to disrobe her they found the portion of the holy sacrament. They took it into their hands and gave it to the judge. The soldiers immediately burst into flames and died; the judge, being partly burned, cried out bitterly. All those who witnessed this marvelous event came to believe in Christ, and they cried out for the holy one to bring back to life those who had been burned by fire. So [Eudocia] prayed and raised them all up, and they believed in Christ.

9. By her prayers [Eudocia] also brought back to life a certain dead woman whose name was Nerfirmina. Both she and her husband Diodoros believed in Christ.

10. Another young man, the only son of a widow, died from the breath of a dragon. The blessed Eudocia directed Diodoros to pray to God on behalf of that one who had died by the dragon, and he, fully confident in Eudocia's holiness, prayed to God and raised up that dead youth; and the dragon was slain, being cleft in two. And many of the pagans came to believe in Christ and were baptized.

11. After Diogenes, Vincentius became judge, and he was informed about the holy Eudocia. He sent soldiers, and they cut off her head on the first of March. She had completed the course of her life in penitence and martyrdom, and her relics were granted the grace to heal every human illness and disease.

The martyrdom of Simon of Cyrene who carried the cross of Christ

12. The holy Simon of Cyrene was a just man who worked in his field and lived in an honest manner. The Jews seized him while he was coming back from his field, and they placed the wooden cross of Christ upon him to carry behind Christ all the way to Golgotha.[3] Then Simon, after he saw the miracles that happened at the time of the crucifixion, came to believe in Christ secretly from the people.

3. Cf. Matthew 27:32 and parallels.

13. *Եւ ոմն մի յաղգականաց իւրոց երթեալ մատնեաց զնա առ Հրեայսն եւ առ քահանայապետսն, եւ նոքա կաչառեցին զՊիղատոս եւ խաչեցին զՍիմոն վասն անուանն Քրիստոսի: Եւ խոցեցին զերկուս կողսն եւ հեղաւ յոյժ արիւնն. եւ աւանդեաց զհոգին բարի խոստովանութեամբ Մարտի Ա, ի փառս Քրիստոսի Աստուծոյ մերոյ:*

13. But one of his relatives went and denounced him to the Jews and to the high priests, and they bribed Pilate and had Simon crucified for the sake of the name of Christ. And they pierced both his sides, and so much blood poured out that he gave up his spirit with a good confession on the first of March to the glory of Christ, Our God.

ՄԵՀԵԿԻ ԻԴ

Մարտի Բ

Տօն է Ամովսայ մարգարէին

1. *Ամովս էր ի Թեկիայ. եւ Ամասիա բազում անգամ կոչկոճէր զնա, յետոյ եւ սպան իսկ զնա Ովսէ որդի նորա բակեղբ ջախջախեալ զծամելիս նորա. եւ ոգւով եկն յերկիր իւր եւ յետ սակաւ աւուրց մեռաւ՝ եւ Թաղեցաւ անդ:*

Յայսմ աւուր վկայութիւն Կոնոնոսի պարտիզպանի

2. *Յաւուրս Դեկոսի անօրէն արքային՝ էր սուրբն Կոնոնոս ի Նազարեթէ Գալիլէացւոց, եւ գնաց ի քաղաքն Մանդնոյ Պամփիւլացւոց բնակեցաւ ի տեղին որ կոչի Կարմենայ եւ եղեւ պարտիզպան:*

3. *Եւ մինչդեռ արբուցանէր զպարտէզն իւր՝ եկին առ նա զօրականք Որոգենէս եւ Նաւոդորոս եւ այլք ընդ նոսա, ի Պուպլիոսէ դատաւորէն Պամփիւլացւոց եւ ասեն կեղծաւորութեամբ. Ողջոյն քեզ Կոնոնոս: Եւ նա ասէ. Ողջոյն եւ ձեզ որդեակք: Ասէ Որոգենէս. Կոչէ զքեզ դատաւորն: Ասէ Կոնոնոս. Զի՞նչ կամի զիս դատաւորն, այր մի օտար գոլով իմ՝ մանաւանդ քրիստոնեայ. եթէ կամի կոչել՝ յիւր նմանեացն կոչեսցէ, եւ ոչ զիս զտառապեալ Հողագործս՝ որ զիմ զաւուրն կերակուր մեծ ջանիւ վաստակիմ:*

March 2

Meheki 24

The feast of the prophet Amos

1. Amos was from Tekoa.[1] Amaziah[2] tortured him many times, and after that his son Hosiah killed him by crushing his jaw with a stick. While still drawing breath, Amos returned to his own country but after a few days he died and was buried there.

On this day is the martyrdom of Kononos the gardener

2. In the days of Decius, the unjust emperor,[3] lived the holy Kononos. From Nazareth of Galilee he went to the city of Magydus in Pamphylia. He took up residence in a place called Karmenay, and he became a gardener.

3. [One day] while he was watering his garden, the soldiers Orogenes and Naodoros, along with others, came to him from Publius, the judge of Pamphylia, and said to him with some insincerity, "Greetings to you, Kononos." And he responded, "Greetings to you also, my children." Orogenes then said, "The judge summons you." Kononos asked, "Why does the judge want me? I am a foreigner, and more than that I am a Christian. If he wishes to summon anyone, let him summon someone of his own rank and not me, a wretched tiller of the earth who earns his daily nourishment only after much labor."

---

1. Amos 1:1.
2. Priest of Bethel, named in Amos 7:10.
3. Decius, the perpetrator of one of the great persecutions against Christians, ruled from 249 to 251.

4. *Յայնժամ հրամայեաց Նաւոդորոս եւ կապեցին զԿոնոնոս յերիվարի խրոմ եւ ի քարշ տարան առ դատաւորն. եւ ստիպէին զնա հայհոյել եւ ուրանալ զՔրիստոս եւ զոհել կռոցն: Եւ նա յոգւոց հանեալ հայեցաւ յերկինս եւ աղօթեաց առ Աստուած, եւ ասէ ցդատաւորն. Ով ամբարիշտ ո՞րպէս իշխեցեր զամենեցունց Աստուածն չար համբաւել եւ հայհոյել, եւ ինձ հրամայես զնոյն առնել, յորոյ ձեռս է շունչ քո. այլ ինձ քաւ լիցի եւ ամենեցուն որ կարդան զանուն նորա ուրանալ, այլ մանաւանդ օրհնել եւ փառաւորել զՔրիստոս Աստուածն մեր:*

5. *Ասէ բռնաւորն. Զարչարեցից զքեզ բազում տանջանօք, յառիծս ընկեցից, եւ ի խաչ հանից, եւ ի բորբոքեալ հուր արկից: Ասէ սուրբն Կոնոնոս. Անմտանաս ով դատաւոր, բանիւք միայն երկուցանես եւ կարծես հաւանեցուցանել զիս. ոչ հաւանիմ եւ ոչ լսեմ քեզ, քաւ լիցի:*

6. *Եւ նոյնժամայն երկաթի բեւեռս հարին յոտսն եւ ընթացուցանէին առաջի երիվարաց դատաւորին: Եւ հասեալ ի գեօղ մի յոյժ աշխատեցաւ սուրբն եւ նուաղեցաւ. եւ կրկնեալ զծունկսն իւր մինչդեռ աղօթէր՝ աւանդեաց զհոգին իւր որպէս նշխար ի ձեռս Աստուծոյ Մարտի Բ:*

Յայսմ աւուր վկայութիւն Սմբատայ սպարապետին Հայոց եւ երկուհարիւր եւ յիսուն վկայիցն որք կատարեցան ի Բուղայէ ամիրաշրէ

7. *Անօրէն իշխանն Իսմայելի Ջափար առաքեաց զօր բազում յաշխարհն Հայոց, եւ այր մի արիւնահեղ եւ աշխարհաւեր Բուղայ անուն զօրագլուխ նոցուն Թուրք ազգաւ:*

4. Naodoros then gave the order, and they tied Kononos to his own horse and dragged him like that to the judge, and they began to force him to blaspheme, to renounce Christ, and to sacrifice to their idols. But [Kononos] gave out a sigh, looked up to heaven, prayed to God, and said to the judge, "O impious one! How do you dare to publicly blaspheme the God of all and command that I do the same to that one in whose hand is your very breath? God forbid that I or anyone who calls out his name should renounce him—rather, we will praise and glorify Christ, our God."

5. That tyrant then retorted, "I will punish you with many tortures: I will throw you to the lions, I will hang you up on a cross, and then I will throw you into a burning fire." The holy Kononos responded, "You are out of your mind, O judge; you try to intimidate me and think you will induce me to believe with words only. I do not believe and I do not even listen to you—God forbid!"

6. So at that very moment they drove iron nails into his feet and made him run in front of the judge's horses. They soon arrived at a small village, and the holy one became extremely exhausted and collapsed; he bent down his knees, and while he was praying he offered up his spirit like a host into the hands of God on the second of March.

On this day is the martyrdom of the Armenian general Smbat and of the 250 martyrs who were put to death by the impious Bugha

7. Djafar, the wicked caliph of the Ishmaelites,[4] sent many soldiers into the land of Armenia with a certain bloodthirsty and land-destroying man, Bugha by name and a Turk by nationality, as leader of the army.

---

4. Djafar al-Mutawakkil was caliph from 847 to 861. He sent Bugha and his soldiers into Armenia in 851. The account of this invasion is told in much greater detail in Tʿovma Artsruni, *History of the House of the Artsrunikʿ*, III.1-8.

8. *Եւ եկեալ յերկիրն Հայոց առ ինքն կոչեաց խաբէութեամբ եւ երդմամբ զՍմբատ սպարապետն Հայոց յազգէ Բագրատունեաց զայր քաջ եւ աստուածապաշտ եւ զայլ նախարարս: Եւ իբրեւ չոգան առ նա ստեաց երդմանն իւրոյ եւ արար զնոսա ի կալանս. եւ առաքեաց զնոսա կապանօք ի Սառամա առ ամիրապետն իւրեանց Ջափար. եւ նա եդ զնոսա ի բանդի, եւ նեղէր ուրանալ զՔրիստոս եւ դառնալ յայլազգութիւն: Եւ ի սաստիկ տանջանացն եւ յանհնարին նեղութեանցն բազումք դրդուեցան եւ ելին ի հաւատոցն:*

9. *Իսկ սպարապետն Սմբատ համբերեալ չարչարանաց եւ տանջանաց՝ քաղցի եւ ծարաւոյ եւ գետնախշտութեան եւ արգելանաց անլուսից վեշտասան ամիս՝ եւ կատարեցաւ նահատակութեամբ: Եւ պատանի մի Միքայէլ անուն նախատէր յայտնապէս զօրէնս նոցա, եւ խոստովանէր զՔրիստոս Տէր եւ Աստուած, զնա ի նմին ժամու սրով սպանին: Եւ այր մի Կոն անուն՝ նոյնպէս խոստովանութեամբ կատարեցաւ:*

10. *Իսկ ամենաչարն Բուղայ գերեաց զաշխարհն Հայոց զարս եւ զկանայս եւ զմանկունս եւ նեղէր զնոսա զի ուրասցին զՔրիստոս: Եւ վկայք երկու հարիւր յիսուն համարձակութեամբ խոստովանեցան զանունն Քրիստոսի. յորոց վերայ սուր եդեալ կատարեցին զնոսա, եւ զայլ բազմութիւնն գերի վարեալ տարան ի Սամառա. եւ բազումք ի ճանապարհին մեռան ի սաստիկ տապոյն եւ ի փութապէս վարելոյն: Եւ կատարի տօն սրբոյն Սմբատայ սպարապետի եւ այլոց սրբոց Մարտի Բ:*

8. When he arrived in the land of Armenia, he summoned to him, with false oaths, Smbat, the general of Armenia, from the house of the Bagratuni, a man courageous and god-fearing, as well as other naxarars. But when they went before him, [Bugha] recanted his oath and put them all under arrest. He then sent them in chains to Samarra to their caliph Djafar, who put them into prison and pressured them to deny Christ and to convert to Islam. Wracked by violent tortures and intolerable afflictions, many of these men turned away from their faith.

9. But the general Smbat endured these tortures and afflictions—hunger, thirst, being forced to sleep on the ground, and being locked up without any light—for sixteen months, and he died as a martyr. A certain young man, Michael by name, openly insulted their laws and confessed Christ as Lord and God; he was immediately put to death by the sword. Another man by the name of Kon was slain after making a similar confession.

10. Then that most wicked Bugha took captive the land of Armenia—men, women, and children—and he pressured them all to renounce Christ. But 250 martyrs boldly confessed the name of Christ. Some of these were put to death by the sword while the majority were led off to prison in Samarra. Many of these died on the way from the excessive heat and from the speed of the march. The feast of the holy general Smbat and these other holy ones is celebrated on the second of March.

ՄԵՀԵԿԻ ԻԵ

Մարտի Գ

Վկայութիւն սրբոցն Եւտրոպիոսի, Կղէոնիկոսի եւ Բասիլիսկոսի

1. *Այս երեք սուրբ վկայքս Քրիստոսի էին ի ժամանակս Մաքսիմիանոսի ամբարիշտ արքային, զօրականք ընկերակիցք եւ ազգականք միմեանց: Եւտրոպիոս եւ Կղէոնիկոս Հօրաքեռ որդիք էին Թէոդորոսի մեծի վկային Քրիստոսի: Իսկ Բասիլիսկոս էր քեռորդի, եւ էին ի Կապադովկեցւոց երկրէն, եւ չարչարեցան ի միասին վասն անուանն Քրիստոսի երեքեանն:*

2. *Զսուրբն Բասիլիսկոս արկին ի բանդ, ի քաղաքին Ամասիա, հրամանաւ դատաւորին. եւ բազում աքանչելիս արարեալ ի բանդին՝ կատարեցաւ ի Քրիստոս:*

3. *Եւ զերկոսեանն կացուցին առաջի Ասկղիպադոտոսի Ամասիոյ դատաւորին, եւ Հարցանէր եթէ զոհեն պիղծ աստուածոցն եւ չահին զկեանս իւրեանց եւ առնուն պատիւս եւ ինչս: Եւ նոքա արհամարհեցին զխոստմունսն եւ անարգեցին զդատաւորն: Եւ դահիճքն Հարկանէին կապարեայ կռանաւ զբերանն Եւտրոպիոսի: եւ ապա գանեցին զերկոսեանն ուժգին: Եւ յաղօթել սրբոցն լուծան ձեռք Հարկանողացն, եւ Տէր երեւեցաւ ընդ սրբոյն Թէոդորոսի եւ առժամայն կապանքն լուծան եւ ողջ մարմնով կանգնեցան եւ ասեն ընդ մերձակայսն. Ահա Թագաւորն մեր Քրիստոս երեւի ընդ սիրելւոյն իւրոյ Թէոդորոսի եւ մեր ազգակցի: Եւ ասէ ցնոսա Տէրն. Տեսանէի զչարչարանսդ զոր կրէք եւ մնայի Համբերութեանդ ձերոյ, եւ արդ եղէց ձեզ օգնական:*

March 3

Meheki 25

The martyrdom of the holy Eutropios, Cleonikos, and Basiliskos

1. These three holy martyrs of Christ lived in the time of the impious emperor Maximinus;[1] they were fellow soldiers, and they were all related: Eutropios and Cleonikos were sons of the aunt of Theodoros, the great martyr for Christ,[2] and Basiliskos was the son of his sister. They were all from the land of Cappadocia, and all three of them were tortured together for the sake of the name of Christ.

2. Basiliskos was thrown into prison in the city of Amasia, at the command of the judge there, and he performed many miracles there in prison and died in Christ.

3. They brought the other two before Asclepiadotos, the judge of Amasia, and he demanded that they sacrifice to their filthy gods; [thus] they would both keep their lives and receive honors and wealth. But they despised such promises and refused the judge. The executioners began to strike Eutropios in the mouth with a hammer, and then they brutally beat [Eutropios and Cleonikos]. While the holy ones were praying, the hands of those beating them went limp, and the Lord appeared to them along with Saint Theodoros; immediately their bonds fell off, and they rose up with their bodies restored to health. They then said to those who were nearby, "Behold, Christ our King has appeared to us with Theodoros, his beloved and our kinsman." And the Lord said to them, "I have seen the tortures that you have borne, and I have been waiting for your endurance, and now I will come to your aid."

---

1. Maximinus Daia was emperor from 305 to 313.
2. The feast day of Saint Theodoros is celebrated on February 17; for that entry, see Mathews, *On This Day: The Armenian Church Synaxarion—February,* 110-15.

4. Իսկ զօրականքն իբրեւ տեսին զսուրբն Թէոդորոս հաւատացին ի Քրիստոս եւ ասեն ցդատաւորն եթէ. Զխորհուրդ յարութեանն տեսաք աչօք մերովք: Եւ նոյնժամայն սրով կատարեցան ամենեքեան ի Քրիստոս:

5. Եւ եդ դատաւորն առաջի Կղէոնիկոսի պարգեւս մեծագինս եւ հանդերձս, եւ ոսկի եւ արծաթ հարիւր եւ յիսուն լիտր, եւ ասէ. Միայն ասա բանիւք վասն ժողովրդեանդ եթէ հաւանեցայ բանից դատաւորին: Իսկ սուրբն որպէս գէշ անկեալ առաջի թուչնոց համարեցաւ զպարգեւսն, եւ զբանս դատաւորին արհամարհեաց:

6. Եւ յորժամ գնաց դատաւորն բազմութեամբ ի տաճար կռոցն զոհս մատուցանել, աղօթեցին սուրբքն եւ եղեւ չարժ եւ անկաւ բագինն Արտեմիդեայ: Եւ ձայն եղեւ յերկնից. Որ Եւտրոպիէ, լսելի եղեն աղօթք քո, եղեցի ի տեղւոջս յայսմիկ եկեղեցի քրիստոնէից: Եւ հրամայեաց դատաւորն եռացուցանել ձիւթ եւ ձէթ՝ երկու կաթսայս, եւ հեղին ի վերայ թիկանց սրբոցն. եւ ի դահճացն այրեցան վեց այր եւ սուրբքն ամբողջ մնացին. ապա երկաթի ճանկօք քերեցին զմարմինս նոցա: Ձայն եղեւ առ նոսա յերկնից եւ ասէ. Որովհետեւ դուք ետուք զանձինս ձեր ի մահ վասն իմ՝ չնորհեցից ձեզ զկեանսն յաւիտենից:

7. Եւ հանեալ ի բանդէն բեւեռեցին ի խաչի: Եւ ձայն եղեւ առ նոսա յերկնից. Ով Եւտրոպիէ եւ Կղէոնիկէ, բարիոք ճգնեցարուք, ընկալարուք զպսակն արդարութեան: Եւ այնպէս աւանդեցին զհոգիս իւրեանց առ Աստուած ի Մարտի Գ:

8. Եւ քրիստոնեայքն եդին զմարմինս նոցա մերձ յԱմասիա քաղաքին, ոչ ի միասին՝ այլ որիչ. զսուրբն Եւտրոպիոս ի Թերմայն, եւ զսուրբն Կղէոնիկոս ի Քոեմայն:

4. When the soldiers saw Saint Theodoros, they came to believe in Christ, and they said to the judge, "We have seen with our own eyes the mystery of the resurrection." And at that very moment all of them were slain by the sword for Christ.

5. The judge set before Cleonikos gifts of great worth—clothing and 150 pounds of gold and silver—and said, "Simply say these words for the sake of your people: 'I consent to the words of the judge.'" But this holy one considered such gifts like a corpse lying before birds, and he disdained the promises of the judge.

6. When the judge then went with a multitude into the temple to offer sacrifices to the idols, the holy ones prayed; and there was an earthquake, and the shrine to Artemis collapsed. A voice came from heaven, "O Eutropios, your prayers have been heard; there will be in this place a church for Christians." The judge ordered [his men] to boil oil and pitch in two cauldrons and to pour it over the backs of these holy ones. Of the executioners, six were burned, but the holy ones remained unharmed. Then they flayed their flesh with iron hooks. A voice came to them from heaven and said, "Because you have handed yourselves over to death for my sake, I will bestow upon you eternal life."

7. They then dragged them out of prison and nailed them to a cross. Again a voice came to them from heaven, "O Eutropios and Cleonikos, you have suffered well, receive now the crown of righteousness." And thus they handed over their spirits to God on the third of March.

8. The Christians deposed their bodies near the city of Amasia, not together but in separate places: Saint Eutropios in Therma and Saint Cleonikos in Ktema.

ՄԵՀԵԿԻ ԻԶ

Մարտի Դ

Վարք սրբոյ հօրն մերոյ Մարկոսի

1. *Այս մեծ բարեսէր եւ աղքատասէր այրս Աստուծոյ Մարկոս
մինչդեռ մանուկն էր, ուսաւ զամենայն Հին եւ Նոր կտակարանս
պատուիրանացն Աստուծոյ, եւ եղեւ կատարիչ Հրամանացն Տեառն,
եւ արժանաւորեցաւ Հոգեւորական չնորհաց: Եւ գրեաց ճառս
զղջման եւ ապաշխարութեան եւ ի սուրբ մկրտութիւնն, եւ վասն
Հոգւոց եւ մարմնոց մարդկան եւ վասն կատարեալ
կենցաղավարութեան, եւ ընդդէմ Հերձուածողացն:*
2. *Եւ յորժամ եղեւ քառասուն ամաց Հրաժարեաց ի բազմաղբաղ
կենցաղոյս, եւ երթեալ բնակեցաւ ի ճգնաւորաց վանս զամս
վաթսուն, եւ ամենեւին յերկիր ոչ եթուք, եւ անկան ամենայն
ատամունք նորա:*

March 4

Meheki 26

The life of Mark, the holy ascetic

1. This great man of God, Mark, was a lover of virtue and a lover of the poor; he learned all the commandments of God, both the Old and the New Testament. He became a perfect practitioner of the commands of the Lord, and he became worthy of spiritual graces. He wrote treatises on compunction and penitence, on holy baptism, concerning the spirit and flesh of man, concerning the life of perfection, and against the heretics.[1]

2. When he reached forty years of age, he renounced his life of wandering and went and dwelt in a monastery of ascetics for sixty years; he never spit on the ground, and all his teeth fell out.

---

1. This enigmatic fifth-century ascetic is traditionally identified with the spiritual writer known as Mark the Monk, or Mark the Hermit. English translations of what remains of his writings have now been conveniently collected in *Mark the Monk: Counsels on the Spiritual Life*.

3. *Պատմեաց մեզ աշակերտն իւր Պափնուտիոս եթէ. Ի միում աւուր նստէր առ դրանն խրճթի նորա եւ ունկն դնէր նորա աղօթիցն, եւ լուայ որ վիճէր ընդ անձին իւրում եւ ասէր. Զի՞նչ աւելի կամիս ով աբեղայ, հարիւր ամաց եղեր եւ ճաշակեցեր ի գինոյ եւ ի ձիթոյ. արդ այլ զինչ արարից քեզ չատակեր եւ որկորագահ աբեղայ: Ի բաց երթ յինէն սատանայ, ծերացար ընդ իս ի տկարութիւն մարմնոյ իմոյ, եւ ետու զմիտս իմ ի կամս քո, եւ հաղորդեցայ ի գինոյ եւ ի ձիթոյ, միթէ այլ ինչ պարտիմ քեզ, ոչինչ գտցես յիս որ կողոպտես: Եւ դարձեալ անգոսնելով ասէր ցանձն իւր. Ով չատակեր ալեւոր, ով որկրամոլ աբեղայ, մինչեւ յե՞րբ եղէց ընդ քեզ: Եւ ելեալ ի խրճթէն երանելին Մարկոս եւ նստաւ ի մէջ սրահին եւ աղօթէր: Եմուտ գազան մի ունելով ի գիրկս իւր զկորիւնն իւր կոյր ծնեալ, ընկէց զնա յոտս երանելոյն, եւ որպէս մարդ երկիր եպագ: Եւ նորա առեալ զկորիւնն աղաչեաց զԱստուած, եւ թքեալ յաչս նորա առժամայն բացան եւ ետես զլոյս: Եւ առեալ գազանն զկորիւնն գնաց: Եւ ի միւս այլ աւուրն եբեր գազանն մեծ խոյենի մորթ երանելոյն տուրս. Եւ նա ոչ առ, եւ ասէ. Ոչ ինչ առնում ի քէն: Եւ գազանն զծունկսն կրկնեալ յերկիր, եւ խոնարհեցուցեալ զգլուխն իւր յերկիր քծնելով երկրպագէր, եւ առեալ զմորթն եդ յոտս երանելոյն: Եւ նա ասէ. Յանձն առ որ ամենեւին մարդոյ վնաս ոչ առնես, ոչ յոչխարսն եւ ոչ յարջառս, ոչ յայգիս եւ ոչ ի պարտէզս: Եւ գազանն իմացաւ զպատուէրն որպէս մտաւոր, եւ գլխովն խոստանայր կատարել զհրամանն: Յայնժամ առեալ զմորթն եւ յուղարկեաց աղախնոյն Աստուծոյ Մելանեայ:*

4. *Երանելին Մարկոս էր կարճահասակ եւ քարձ, եւ ի վեր ի շրթունսն ունէր սակաւ մի մօրուս եւ ի ներքոյ կլափանն. եւ ի բազում ճգնութենէն հեր գլխոյն ոչ աճէր:*

5. *Պատմեաց մեզ երանելի քահանայն Մակար մեծ սքանչելիս վասն երանելի հօր մերոյ Մարկոսի եթէ. Ամենեւին ի ձեռաց իմոց զպատուական օրէնսն ոչ առ, այլ ի ձեռաց հրեշտակին եւ յամենայն տօնի ես ինքնին տեսանէի աչօք իմովք թաթ ձեռին ի վերայ սրբոյ սեղանոյն, եւ առնոյր ի ձեռաց իմոց զօրէնսն, եւ արկանէր ի բերան Մարկոսի:*

6. *Այլ վասն բազում ճգնութեանն եւ առաքինի վարուց նորա ո՞ կարէ պատմել, ի մեծամեծ սքանչելեաց նորա գիտեմք որ առաւել քան զբնութիւն մարդկան ջանաց հաճոյանալ Աստուծոյ: Եւ ի կատարել զհարիւր ամն բարի հանգստեամբն ննջեաց ի Քրիստոս ի Մարտի Դ:*

3. His disciple Paphnutius told us the following story: "One day I was sitting at the door of his cell, and I was listening to him praying; and I heard him arguing with himself and saying, 'What more do you want, O monk? You are now a hundred years old and you have consumed both wine and oil; what else might I do for you, O gluttonous and indulgent monk? Go away from me, Satan; you have grown old with me in the weakness of my flesh, and I have handed my mind over to your will. I have partaken of both wine and oil. Do I owe you anything else? You will find nothing else to plunder from me.' He then rebuked himself again and said to himself, 'O gluttonous old man, O insatiable monk, how long will I be with you?' Then the blessed Mark went out from his cell and sat in the middle of the common room and began to pray. A wild animal ambled in, holding in its arms its newborn blind cub, and tossed it at the feet of the holy one and, like a human, prostrated itself. [Mark] took up the cub, prayed to God, and spit into its eyes. Immediately they opened, and it saw light. The wild animal then took up its cub and went off. On yet another day that wild animal brought to the holy one a large skin of a ram as a gift. But he did not take it and said, 'I will take nothing from you.' But the wild animal bent its knees along the ground and lowered its head to the ground, prostrated itself, and while nuzzling him took the skin and set it at the feet of the blessed one. He then said, 'Promise never to do any harm to a human being, nor to any sheep or oxen, nor to any vines or gardens.' The wild animal understood the command as if it were intelligent and, by a nod of its head, vowed to carry out that order. Then [Mark] accepted the skin, and he sent it to Melania, the handmaid of God."

4. The blessed Mark was short of stature and had a thin beard with hair above his lips and beneath his jaw, and because of his great asceticism the hair on his head no longer grew.

5. The blessed priest Makarios recounted to us this great miracle concerning our blessed father Mark: "He never received the holy sacrament from my hands, only from the hand of an angel; on every feast day I would see with my own eyes a palm of a hand above the holy altar. It would take the host from my hands and put it into the mouth of Mark."

6. But who is able to recount his great asceticism or his virtuous life? We know from his wondrous miracles beyond human nature that he strove to make himself pleasing to God. When he completed one hundred years, he fell peacefully asleep in Christ on the fourth of March.

Յայսմ աւուր յիշատակ է Երանելւոյն Մակարայ անապատականին

7. *Երանելին Մակար եգիպտացի էր ազգաւ, եւ ճգնաւոր
խստակրօն, եւ զքառասուն օր եւ զգիշեր յոտն կալով աղօթեաց,
եւ ի կիւրակէն միայն կոճ մի կաղամբ ուտէր, եւ զքառասուն օր
եւ զգիշեր ոչ ննջեաց եւ յաղթեաց քնոյ:*
8. *Սա գնաց ի դրախտն կախարդացն Փարաւոնի՝ Յաննեսի եւ
Յամրէսի՝ զոր դեւքն ունէին, եւ ի վառել դիւացն ընդդէմ. Մտանեմ,
ասէ, տեսանեմ, եւ ոչ բնակեմ այլ ելանեմ: Եւ արար այնպէս:*
9. *Սա ի պատերազմել պոռնկութեան դիւին՝ զկորիւն իժի արկ ի
ծոց իւր եւ ոչ վնասեաց նմա: Սա գրեաց բազում խրատս
ոգեշահս կրօնաւորաց: Հայրն Մակար ոչ ծիծաղեցաւ զամենայն
ժամանակս կենաց իւրոց, եւ յաւուր միում ժողովեալ ամենայն
դիւացն հնարս նիւթեցին այնմիկ. բերին կառանս մեծամեծս,
կապեցին ի չնչին փետուրս կրծից ճնճղկի միոյ, եւ բուռն հարեալ
ամենեքեան զօրութեամբ մեծաւ՝ զաղաղակ բարձեալ ասէին.
Քարշեցէք մանկտի, քարշեցէք: Եւ ոչ կարացին շարժել ամենեւին:
Եւ զայս տեսեալ Մակարի ժպտեցաւ: Եւ նոցա ծափս ծափի
հարեալ. Ծիծաղեցաւ, ասեն Մակար: Եւ նա ասէ. Ոչ այլ զինչ
զանմտութիւն ձեր եւ զտկարութիւն:*
10. *Սա եղեւ եպիսկոպոս կամօքն Աստուծոյ, եւ արար բազում
սքանչելիս, եւ հանգեաւ խաղաղութեամբ ի Քրիստոս:*

On this day is the memorial of the blessed anchorite Makarios

7. The blessed Makarios was an Egyptian by nationality and an austere ascetic. He would stand on his feet in prayer for forty days and nights; only on Sundays would he eat a chunk of cabbage. And for forty days and nights he would not rest but overcame sleep.

8. He went to the garden of the enchanters of Pharaoh, Jannes and Jambres, whom demons possessed. When these demons rose up against [Makarios], he said, "I enter and I see; I will not dwell here, but I will go away." And he did just that.

9. After he fought with a demon of fornication, he placed a young viper against his chest, but it did him no harm. He wrote numerous spiritual counsels for the ascetics. Father Makarios never laughed during the whole time of his life, but one day all the demons gathered in order to lay a trap for him in that regard. They brought some huge cables and tied them onto some tiny breast feathers of a sparrow, and the [demons] all took hold with great force and cried out saying, "Pull, children, pull!" But they were unable to move it at all. Upon seeing this, Makarios smiled. And they all applauded and said, "Makarios has laughed!" But he retorted, "Not for any other reason than your lack of intelligence and your powerlessness."

10. [Makarios] became a bishop by the will of God. He performed many miracles and fell peacefully asleep in Christ.

ՄԵՀԵԿԻ ԻԷ

Մարտի Ե

Վկայաբանութիւն սրբոյն Կոնոնայ Իսաւրացւոյ

1. *Յաւուրս սրբոց առաքելոցն էր Կոնոնոս ի գեղջէն Եղանիս՝ ութ*
եւ տասն ասպարիսաւ հեռի ի քաղաքէն Իսաւրիոյ, եւ անուն հօրն
Նեստորիոս եւ մօրն Նադաս.
2. *Եւ յորժամ եղեւ ի չափ հասակի, խօսեցան ծնօղքն իւր նմա*
կին, որոյ անուն էր Աննա: Եւ նախ քան զհարսանիսն երեւեցաւ
Կոնոնոսի հրեշտակապետն Միքայէլ որպէս ահաւոր այր պայծառ
հանդերձիւք, եւ ուսոյց նմա զբարեպաշտութեան հաւատն
Քրիստոսի. եւ տարեալ ի ջուր՝ մկրտեցաւ յանուն սրբոյ
Երրորդութեանն, եւ հաղորդեցոյց զնա ի սուրբ խորհրդեանն, եւ
վերացաւ յերկինս, եւ յամենայն ժամ աներեւոյթաբար էր ընդ
նմա:
3. *Եւ յորժամ եղեն հարսանիքն եւ եմուտ յառագաստն ընդ*
հարսինն ունելով զերկիւղն Աստուծոյ ի սրտի իւրում՝ առեալ ճրագ
ելոյց եւ եդ ի ներքոյ գրուանի, եւ ասէ ցհարսն. Ով կին, ասա
ինձ, ո՞ր լաւ է՝ լոյսն թէ խաւարն: Եւ նա ասէ. Լոյսն: Եւ բազում
բանիւք եցոյց նմա զբանս ճշմարտութեան, եւ հաւանեցոյց զի
անարատ կացցեն ընդ միմեանս: Նոյնպէս եւ զծնօղսն հաւանեցոյց,
եւ հաւատացին ի Քրիստոս եւ մկրտեցան. որ եւ յետոյ հայրն իւր
Նեստորիոս մարտիրոսացաւ: Եւ երանելին Կոնոնոս պահօք եւ
աղօթիւք ճգնէր եւ զբազումս ի հեթանոսաց դարձուցանէր ի
հաւատս:

March 5

Meheki 27

The martyrdom of the holy Kononos the Isaurian

1. Kononos lived in the days of the holy apostles in the village of Etena, eighteen miles from the city of Isauria; the name of his father was Nestorios and that of his mother Nadas.

2. When Kononos came of age, his parents betrothed him to a wife, whose name was Anna. But before the wedding the archangel Michael appeared to Kononos in the guise of an awe-inspiring figure clothed in luminescent garments. He taught Kononos the faith and worship of Christ. He then brought him to water, baptized him in the name of the Trinity, and served him holy communion. Then he rose up to heaven. During this entire time he had been invisibly with him.

3. When the marriage had taken place and he entered into the bridal chamber with his wife—and possessing the fear of God in his heart—he took up a lantern, lit it, set it underneath a bushel basket, and said to his wife, "O my wife, tell me. Which is better, the light or the darkness?" And she responded, "The light." And with much discussion, he demonstrated to her the words of truth, and he persuaded her that they should remain pure with each other. In the same manner, he also persuaded his parents, and they believed in Christ and were baptized. Sometime later his father Nestorios suffered martyrdom. And the blessed Kononos lived an ascetic life in fasting and prayer, and he converted many of the pagans to the faith.

4. *Եւ յաւուր միում տօն կատարէին կռապաշտքն եւ տօնէին ի տեղւոջ նսեմ եւ մթին. եւ երանելին խրատ տայր ժողովրդեանն ի բաց կալ ի մոլորութենէն եւ դառնալ ի լոյս աստուածգիտութեանն. եւ նոքա ծանրանային եւ խնդրէին ի նմանէ նշան տեսանել. եւ տեղին յորում կամէին զոհս մատուցանել՝ հեռագոյն էր: Ասէ ցնոսա Կոնոնոս. Դուք արք էք զօրաւորք եւ երիվարօք, եւ ես այր տկար եւ հետեւակ. ընթանամք ի միասին, եւ որ յառաջ հասցէ ի տեղի զոհից ձերոց՝ զնորա աստուածն պաշտեսցուք: Եւ նոքա հաճեցան ի բանս նորա: Կարգեցան հաւասարք միմեանց, նոքա երիվարօքն եւ Կոնոնոս հետեւակ, եւ ընթացան ամենեքեան: Եւ հրեշտակապետն զօրացոյց զընթացսն Կոնոնոսի եւ յառաջ հասոյց ի տեղին, եւ կալով մնայր նոցա. եւ նոքա եկեալ զարմացան՝ այլ ոչ հաւանեցան նմա: Ասէ ցնոսա Կոնոնոս. Հարցից ցբագինս ձեր՝ եւ զոր նա ասէ եթէ իցէ ճշմարիտ աստուած, զնա արժան է պաշտել: Եւ նոքա յանձն առին:*

5. *Ասէ Կոնոնոս ցբագինն որ ի բարձրաւանդակին կայր. Քեզ հրամայէ Յիսուս Քրիստոս Աստուածն իմ, մարմարիոնեայ բագին, էջ ի բարձր տեղւոջէդ եւ կացջիր առաջի մեր: Եւ առժամայն անկաւ բագինն եւ գլորեցաւ առաջի նոցա. եւ դարձեալ կանգնեցաւ: Եւ սարսեցին հեթանոսքն, եւ յահէն աղաղակէին: Եւ խստասրտութեամբ ասէ սուրբն ցբագինն. Դո՞ւ ես աստուածն՝ եթէ Քրիստոս զոր ես քարոզեմ: Ասէ բագինն մարդկային բարբառով. Միայն Աստուած նա է զոր դու քարոզես Յիսուս Քրիստոս: Յայնժամ բազմութիւն ամբոխին աղաղակէին մեծաւ բարբառով. Միայն Աստուածն Կոնոնոսի յաղթեաց: Եւ զայս բարբառ մինչեւ ցայսօր՝ յաւուր տօնի սրբոյն Կոնոնոսի ժողովին Իսաւրացիքն յեկեղեցին եւ մեծաձայն աղաղակեն զնոյն բնաս: Ընթացան ժողովուրդքն եւ խորտակեցին զբագինսն մանր:*

6. *Այս երանելի վկայս Քրիստոսի զդեւսն հնազանդեցոյց ի ծառայութիւն, եւ նորին հրամանաւն վաստակէին զերկիր, եւ բրէին արտորայս եւ այգիս եւ պարտէզս:*

7. *Ի միում աւուր աւազակք դիմեցին ի վերայ սրբոյն, եւ դիւացն կալեալ զնոսա զան հարին ուժգին, եւ վառեցին թոնիր զի այրեսցեն զնոսա: Եւ սաստեաց նոցա սուրբն եւ արձակեցին զաւազակսն, եւ պատուիրեաց նոցա զի չար ումեք ոչ արասցեն:*

4. One day the idolaters were celebrating one of their feasts, and they were celebrating it in a dark and gloomy place. The blessed one counseled the people to turn away from their error and to turn to the light of the knowledge of God. But they became enraged, and they sought to see some sort of sign from him. The place where they were intending to offer their sacrifice was far off. Kononos said to them, "You men are soldiers and are on horses; I, however, am a weak man and on foot. Whoever arrives first at the place of your sacrifices, his god we will worship." They agreed to his proposal. They lined themselves up alongside each other, they on their horses and Kononos on foot, and they all ran off. Now an archangel gave strength to Kononos's running, and he arrived at the place first, and he stood there waiting for them. When they came, they were stupefied, but they did not yield to him. Kononos then said to them, "Let me pose the question to your idol, and whichever he says is the true god, that one will be worthy of our worship." They again agreed.

5. So Kononos said to the idol that had been set up on a high point, "My God, Jesus Christ, commands you, O marble idol, to come down from that high place and stand before us!" And immediately the idol fell over, rolled down in front of them and then again took an upright position. The pagans trembled and screamed in fear. With adamant demeanor, the holy one said to the idol, "Are you god, or is Christ whom I preach?" The idol, with a human voice, responded, "The only God is the one whom you preach, Jesus Christ." Then those many who had assembled all cried out in a loud voice, "The God of Kononos alone has won the victory." (To this day, the Isaurians who gather in the church on the feast day of Saint Kononos say these words in a loud voice.) Then the people ran and smashed the idols to bits.

6. This blessed martyr of Christ subdued the idols into servitude, and at his command they began to till the earth, to plow the fields, the vineyards, and the gardens.

7. One day some thieves fell upon the holy one, but demons came, seized those [thieves], and brutally beat them. They even heated up an oven so that they might burn them. But the holy one rebuked them, so they freed the thieves. He then commanded them never again to do harm to anyone.

8. *Արտ մի հասեալ սխռան զոր վաստակեցին դեւքն, եմուտ գողն եւ փետեաց եւ եբարձ յոյժ. եւ դեւքն աներեւոյթաբար ասեն ցնա բարձր բարբառով. Կեր որչափ կարես եւ բարձ զչափսն եւ մի անյագութեամբ: Եւ նա ոչ լուաւ նոցա: Եւ դեւքն առին զնա բեռամբն եւ տարան առաջի Կոնոնոսի. եւ նա խրատ տուեալ նմա արձակեաց բեռամբն: Եւ մինչեւ ցայժմ ոչ ոք իշխէ յափշտակել կամ գողանալ յընչից եկեղեցւոյ սրբոյն Կոնոնոսի, ապա եթէ յանդգնի ոք տանջի ի դիւաց:*

9. *Յայլ աւուր գայլ յափշտակեաց զայրւոյ միոյ տղայ զաւակ, եւ յոյժ ողբայր եւ հառաչէր կինն. եւ լուաւ սուրբն զողբսն. Հրամայեաց դիւացն եւ հասին գայլոյն. եւ կալան կէսքն զականջացն այլք զագւոյն, այլք ձաղկէին եւ քարշէին առաջի սրբոյն Կոնոնոսի. եւ ընկէց զտղայն անվնաս, եւ դարձաւ գայլն ի տեղւոյն: Իսկ երանելին զհասարակ դիւին հալածեաց, եւ զայլսն արգել ի խեցի սափորս, եւ կապարեայ մատանեաւ կնքեաց, եւ փորեաց վիհ ի հիմանս տան իւրոյ եւ թաղեաց անդ:*

10. *Եւ ընդ աւուրսն ընդ այնոսիկ եհաս Մագնոս դատաւորն, եւ ունէր հրամանս ի թագաւորէն զի զքրիստոնեայսն որ ոչ ուրասցին զՔրիստոս եւ զոհեսցեն կռոցն խիստ տանջանօք կորուսցէ: Եւ կալեալ զսուրբն Կոնոնոս՝ կուտեաց առաջի նորա զամենայն մեքենայս տանջողական, եւ բազում խստութեամբ եւ սպառնալեօք պատուէր տայր եւ ոչ հաւանեցոյց: Եւ ապա ողոքանօք եւ քաղցրութեամբ խրատ տայր եւ խոստանայր պարգեւս եւ պատիւս. եւ ամենեւին ոչ կարաց խախտել զնա ի հաւատոցն Քրիստոսի: Հրամայեաց եւ այնչափ գանեցին զնա մերկ մինչեւ ամենայն մարմինն գզեցաւ:*

11. *Եւ լուեալ ժողորրդեանն ընթացան ըմբռնել զդատաւորն. եւ նորա գիտացեալ զյարձակումն ամբոխին ի վերայ՝ վաղվաղակի փախեաւ: Եւ գտին զսուրբն կապեալ եւ կիսամահ լեալ, լուծին եւ բարձեալ լալագին ողբովք տարան ի տունն իւր: Եւ կեցեալ ցաւագին ի չարաչար վիրացն զամս երկու՝ գոհութեամբ փառաւորելով զԱստուած՝ հանգեաւ մարտի Ե: Եւ եդին ի տապանին յորում թաղեալ էին զմայրն եւ զկուսան կինն իւր:*

8. Coming upon a field of peas that the demons had tilled, a thief entered in, picked and carried off a large amount of them. The demons, though invisible, said to him in a loud voice, "Eat as much as you can, but only take them according to your needs, not out of greed." But he paid no attention to them. So the demons took him, along with what he had taken, and they brought him to Kononos, who reprimanded him and then let him depart with what he had taken. And up until now, no one has dared to rob or to steal anything from the Church of Saint Kononos, and whoever dares to try is tortured by demons.

9. At another time a wolf snatched a young infant from a widow, and the woman wept and groaned violently. The holy one heard her weeping and commanded the demons, who overtook the wolf. Half of them took him by the ears, others by the tail, yet others beat him and dragged him back to the holy Kononos. The wolf tossed the child down unharmed and went back to where he came from. Then the blessed one chased away most of those demons, and the others he enclosed in earthenware jugs. He secured them with lead seals, and he dug out a hole in the foundation of his house and buried them there.

10. In those days Magnus the judge came there, and he had an order from the emperor to put to death by cruel tortures those Christians who would not renounce Christ and worship the idols. He had the holy Kononos seized, and he lined up in front of him all his instruments of torture. With great force and many threats he ordered [Kononos to renounce Christ and sacrifice to the idols], but he would not comply. Then [Magnus] tried to counsel him with gentle, kind, persuasive words, but he was completely unable to turn him away from his faith in Christ. So he commanded that Kononos be scourged naked to such a degree that his entire body was shredded.

11. When the people heard this, they ran to seize the judge, but he had learned about the mob's attack and promptly took flight. They found the holy one bound up and nearly dead. They untied him, and full of tears and wailing, they took him up and brought him back to his own house. He lived full of pain from his cruel wounds for another two years, and glorifying and praising God, he fell asleep on the fifth of March. They deposed him in the grave in which his mother and his virgin wife were buried.

12. *Եւ յետ ժամանակաց կամեցան քրիստոնեայքն աւերել զտուն եւ շինել եկեղեցի. եւ փորեալ զհիմունսն գտին զսափորսն կապարով կնքեալ. ի ծանրութենէն կարծեցին եթէ գանձ իցէ, բացին զմին ի սափորացն, եւ ելին որպէս տարափ դեւքն. եւ նոքա յերկեղէն ընկեցին յերկիր եւ փախեան։ Եւ յորժամ արեգակն յերեկոյն մտանէր ոչ ոք իշխէր անցանել ընդ այն սահմանն, եւ ի բաց թողին զշինումն եկեղեցւոյն։*

13. *Եւ յետոյ հրամանաւ սրբոյն Կոնոնոսի տեսլեամբ՝ կործանեցին զաւերակսն, եւ փորեցին վիհս խորս եւ թաղեցին զմնացեալ կնքեալ սափորսն. եւ շինեցին զեկեղեցին յանուն սրբոյն Կոնոսի. եւ բազում նշանք լինին ի սուրբ նշխարացն։*

14. *Յայսմ աւուր կռապաշտ դատաւորն Մագնոս զՔրիստոսի վկայն զՆերսիոն կալաւ ի գեօղն Սորուստի, եւ բազում եւ խիստ տանջանօք սպան վասն զի ոչ ուրացաւ զՔրիստոս, եւ ոչ զոհեաց կռոցն։*

12. Some time later the Christians wanted to demolish his house and build a church there. When they dug out the foundations, they found the jugs sealed with lead. From their weight they thought that it was some sort of treasure, so they opened one of the jugs, and demons came forth like a rain shower. [The Christians] then tossed the jug to the ground in their fear and fled. When the sun reached evening, no one would yet dare to pass through this area, and they gave up the [idea of] building a church.

13. Yet later, at the command of Saint Kononos in a vision, they hauled away the ruins, and they dug out deep holes, and they buried the remaining sealed jugs. Then they built a church in the name of Saint Kononos, and many miracles were performed through his holy relics.

14. On this day the idolatrous judge Magnus seized the martyr of Christ Nersion from the village of Soroust, and he had him killed by many cruel tortures because he would neither renounce Christ nor sacrifice to the idols.

ՄԵՀԵԿԻ ԻԸ

Մարտի Զ

Վարք երանելոյն Պորփիւրոսի Գազայ եպիսկոպոսի

1. *Երանելին Պորփիւրոս էր ի Թեսաղոնիկեցւոց քաղաքէն, յաւուրս բարեպաշտ արքայիցն Արկադիոսի եւ Ոնորիոսի: Եւ մինչդեռ պատանին էր գնաց յԵգիպտոս եւ եղեւ կրօնաւոր ի Սկիւթ վանս. եւ զհինգ ամ կացեալ առ սուրբ հարցն՝ ուսաւ զամենայն ճգնողական ժուժկալութիւնսն: Եւ գնաց յԵրուսաղէմ, եւ երկիր եպագ սուրբ տեղեացն: Եւ առաքեաց զՄարկոս զհաւատարիմ ծառայն իւր ի Թեսաղոնիկէ եւ վաճառեաց զհասեալ բաժին նորա յընչից իւրոց ի չորեք հազար եւ չորեք հարիւր դահեկան, եւ տարաւ առ Պորփիւրոս, եւ նա բաշխեաց զամենայն աղքատաց եւ կրօնաւորաց:*

2. *Եւ էր երանելին Պորփիւրոս լերդացաւ: Եւ ետես յանուրջս զՔրիստոս բեւեռեալ ի խաչին եւ զմի յաւազակացն յայլ խաչի բեւեռեալ, եւ աղաղակեաց առ Քրիստոս. Յիշեա զիս Տէր յարքայութեան քում: Ասէ Փրկիչն ընդ աւազակն. էջ ի խաչէդ եւ բժշկեա զդա: Եւ իջեալ կալաւ զձեռանէ նորա եւ տարաւ առ Փրկիչն. եւ էջ Քրիստոս ի խաչէն եւ մերձեցաւ յաջակողմն, կողից նորա, եւ ետ ի նա զխաչն իւր եւ ասէ. Պահեա ինձ զփայտս զայս, որով եւ դու ողջացար ի ցաւոց քոց: Եւ զարթեաւ ողջացեալ:*

3. *Եւ երանելին ոչ դադարէր ի յանդիմանելոյ զհրէայս եւ զհեթանոսս, եւ զհերձուածողս, եւ ուսուցանէր եւ լուսաւորէր զբազումս վարդապետութեամբ իւրով:*

March 6

Meheki 28

The life of the blessed Porphyry, bishop of Gaza

1. The blessed Porphyry was from the city of Thessalonica. [He lived] during the time of the pious emperors Arcadius and Honorius.[1] While he was still a youth, he went to Egypt and became an ascetic in the monasteries of Scetis. He remained for five years among the holy fathers and learned every austerity of the ascetical life. He then went to Jerusalem and worshipped there at the holy places. He sent Markos, his faithful servant, to Thessalonica where he sold the portion of possessions that had come to him for 4,400 dahekans. He brought this money to Porphyry, who distributed it all among the poor and the ascetics.

2. The blessed Porphyry suffered from consumption. In a dream he saw Christ nailed to the cross with that thief who was nailed upon another cross and who cried out to Christ, "Remember me, O Lord, in Your kingdom" (Luke 23:42). The Savior said to the thief, "Get down from your cross and heal [Porphyry]." He then descended, took [Porphyry] by the hand, and brought him to the Savior. Christ then also descended from the cross and drew near to his right side, gave to him His cross, and said, "Keep this cross for me, and by it you will be healed of your illnesses." And he awoke healed.

3. The blessed one never ceased from remonstrating against the Jews, the pagans, and the heretics. He taught and enlightened many by his teaching.

---

1. Upon the death of Theodosius I, Arcadius became ruler of the Eastern empire from 395 to 408, while his brother Honorius ruled the western part of the empire from 395 to 423.

4. *Ձեռնադրեաց զնա Պռայլոս Երուսաղեմայ Հայրապետն քահանայ, եւ արար զնա պահապան սրբոյ խաչին Քրիստոսի: Եւ էր կերակուր հաց եւ բանճար եւ ջուր ի մտանել արեգականն:*

5. *Եւ եղեւ ի մեռանել Գազայ եպիսկոպոսին առաքեաց զնա Հայրապետն Երուսաղեմի թղթով առ մետրապօլիտն Կեսարիոյ Պաղեստինացւոց: Եւ երեւեցոյց Աստուած մետրապօլտին զՊորփիւրոս ի տեսլեան եթէ. Սա է արժանի: Եւ յորժամ ետես՝ ծանեաւ ի տեսլենէն, եւ ձեռնադրեաց զնա եպիսկոպոս Գազայ:*

6. *Եւ ի քաղաքին յայնմիկ դեռ եւս կային կռապաշտք եւ տաճարք բագնաց, զի վասն բազում հարկաց զոր տային յարքունիս՝ թողին զնոսա ի կռապաշտութեանն, եւ համարձակութեամբ զոհէին ի տաճար կռոցն: Եւ երանելի եպիսկոպոսն բազում նեղութիւնս կրեաց ի նոցանէ, եւ ոչ կարաց ժուժկալել յանարգանս տեսանելով զանունն Քրիստոսի: Գնաց առ մետրապօլիտն իւր ի Կեսարիա, եւ խորհեցան ի միասին. եւ մտեալ ի նաւ գնացին ի Կոստանդինուպօլիս, երկիր պագին սրբոյն Յովհաննու Ոսկեբերանին որ յայնժամ պատրիարք էր Կոստանդինուպօլսի, եւ նա ի ձեռն ներքինոյ սենեկապետին եմոյծ զնոսա առաջի թագուհւոյն Եւդոքսիայ: Եւ երանելին Պորփիւրոս ասէ ցթագուհին. Եթէ կործանես զտաճար կռոցն եւ խափանես զհամարձակութիւն կռապաշտիցն՝ ծնցես արու մանուկ: Եւ նա յանձն էառ, եւ էր մերձ ի ծնունդ. եւ յետ սակաւ աւուր ծնաւ զՓոքր Թէոդոս: Եւ աղաչեաց զթագաւորն յաւուր յորում մկրտեաց զմանուկն Ոսկեբերանն:*

7. *Եւ առաքեաց թագաւորն զոմն Կինիգոս անուն հրամանօք, տուեալ եւ թագուհին հարիւր լիտր գանձ ի Պորփիւրոս զի շինեսցէ ի մէջ քաղաքին եկեղեցի: Եւ յորժամ գնացին կործանեցին զբագինս կռոցն եւ զտաճարսն հրով այրեցին, եւ շինեցին զեկեղեցին խաչանշան: Եւ զբազումս ի կռապաշտիցն դարձոյց Պորփիւրոս ի Քրիստոսի հաւատն եւ մկրտեաց:*

4. Praylios, the patriarch of Jerusalem,[2] ordained him a priest and appointed him as custodian of the holy cross of Christ. His food consisted of bread, vegetables, and water, [which he consumed only] after the setting of the sun.

5. When the bishop of Gaza died, the patriarch of Jerusalem sent [Porphyry], accompanied with a letter, to the metropolitan of Caesarea in Palestine. God had Porphyry appear to the metropolitan in a vision [and said], "This one is worthy." When he saw [Porphyry], the metropolitan recognized him from the vision and ordained him as bishop of Gaza.

6. In that city there were still idolaters and temples with altars to the idols, for they left them to their idolatry because of the many taxes that [the people] were paying to the palace, and they openly offered their sacrifices in the idol temples. The holy bishop endured much suffering from them, and he was unable to oppose the indignities that he saw [being done] to the name of Christ. He then went to his metropolitan in Caesarea, and they took counsel together. They boarded a ship and went to Constantinople, where they humbly presented themselves to Saint John Chrysostom, who was at the time the patriarch of Constantinople. He then, through the intercession of the eunuch who was high chamberlain, brought them before the empress Eudoxia.[3] And the blessed Porphyry said to the empress, "If you destroy the temple of idols and suppress the unrestrained liberty of the idolaters, you will give birth to a male child." She consented to this as she was near to giving birth. A short time later she gave birth to Theodosius the Younger.[4] She made her plea to the emperor on the very day that Saint John Chrysostom baptized the child.

7. The emperor dispatched a certain Cynegios with the royal command, and the empress gave to Porphyry a sum of one hundred gold solida from the treasury so that he might build a church in the middle of the city. When they arrived, they destroyed the altars to the idols and burned down the temples and there built a cruciform church. Then Porphyry converted many of those idolaters to the faith of Christ and baptized them.

---

2. Praylios was patriarch of Jerusalem from 417 to 422.
3. Eudoxia was the wife of the emperor Arcadius and mother of the future emperor Theodosius II.
4. Theodosius II (the Younger) would be emperor from 408 to 450.

8. Եւ ամբաւ նշանս եւ սքանչելիս արար որք գրեալ են ի կատարեալ պատմութեանն իւրում: Եւ կեցեալ յաթոռ եպիսկոպոսութեանն ամս քսան եւ հինգ երանելի մահուամբ ննջեաց ի Քրիստոս Մարտի Զ:

Յայսմ աւուր կատարեցան քառասուն եւ երկու վկայքն ի Տաճկաստան, ի Սամառա քաղաքին վասն Քրիստոսի աստուածութեանն

9. Քառասուն եւ երեք քրիստոնեայս տարան ի գլխատումն ի Սամառա, եւ մինն տաճկացաւ. եւ հատին զքառասուն եւ երկու սրբոցն զգլուխսն: Եւ ասէ Ամիր Իլմումնի եթէ. Որպէս զիւր հաւատն ոչ պահեաց եւ ոչ զմերս պահեսցէ, եւ հրամայեաց եւ զնա գլխատեցին, եւ կորեաւ ի խաւարն արտաքին:

10. Յայսմ աւուր Գիւտ նշխարաց Գրիգորիսի Աղուանից կաթողիկոսի, եւ վարք Վարոսի եւ Թաթլոյ:

11. Ի նմին աւուր ստուգապէս եւ ճշմարիտ Գիւտ է սուրբ եւ պատուական եւ կենդանարար երանելի խաչափայտին Քրիստոսի Աստուծոյ մերոյ. որ թէպէտ յայլ տեղիս յիշատակի, այլ գիւտն աստ եղեւ:

8. He performed innumerable signs and miracles that are all written in his complete biography.[5] He occupied the episcopal throne for twenty-five years; then with a blessed death he fell asleep in Christ on the sixth of March.

On this day forty-two martyrs were killed in Muslim territory, in the city of Samarra, over the divinity of Christ

9. Forty-three Christians were brought to Samarra for decapitation, of whom one converted to Islam. They cut off the heads of the other forty-two holy ones. The emir Al-Maʿmun said, "As he did not keep his own faith, he shall not keep ours either." So he gave the command, and they cut off his head as well, and it was lost in the darkness outside.[6]

10. On this day is the discovery of the relics of Gregory, the catholicos of the Albanians, as well as the life of Varos and of Tatoul.

11. On this same day is the discovery of the authentic, true, holy, venerable, life-giving blessed wood of the cross of Christ our God. Although its memorial is celebrated at another time, its discovery occurred on this day.[7]

---

5. This complete biography is probably that composed by Mark the Deacon; see the *Life of Porphyry*.

6. The traditional date for this mass martyrdom is 845.

7. This feast celebrates the discovery of the cross by Queen Helena, mother of the emperor Constantine. The other memorial referred to here is, of course, the great feast of the Exaltation of the Cross, generally celebrated (as according to this *Yaysmawurkʿ*) on September 14, but celebrated now in the Armenian church on the Sunday closest to that date.

ՄԵՀԵԿԻ ԻԹ

Մարտի Է

Վկայութիւն Վասիլիոսի եպիսկոպոսի որ Խերսոնի քաղաքի

1. *Ի վեշտասաներորդի ամի Թագաւորութեանն Դիոկղետիանոսի կռապաշտ արքային՝ երանելին Երմոն Հայրապետն Երուսաղեմի առաքեաց ի բազում գաւառս եպիսկոպոսունս քարոզել յայլազգիս զբանն կենաց, եւ դարձուցանել զանհաւատս ի գիտութիւն ճշմարտութեան:*

2. *Առաքեաց զԵփրեմ ի Թուրքաստան, եւ զՎասիլիոս ի Քերսոն քաղաք: Եւ երթեալ քարոզէր զաւետարանն Քրիստոսի, եւ բազում նեղութեանց եւ տանջանաց համբերեաց վասն անուանն Քրիստոսի: Եւ ելեալ բնակէր ի քարայր մի լերինն որ կոչի Պարթենիոն: Դէպ եղեւ մեռանել որդւոյ իշխանի քաղաքին, եւ յորժամ թաղեցին՝ զօրն զայն եւ զգիշերն ի գերեզմանէն ոչ որոշէին ծնօղքն, այլ անմխիթարելի լային զզաւակն իւրեանց, եւ ի բազում տքնութենէն ննջեցին ի վերայ տապանին: Եւ տեսանէին յերազի զորդին իւրեանց որ ասէր. Ընդէ՞ր լայք զիս: Եթէ կամիք որ ես կենդանի լինիմ՝ անկերուք յոտս արդար առն զոր չարաչար տանջեցէք, թերեւս աղաչեսցէ զԱստուածն իւր վասն իմ եւ դուք հաւատացէք բանից նորին, եւ կատարին խնդրուածք ձեր. քանզի ստոյգ տեսի եւ գիտացի զի աստուածքն մեր դեւք են, եւ ամենեւին մարդոյ օգնել ոչ կարեն:*

March 7

Meheki 29

The martyrdom of the bishop Basil, which is translated "king"

1. In the sixteenth year of the reign of the impious emperor Diocletian,[1] Germanion the patriarch of Jerusalem sent bishops into many provinces to preach the word of life to pagans and to convert unbelievers to the knowledge of the truth.

2. [Patriarch Germanion] sent Ephrem to Turkestan[2] and Basil to the city of Cherson.[3] When [the latter] arrived, he began to preach the gospel of Christ, and he endured many tribulations and much suffering on behalf of the name of Christ. He went and dwelt in a mountain cavern that was called Parthenion. It happened that the son of the prince of the city had just died. After he was buried, his parents did not depart from the tomb that entire day and night, weeping inconsolably for their child; and after much sleeplessness, they fell asleep on top of the coffin. They saw their son in a dream, and he said, "Why are you weeping for me? If you wish that I live, fall at the feet of that just man whom you tortured so cruelly; perhaps he will beseech his God on my behalf. And if you believe his words, then that which you seek will also come to pass. For I have truly seen and have come to know that our gods are demons and are completely incapable of helping anyone."

---

1. Diocletian, perpetrator of the great persecution against Christians, was emperor from 284 to 305.
2. The area in central Asia east of the Caspian Sea.
3. Ancient Greek city on the southwestern shore of the Crimean Peninsula.

3. *Եւ զարթուցեալք գնացին առ եպիսկոպոսն Վասիլիոս եւ աղաչէին զնա վասն որդւոյն իւրեանց: Ասէ ցնոսա երանելի եպիսկոպոսն. Եթէ հաւատայք ի Քրիստոս կարող է զայդ առնել: Եւ նոքա յանձն առին եւ խոստովանեցան հաւատով: Եւ յարուցեալ գնաց նոքօք ի գերեզմանն, եւ արարեալ զաղօթս մկրտութեանն ի վերայ ջրոյ՝ եհեղ ի վերայ մեռելոյն յանուն սրբոյ Երրորդութեանն, առժամայն կենդանացաւ, եւ ետուն փառս Աստուծոյ, եւ մկրտեցան ամենեքեան ազգակցօք եւ ընտանեօք:*

4. *Իսկ այլ կռապաշտքն եւ քաղաքին Հրէայքն նախանձու լցեալք՝ ժողովեցան ի միասին, եւ բարկութեամբ դիմեցին ի վերայ սրբոյն Վասիլիոսի, ընկեցին յերկիր, կապեցին պարան յոտս նորա եւ քարշեցին ընդ մէջ քաղաքին, եւ փայտիւ եւ քարամբ հարկանէին. եւ այնպիսի տանջանօք աւանդեաց զհոգին իւր առ Աստուած՝ Մարտի է: Եւ զմարմինն ընկեցին արտաքոյ քաղաքին, եւ ի ցերեկն պահէր զսուրբ մարմինն արծիւ, եւ ի գիշերի գայլ, մինչեւ եկեալ քրիստոնէիցն գաղտ թաղեցին:*

5. *Եւ մի ոմն յորոց էին ի Քերսոն ընդ սրբոյն Վասիլիոսի, նաւեաց յայնկոյս յԵլենիոպոնտոս, եւ եգիտ այլ երեք եպիսկոպոսունս որ երթեալ էին յԵրուսաղէմայ քարոզել զաւետարանն Քրիստոսի, զԵւգինիոս, զԱգաթոդորոս եւ զԵլպիոս, եւ պատմեաց նոցա զմարտիրոսութեամբ մահն սրբոյն Վասիլիոսի, եւ գոհութեամբ փառս ետուն Աստուծոյ: Եւ մտեալ ի նաւ գնացին ի Քերսոն, եւ քարոզէին հրապարակաւ զանուն Տեառն Յիսուսի: Եւ զնոսա կալան քաղաքացի կռապաշտքն, կապեցին եւ ուժգին ձաղկեցին հաստ մահակօք մինչեւ զհոգիս իւրեանց աւանդեցին առ Աստուած: Եւ քարշեցին զմարմինս նոցա արտաքոյ քաղաքին, եւ քրիստոնեայք թաղեցին զնոսա ի ծածուկ. եւ են մեզ բարեխօս առ Քրիստոս:*

3. When they awoke, [his parents] went to the bishop Basil, and they begged him on behalf of their son. The blessed bishop said to them, "If you believe in Christ, he is able to do this." They both consented and confessed in faith. Then [Basil] rose up and went with them to the tomb; he recited the prayers of baptism over the water and poured it over the dead child in the name of the Holy Trinity, and he was immediately restored to life. And they gave glory to God, and they too were baptized along with their parents and their families.

4. Then other idolaters and the Jews of the city, filled with anger, assembled together; and mad with rage, they attacked the holy Basil. They threw him to the ground, tied a rope around his feet, and dragged him through the middle of the city; then they beat him with sticks and rocks. Due to such tortures, he committed his soul to God on the seventh of March. They then threw his corpse outside the city. But an eagle kept watch over his holy flesh during the day and a wolf during the night until the Christians came and secretly buried him.

5. One of those who was with the holy Basil in Cherson sailed across to Helenespont, and he found three other bishops who had come from Jerusalem to preach the gospel of Christ: Eugenios, Agathodoros, and Elpidios. He recounted to them the martyrdom of the holy Basil, and they gave glory and praise to God. They embarked once again by ship and returned to Cherson, and they began publicly to preach the name of the Lord Jesus. The idolaters of that city seized them, bound them, and flogged them so severely with thick clubs that they committed their souls to God. They then dragged their corpses outside the city, and the Christians buried them in secret. They are now our intercessors before Christ.

ՄԵՀԵԿԻ Լ

Մարտի Ը

Վարք սրբո–հ–ւոյն Եփրոսինեայ

1. *Յաւուրս Փոքր Թէոդոսի բարեպաշտ արքային էր այր մի մեծատուն որոյ անուն էր Պափնոտիոս, ի քաղաքէն Աղեկսանդրիայ. եւ ունէր դուստր մի ամաց երկոտասանից որոյ անուն էր Եփրոսինէ, որ թարգմանի ուրախութիւն: Եւ ուսուցեալ էր նմա գիր, եւ կրթեալ էր նա յերկիւղ Տեառն պարկեշտութեամբ, եւ ի պահս եւ յաղօթս. եւ եղեւ Եփրոսինէ բարի բնութեամբ եւ գեղեցիկ տեսլեամբ:*

2. *Եւ մի ոմն ազնուական եւ մեծատուն իշխան խնդրեաց զնա հարսն յորդին իւր. եւ հաւանեցաւ Պափնոտիոս, եւ առնէին զհաստատութիւն խնամութեանն: Եւ Եփրոսինէ ունելով զերկիւղ Աստուծոյ ի սրտի իւրում՝ ոչ կամէր չաղախիլ ի յանցաւոր ցանկութիւնս, այլ փափաքէր պահել զկուսութիւնն իւր մաքուր եւ հարսնանալ Քրիստոսի:*

3. *Եւ ի միում աւուր կոչեցին զՊափնոտիոս ի վանս վասն ուխտի տօնի վանացն. եւ երթեալ անդ արար աւուրս երիս ուրախանալով ընդ կրօնաւորսն: Իսկ Եփրոսինէ գաղտ գերծեաց զգլուխ իւր եւ զգեցաւ հանդերձ առնն, եւ առ ընդ ինքեան հինգ հարիւր դահեկան, եւ յորժամ գիտաց վասն հօրն իւրոյ եթէ գնաց ի վանացն՝ եմուտ ի նաւ եւ գնաց ընդ այլ ճանապարհ ի վանսն: Քանզի ասէր ի մտի իւրում. Եթէ երթայց ի կանանց վանսն՝ գտանէ զիս հայրն իմ եւ բռնութեամբ հանէ վասն խօսեցեալ փեսային:*

March 8

Meheki 30

The life of Saint Euphrosyne

1. In the days of the pious emperor Theodosius the Younger, there was a wealthy man, whose name was Paphnutius, from the city of Alexandria. He had a twelve-year-old daughter, whose name was Euphrosyne, which is translated "Joy." He taught her to read and write, and he trained her in chastity and in the fear of the Lord, as well as in fasting and prayer. Euphrosyne grew up with a good nature and a beautiful figure.

2. A certain noble and wealthy prince sought her as a bride for his son. Paphnutius gave his consent, and the two of them ratified their union. Euphrosyne, however, with the fear of God in her heart, did not wish to soil herself in such ephemeral pleasures. She desired rather to keep her virginity pure and to betroth herself to Christ.

3. One day, Paphnutius was invited to the monastery for the monastery's communal feast. He went there and spent three joy-filled days with the monks. But Euphrosyne [still at home] secretly shaved her head and put on the garments of a man and collected together five hundred dahekans. When she learned that her father had returned from the monastery, she got on a ship and went by a different path to the same monastery, for she said to herself, "If I were to go to a women's convent my father would recognize me and remove me forcibly for the sake of my intended."

4. *Գնաց ի վանսն եւ եւտ ողջոյն Հօր վանացն եւ ասէ. Ես ներքինի եմ ի տանէ թագաւորին Թէոդոսի եւ ցանկացայ կրօնաւորական վարուց, եւ ի քաղաքին մերոյ կրօնաւորք խաղաղութեամբ ի վանս որպէս աստ ոչ գտանին. եւ լուայ վասն աստուածահաճոյ վարուց սրբութեան ձերոյ, եւ եկի առ ձեզ զի կեցուցից զոգի իմ. ունիմ ինչս բազումս եւ եթէ օգտեցայց ինչ հոգւով՝ տաց զայն վանացս: Եւ հանեալ զհինգ հարիւր դահեկանն ետ ցհայրն:*

5. *Ասէ հայր վանացն. Բարի եկիր որդեակ, եթէ հաճոյ է քեզ վանքս՝ կեցջիր ընդ մեզ: Եհարց եւ զանունն: Եւ նա ասէ. Սմարագդոս, որ թարգմանի զմրուխտ: Ասէ հայրն. Վասն զի դեռ մանուկ ես չէ պարտ միայն կեալ քեզ, այլ վերակացու քեզ տաց որ ուսուցանէ քեզ զկարգ եւ զգիր կրօնաւորական ժուժկալութեան: Ասէ Սմարագդոս. Որպէս հաճոյ է քեզ այնպէս արասջիր, զի ես պատրաստ եմ կատարել զհրամայեալսն ի քէն:*

6. *Եւ կոչեաց հայրն կրօնաւոր մի Ագաբիոս անուն, այր ճգնաւոր եւ աստուածահաճոյ, եւ ասէ. Առ զտէր Սմարագդոս քեզ աշակերտ եւ որդի, եւ այնպէս արասցես զդա իբրեւ զքեզ: Եւ յետ եօթն աւուր արար զնա կրօնաւոր: Իսկ այլ կրօնաւորքն տեսանէին զգեղեցկութիւն երեսացն Սմարագդոսի, տրտնջէին զհօրէն եթէ չէր պարտ այնպիսի տեսլեամբ մանուկ արկանել ի վանս վասն սատանայական հնարիցն:*

7. *Եւ գիտացեալ հօրն կոչեաց զԱգապիոս եւ պատուիրեաց նմա յարգելական եւ ի նսեմ խցի փակել զՍմարագդոս, եւ անդ միայն տալ աղօթել եւ ճաշակել, եւ ոչ յեկեղեցին եւ ոչ ի սեղանն ելանել: Եւ յոյժ ուրախ եղեւ Սմարագդոս: Եւ արարին այնպէս. արգելին զնա ի մթին խրճիթ, եւ այնչափ ճգնութիւն ստացաւ Սմարագդոս պահօքն եւ աղօթիւք եւ տքնութեամբ՝ որ զարմանայր Ագապիոս եւ պատմէր հօրն եւ եղբարցն, եւ որպէս զհրեշտակ ընդունէին զնա:*

4. So [Euphrosyne] went to the monastery, greeted the abbot of the monastery, and said, "I am a eunuch from the court of Emperor Theodosius, and I am longing for the monastic life. In our city the monks are found to be not so happy in the monasteries as they are here. I heard about the God-pleasing holiness of your lives, and so I came to you that I may save my soul. I have considerable wealth, and if I find any profit for my soul, I will give it to this monastery." She then pulled out the five hundred dahekans and gave it to the abbot.

5. The abbot of the monastery responded, "Welcome, my son. If this monastery is agreeable to you, you may live with us." He then asked him for his name, and she replied, "Smaragdos," which is translated "Emerald." The abbot said, "Because you are still a youth, it is not permitted for you to live alone, so I will appoint a guardian for you who will teach you the order and the rule of the monastic discipline." Smaragdos responded, "Do as you wish, for I am ready to carry out whatever you demand from me."

6. The abbot then summoned a monk, Agapius by name, very ascetic and pleasing to God, and said, "Take Smaragdos here as your disciple and son, and make him such as yourself." Seven days later [the abbot] made [Smaragdos] a monk. But when the other monks beheld the beauty of the visage of Smaragdos they began to complain to the abbot that it was not right to admit a youth of such beauty into the monastery on account of the wiles of the devil.

7. When the abbot perceived this, he summoned Agapius and ordered him to confine Smaragdos to an enclosed and sequestered cell, to allow him to pray and take his meals alone there but not to go into the church or into the refectory. Smaragdos was quite happy about this. And so they carried this out and enclosed him in a remote hut. Smaragdos acquired such asceticism by his fasts, prayers, and vigils that Agapius marveled and told the abbot and his brothers, and they received him like an angel.

8. Իսկ Պափնուտիոս Հայրն իւր գնաց ի տուն, եւ մտեալ ի սենեակ զԵփրոսինէ ոչ եգիտ, եւ սկսաւ այլագունել երեսք իւր․ Հարցանէր ընդ ծառայսն եւ ընդ աղախնայսն եթէ ու՞ր իցէ կամ զինչ եղեւ։ Եւ նոքա ասեն եթէ․ Երէկ ի տանս էր, բայց այսօր զնա ոչ տեսաք։ Եւ նա կարծեաց եթէ ի տան ուր խօսեցեալն էր՝ եկեալ տարան զնա։ Եւ յղեաց փութապէս ծառայս առ ի տեղեկանալ։ Եւ նոցա լուեալ՝ եկին յրնթացս ի տունն Պափնուտիոսի, եւ ի տարակուսի լեալ՝ առաքեցին ծովով եւ ցամաքաւ երիվարօք ի դրացիս ի քաղաքս եւ ի գաւառս ի չէնս եւ ի կղզիս, ի վանորայս յանապատաւորս․ եւ յորժամ ոչ գտին եւ անցին բազում աւուրք՝ յուսահատեցան։

9. Փետտեաց Պափնուսիոս զմօրուսն եւ զհերս գլխոյն եւ անկաւ ե վերայ մոխրոյ, եւ բաղխէր զերեսն։ Ողբայր մեծաւ հառաչմամբ զդուստրն իւր եւ ասէր․ Վայ ինձ քաղցր զաւակ իմ, վայ ինձ լոյս աչաց իմոց, վայ ինձ ցուպ ծերութեան իմոյ, վայ ինձ զի ոչ գտանեմ ուրախութիւն տրտմութեանս։ Ով զգանձն իմ կողոպտեաց, ո՞վ զմեծութիւն իմ յափշտակեաց, ո՞վ զմարգարիտն իմ ցրուեաց, ո՞վ զճրագն իմ շիջոյց․ ո՞վ զփառս տանն իմոյ գողացաւ, ո՞վ զվայելչութիւն անձին իմոյ ջնջեաց․ ո՞ր գայլ զգառն իմ գիշատեաց, ո՞ր տեղի թագոյց զարեգակնանման տեսութիւնն, ո՞վ գերեաց զթագաւորական գեղեցկութիւնն, ո՞վ սպան զտրտմութեան իմոյ լուծիչն։ Նա էր նեղսրտութեան իմոյ անդորրիչ, նա էր ծանրութեանս իմոյ թեթեւացուցիչ։ Հող երկրի մի ծածկեր զարիւն մարմնոյ իմոյ, մինչեւ գիտացից թէ զինչ եղեւ զաւակն իմ Եփրոսինէ։

10. Եւ յետ բազում աւուրց եմուտ ի նաւ եւ գնաց ի վանսն յորում էր Եփրոսինէ, եւ անկաւ յոտս հօր վանացն պատմեաց նմա զյանկարծակի կորուստ դստերն իւրոյ։ Եւ յոյժ տրտմեցաւ նա եւ հրամայեաց եղբարցն պահօք եւ աղօթիւք զեօթն օր ուխտ կատարել եւ տքնութեամբ զԱստուած աղաչել զի յայտնեսցէ նոցա զզաւակն նորա։ Եւ ամենեւին ոչ երեւեցոյց Աստուած ումեք՝ վասն զի աղօթք Սմարագդոսի ծածկէր զաղօթս կրօնաւորացն, զի աղաչէր զԱստուած որպէս զի ի կենդանութեան իւրում մի ումեք երեւեսցի։

8. Meanwhile her father Paphnutius returned to his home and entered her room, but when he did not find Euphrosyne, his face began to lose its color. He began to question the servants and the maids about where she was or what had happened to her. They responded, "She was here in the house yesterday, but we have not seen her today." He then thought that perhaps someone had gone to the house of her intended in order to bring her back, so he quickly sent servants to find out. When they heard [what had happened], they went with haste to the house of Paphnutius. They became quite anxious and sent men out on horseback by sea and by dry land, to neighbors, to cities, to villages, to towns, to islands, to monasteries, to desert areas, but when after many days they still did not find her, they began to lose all hope.

9. Paphnutius tore out his beard and the hairs from his head and threw himself upon an ash heap and began to strike his face. He lamented his daughter with much groaning, and he said, "Woe to me, my sweet child! Woe to me, light of my eyes! Woe to me, staff of my old age! Woe to me, who finds no joy in these sufferings. Who has stolen my treasure? Who has plundered my wealth? Who has run off with my pearl? Who has extinguished my lamp? Who has robbed me of the glory of my house? Who has wiped away the delight of my face? What wolf has ravaged my lamb? What place has concealed her radiant visage? Who has taken captive her royal beauty? Who has killed her who takes away my every sorrow? She was the one who stilled my irascibility and who lightens my every burden. O soil of the earth, do not cover up the blood of my flesh until I discover what has happened to my child, Euphrosyne."

10. Many days later he boarded a boat and went to the monastery where Euphrosyne was. There he fell at the feet of the abbot of the monastery and informed him of the sudden loss of his daughter. He was greatly saddened, and he commanded the brothers to make a pledge to fast and to pray and to keep vigil for seven days, praying to God that He might reveal to them [the whereabouts of Paphnutius]'s daughter. But God did not reveal anything to anyone because the prayers of Smaragdos, who was praying that God would reveal to no one that she was still alive, were eclipsing the prayers of the monks.

11. Եւ յետ եօթն աւուր ասէ Հայր վանացն. Գիտասջիր տէր Պափնոտիոս որ եթէ ի չարիս տուեալ էր զանձն իւր՝ Աստուած յայտնէր մեզ, այլ նա ըստ հաճոյիցն Աստուծոյ գնաց, եւ դու գոհացիր զԱստուծոյ: Եւ սակաւիկ մի մխիթարեցաւ ի բազում սգոյն, գնաց ի տուն իւր եւ գոհանալով փառաւորէր զԱստուած, եւ բաշխէր զինչս իւր կարօտելոց: Եւ յամենայն տարի երկիցս եւ երիցս երթայր Պափնոտիոս ի վանսն եւ խօսէր ընդ Սմարագդոսի բանս հոգեկանս եւ մխիթարէր յանձն իւր: Եւ ասէ ցհայրն. Յոյժ օգտիմ ի բանից արգելական կրօնաւորին, եւ մեծապէս մխիթարի անձն իմ: Եւ դառնայր ի տուն իւր:

12. Եւ արար Սմարագդոս ի վանսն մեծ եւ առաքինի ճգնութեամբ ամս երեսուն եւ ութ յարգելական խցին. եւ գիտաց զվախճանն իւր մերձեալ: Եւ եղեւ գնալ ի վանսն Պափնոտիոսի. եւ երթեալ առ Սմարագդոս կօսէր եւ լսէր ի նմանէ բան մխիթարութեան եւ փրկութեան. եւ ասէ Պափնոտիոս. Յոյժ տրտում եմ, սուրբ Հայր, վասն դստերն իմոյ Եփրոսինեայ որ ոչ գիտացի թէ զինչ եղեւ: Ասէ Սմարագդոս. Համբերեա ի վանս զերիս աւուրս եւ Աստուած ծանուցանէ քեզ եթէ որպէս կամեցաւ առնել ի զաւակն քո: Եւ յորժամ ծանրացաւ կոչեաց զհայրն իւր միայն առանձինն եւ ասէ. Քանզի արար յիս Աստուած որպէս կամեցաւ, եւ կատարեաց զցանկութիւնս իմ, այժմ կամիմ զքեզ մխիթարել վասն զաւակին քո որ ոչ տրտմեցիս: Ես եմ Եփրոսինէ դուստրն քո, տես եւ հաւատովք մխիթարեաց: Եւ վասն զի յանձին կալայ հօր վանացս տալ ի յընչից իմոց՝ դու զբաժինն զոր խոստացար տալ փեսային վասն իմ, տուր ի վանքս: Եւ դու քո ինքնին ձեռօքդ մազեղինաւս իմով թաղեա զիս յորժամ պատեսցես զմարմինս իմ: Եւ զայս ասացեալ՝ աւանդեաց զհոգին իւր առ Աստուած Մարտի Ը:

13. Եւ յորժամ լուաւ Պարփնոտիոս յահագին հիացմանէն լուծաւ եւ անկաւ յերկիր որպէս մեռեալ: Եւ ընթացաւ Ագապիոս ցանեաց ջուր յերեսն, յարոյց եւ հարցանէր եթէ. Զի՞նչ եղեւ քեզ: Ասէ. Թոյլ տուք ինձ աստ մեռանել, զի տեսի այսօր զարմանալի սքանչելիս: Եւ քակեցին զտախտակս արգելական խցին, եմուտ Պափնոտիոս եւ անկաւ ի վերայ լանջացն, եւ արտասուօքն լուաց զերեսս երանելոյն:

11. After those seven days, the abbot of the monastery said, "Know, Lord Paphnutius, that if any evil had befallen her soul, God would have revealed it to us. She has gone according to the pleasure of God, so you should give praise to God." Thus he was given a little comfort from his great sorrow. He returned to his home and with praise gave glory to God, and he distributed his wealth to those in need. Every year thereafter Paphnutius would go two or three times to the monastery, and he would converse with Smaragdos on spiritual matters and would receive much consolation for his soul. And he said to the abbot, "I have profited from the words of that cloistered monk, and my soul is greatly comforted." And he returned to his home.

12. Smaragdos passed thirty-eight years in that monastery in his cloistered hut [practicing] great and heroic asceticism, when he realized that his death was approaching. It happened then that Paphnutius came to the monastery to speak to Smaragdos and to hear from him words of comfort and salvation. Paphnutius said to him, "I am very said, Holy Father, because I have never learned what happened to my daughter Euphrosyne." Smaragdos replied, "Wait here in the monastery for three days, and God will reveal to you just what He had wished to do to your child." And when her condition had worsened, she summoned her father alone and said to him, "Because God has done to me what He wanted and He fulfilled all my desires, now I wish to give you comfort concerning your child so that you need not be sad any longer. I am your daughter Euphrosyne; look and with faith be comforted. Because I had agreed with the abbot of the monastery to donate some of my wealth, whatever portion you had promised to give to my fiancé on my behalf, please give it now to the monastery. And as for you, bury me in this haircloth with your own hands when you inter my body." As soon as she had said this, she committed her soul to God on the eighth of March.

13. When Paphnutius heard this, he was overcome with alarming astonishment, and he fell to the ground as if he were dead. Agapius quickly splashed water on his face, sat him up, and asked, "What has happened to you?" He responded, "Let me die right here, for today I have seen a wondrous miracle." They then took down the wooden planks from the enclosed hut and Paphnutius went in, threw himself upon her bosom, and with his tears washed the face of the blessed one.

14. *Գնաց Ագապիոս եւ պատմեաց Հօր վանացն եւ եղբարցն, եւ ամենեքեան անդ ժողովեցան։ Եւ Հանեալ զմարմինն եդին առաջի դրան եկեղեցոյն, եւ ողբայր Պափնուտիոս լալագին արտասուօք. Վայ ինձ դուստր իմ Եփրոսինէ, ընդէ՞ր ոչ նախ ասէիր ինձ զխորՀուրդ քո, որ եւ ես ընդ քեզ մեռանէի. եւ եթէ ո՞րպէս կրեցեր զգաղտնի խայթոցս սատանայի, եւ անցեր ընդ պետութիւնս եւ ընդ իշխանութիւնս. եւ մտեր յանանց կեանսն եւ յանստուեր լոյսն, եւ յանտրտում ուրախութիւնսն։*

15. *Նոյնպէս եւ Հայր վանացն եւ կրօնաւորքն ողբալով աղաղակէին. Ով Հարսն Քրիստոսի մի մոռանար զընկերակիցքս քո, այլ աղօթիւք քո տացի մեզ զգաստութիւն եւ զօրութիւն կեալ ըստ Հաճոյից Աստուծոյ եւ Հասանել մասին սրբոցն։*

16. *Եւ ժողովեցան անդ բազմութիւն կրօնաւորաց յայլ եւ այլ վանօրթից, եւ զարմանային ընդ ժուժկալութիւնն Եփրոսինեայ եւ փառաւորէին զԱստուած։*

17. *Եւ մի ոմն կրօնաւոր միականի եդեալ զերեսն ի վերայ երեսացն արտասուօք Համբուրէր զաչսն, եւ առժամայն բացաւ խաւարեալ ակն։ Եւ այսու առաւելապէս փառաւորեաց Աստուած յերկրի զաղախինն իւր։*

18. *Եւ ըստ արժանեացն սաղմոսիւք եւ օրՀնութեամբ եդիր Հայրն իւր զնշխարս նորա մազեղինաւն ի տապանի։*

19. *Յայսմ աւուր երանելին Թէոփիլաքտոս, որ թարգմանի աստուածապաՀ, Նիկոմիդացւոց արքեպիսկոպոսն, Հանգեաւ յաքսորս. զոր ընկէց յաթոռոյն Լէոն Հերձուածող արքայն, վասն զի պատուէր զոր նա անարգէր՝ զտէրունական եւ զսրբոց պատկերս։*

20. *Եւ յայսմ աւուր պարոն Կոստանդին որդի Լեւոն թագաւորի բարի վարուք փոխեցաւ ի Քրիստոս, եւ կայ ի Կոստանդինուպօլիս։*

14. Agapius went and told the abbot of the monastery and the brothers, and they all gathered together in that place. They took her corpse and set it in front of the doors to the church, and Paphnutius wailed with tears and lamentation. "Woe to me, Euphrosyne, my daughter! Why did you not tell me your secret before so that I might have died with you? How you trampled down the hidden stings of Satan and surpassed the powers and dominions and have now entered into everlasting life and into that light without shadow and that joy with no sadness!"

15. In the same fashion, the abbot of the monastery and the monks cried out in lamentation. "O bride of Christ, do not forget your close companions; may your prayers give to us the watchfulness and strength to live according to the will of God and to attain the lot of the saints."

16. A multitude of monks then began to gather there from other places and from other monasteries, and they all marveled at the perseverance of Euphrosyne and gave glory to God.

17. A certain monk, who had only one [good] eye, pressed his face against the face [of Euphrosyne], and full of tears kissed her eyes. Immediately his darkened eye was opened. In this way, God greatly glorified his handmaiden upon the earth.

18. Then, with suitable psalms and benedictions, her father clothed her in her haircloth and deposed her remains into the coffin.

19. On this day the blessed Theophylactos, which is translated "guarded by God," the archbishop of Nicomedia, departed this life in exile. Leo, the schismatic emperor,[1] deposed him from his seat because he had venerated the images of the Lord and of the saints, which he himself had despised.

20. And on this day Baron Constantine, son of King Levon,[2] passed on to Christ after a good life. [His body] is in Constantinople.

---

1. Leo V, known as "the Armenian," and also a spirited iconoclast, ruled as emperor from 813 until his assassination on Christmas Day, 820.

2. This is presumably Constantine I, one of many sons of King Levon II, who was king of Cilicia from 1270 to 1289. A decade after King Levon's death, Constantine was exiled to Constantinople by his brother Hetum II who—not without family intrigue—had succeeded their father.

Արեգի Ա

Մարտի Թ

Տօն է սրբոց Քառասնիցն որք ի Սեբաստիա վկայութեամբ նահատակեալ կատարեցան

1. *Սուրբ եւ փառաւորեալ քառասուն վկայիցն անուանքն են այսոքիկ. Դոմետիանոս, Կիւրղոս, Ուվաղէս, Եւտիքիոս, Իւսիքիկոս, Եւնոյիկոս, Եղիանոս, Փլաւիոս, Սմարագդոս, Քսանթիոս, Սիսինիոս, Ղեւոնդիոս, Մելիտոն, Սեւերիանոս, Փիլոքտեմոն, Անկէաս, Իրակլոս, Եքտիկիոս, Կիւրիոն, Այետիոս, Ալեկսանդրոս, Ակակիոս, Վաղերիանոս, Նիկոլայոս, Եւտիւքիոս, Յովհաննէս, Բեբիանոս, Քուդիոն, Լուսիմաքոս, Գայիոս, Ագդիոս, Իլիոդէս, Դոմնէս, Աթանասիոս, Պոխսկոս, Կանդիտոս, Սակերդոն, Գորգոնիոս, Թէոդուլոս, Թէոփիլոս:*
2. *Սոքա էին ի Կապադովկացւոց երկրէն, ի մի գունդս դասեալք էին, զօրականք Լիկիանոսի արքային:*
3. *Իսկ դատաւորն Ագրիկողայոս տարաւ զնոսա ի քաղաքն Սեբաստիոյ, եւ յոյժ բռնադատէր զնոսա զոհել կռոցն, եւ ամենեւին ոչ կարաց մեկնել զնոսա ի Քրիստոսի հաւատոցն: Արկ զնոսա ի բանդ, եւ յաղօթելն նոցա երեւեցաւ Փրկիչն եւ քաջալերեաց զնոսա:*
4. *Եւ յետ ութ աւուր հասաւ դուքսն ի Կեսարիոյ, եւ նստան ի միասին յատենի, եւ տարան զնոսա առաջի, եւ հարցանէին վասն հաւատոցն Քրիստոսի եթէ ուրանան եւ զոհեն կռոցն: Եւ սուրբքն որպէս ի միոյ բերանոյ յանդիմանեցին աստուածային բանիւք զանաստուած մոլորութիւն կռապաշտիցն:*

March 9

Areg 1

The feast of the forty saints who died bravely by martyrdom

1. The names of these forty glorified martyrs are Dometianos, Cyril, Valens, Eutychius, Hesychius, Eunoichos, Aelianos, Flavius, Smaragdos, Xanthios, Sisinnios, Leontius, Meletios, Severianos, Philoctemon, Aggias, Heraclios, Ecdikios, Kyrion, Aetios, Alexander, Akakios, Valerianus, Nikolaos, Claudius, John, Vivianos, Choudion, Lysimachos, Gaius, Aglios, Elias, Domnos, Athanasios, Priscus, Candidus, Sakerdon, Gorgonios, Theodoulos, and Theophilos.

2. These men were all from the region of Cappadocia and were enrolled in the same legion as soldiers of the emperor Licinius.[1]

3. The judge Agricolaos led them to the city of Sebaste and put great pressure on them to sacrifice to the idols, but he was completely unable to separate them from their faith in Christ. He threw them into prison, and while they were praying, the Savior appeared to them and encouraged them.

4. After eight days the general arrived from Caesarea, and he [and the judge] sat down together in the tribunal and had [the forty] brought in before them. They then asked them to renounce their faith in Christ and to sacrifice to the idols. Those holy ones, as if with one mouth, repudiated with godlike speech the errors of those godless idol worshippers.

---

1. Licinius was Roman emperor from 308 to 324.

5. Եւ հրամայեցին քարամբք զբերանս նոցա խորտակել, եւ զօրականքն սկսան զմիմեանս քարկոծել: Եւ առեալ վէմ մի պիղծ դուքսն ձգեաց ի վերայ սրբոցն եհար զդատաւորն եւ խորտակեաց զերեսն: Արկին զնոսա ի բանդ. եւ յաղօթել նոցա երեւեցաւ դարձեալ Փրկիչն եւ ասէ. Որ հաւատայ յիս թէպէտ եւ մեռանի՝ կեցցէ. քաջալերեցարուք եւ մի երկնչիք ի չարչարանաց նոցա զի առ ժամանակ մի են, համբերեցէք սակաւիկ մի եւ յերկնից պսակս ընկալջիք:

6. Եւ ընդ առաւօտն կացուցին զնոսա առաջի բռնաւորին, եւ ասեն. Զոր ինչ առնելոց էք՝ արարէք, զի մեք զՔրիստոս ոչ ուրանամք: Յայնժամ կապեցին չուանօք զպարանոց եւ զձեռս նոցա, եւ տարան զամենեսեան ի լիճն, եւ ընկեցին մերկս ի մէջ ջրոցն յաւուրս ձմերայնոյ: Եւ սառուցեալ յոյժ լճին պատառեցան մարմինք նոցա ի խիստ սառուցմանէն, եւ հեղոյր արիւնն ի վերայ ոտից իւրեանց յառաջին պահու գիշերոյն, եւ սուրբքն յաղօթից ոչ դադարէին:

7. Մի ոմն ի նոցանէ ոչ կարաց ժուժել յուժգին սառուցմանէն, ելեալ ի լճէն եմուտ ի բաղանիսն զոր պատրաստեցին նոցա անօրէնքն, եւ առժամայն ի ջերմութենէ բաղանեացն լուծեալ հալեցաւ:

8. Եւ յերրորդ ժամու գիշերոյ ծագեաց ի վերայ նոցա արեւ որպէս յամարայնոյ ի ջերմութենէ հալեցան սառուցեալ ջուրքն: Եւ մի ոմն ի զօրականացն որք պահէին զսուրբսն յարթնութեան էր, եւ նայէր թէ ուստի իցէ լոյսն: Եւ տեսանէ երեսուն եւ ինն պսակս իջեալ ի վերայ գլխոց մարտիրոսացն, եւ գիտաց եթէ որ փախեաւն ի բաղանիսն ի թիւ քառասնիցն ոչ դասեցաւ, մերկացաւ զհանդերձսն վազեաց ի ներքս ի լիճն, եկաց ի մէջ սրբոցն, աղաղակեաց եւ ասէ, Քրիստոնեայ եմ:

9. Եւ ընդ առաւօտն հանին զնոսա ի լճէն յեզր, եւ հաստ բրովք զանձինս եւ զոլոքս նոցա ջարդեցին սաստիկ. եւ առ հասարակ ի միասին աւանդեցին զհոգիս իւրեանց Մարտի Թ: Բայց մի ոմն որոյ անունն էր Մելիտոն՝ դեռ եւս կենդանի էր. եւ մայրն աղաչէր զնա եւ խրատ տայր. Քաղցրիկ որդեակ իմ, սակաւիկ մի համբերեա եւ կատարեացիս ընդ սրբոցն. եւ մի երկնչիր զի Քրիստոս եկեալ է քեզ յօգնականութիւն:

5. The [prince and judge] then gave the order to break their jaws with rocks, but the soldiers began to stone each other. That abominable general then grabbed a rock and hurled it at the holy ones, but it struck the judge and broke his jaw. They threw the [forty] into prison, and while they were praying, the Savior again appeared to them and said, "Whoever believes in me, even though he dies, he shall live (John 11:25). Be courageous and do not fear their tortures, for they are but momentary; endure for a little while, and you will receive crowns from heaven."

6. In the morning the [forty] were brought before that tyrannical [general], and they said, "Whatever you are going to do, do it, for we are not going to renounce Christ." So they were bound with ropes about their necks and their hands, and they were all brought to a lake where they were thrown naked into the waters on a harsh winter day. The lake was so cold that their flesh cracked open from the bitter cold, and their blood poured out all over their feet by the first watch of the night, but these holy ones never ceased from their prayers.

7. A certain one of them was unable to endure such extreme cold, so he removed himself from the lake and went into a bath that the lawless ones had prepared for them; he was immediately relieved and thawed by the warmth of the bath.

8. At the third hour of the night the sun rose over them as if in summertime, and from its heat the frozen waters melted. One of the soldiers who was on watch guarding these holy ones was gazing upon [the place] whence the light had come. He saw thirty-nine crowns descending upon the heads of the martyrs, and he knew that the one who had fled into the bath was no longer included in the number forty. Therefore, he stripped off his clothes, ran out into the middle of the lake, went in among those holy ones, and said, "I am a Christian."

9. At dawn they removed them from the lake to the shore, and with thick rods they violently beat their bodies and their shinbones, and they all together committed their souls [to God] on the ninth of March. But one of them, whose name was Meletios, remained alive. His mother began to implore him and to exhort him: "My sweet son, endure a little longer and you will end your life among the saints; do not fear, for Christ is coming to your assistance."

10. *Եւ զօրականքն եկին եւ բերին սայլս, եդին զմարմինս նոցա ի վերայ զի տարցեն յայրումն, եւ զՄելիտոն զի դեռ եւս կենդանի էր Թողին: Եւ մայրն բարձեալ յուսն զորդին ընԹանայր զկնի սայլիցն. եւ նոյնժամայն ի վերայ ուսոյ մօրն աւանդեաց զհոգին իւր, եւ ընկէց զնա մայրն ի վերայ այլ սրբոցն: Եւ յորժամ այրեցին զմարմինս նոցա ընկեցին ի մերձակայ գետն, եւ ամենեւին ոչ ցրուեցան այլ ի միում տեղւոջ ժողովեցան:*

11. *Եւ յետ երից աւուրց երեւեցան սուրբքն Սեբաստիոյ եպիսկոպոսին Պետրոսի եւ ասեն. Պահեալ կան մարմինք մեր յայս նիշ տեղի ի մերձակայ գետն, եկ եւ հան զմեզ: Եւ առեալ եպիսկոպոսին զաղտ զուխտ եկեղեցւոյն գնաց ի գիշերի յեզր գետոյն, եւ փայլէին նշխարք սրբոցն ի մէջ ջրոցն որպէս աստեղք: Ժողովեցին զնոսա եւ եԹէ մնացեալ էր ուրեք ի նշխարացն՝ ի ճաճանչից փայլմանցն գտանէին. եւ առեալ եդին ի տապանս:*

10. The soldiers returned and brought wagons with them. They threw the corpses onto them to carry them off to be burned, but they left Meletios there since he was still alive. Then the mother threw her son over her shoulder and ran after the wagons, and at that moment, while he was over the shoulder of his mother, he committed his soul [to God], and his mother threw him upon the other holy ones. After they had burned their bodies, they threw them into a nearby river. They did not float off in separate directions but all gathered into one place.

11. Three days later those holy ones appeared to Peter, the bishop of Sebaste, and said, "Our bodies have been preserved in such-and-such a place in the nearby river. Go and take them out." The bishop secretly took some clergy of the church and went at night to the bank of the river, and the remains of the saints were shining as bright as stars in the middle of the water. [The bishop and clergy] gathered them all up and found every fragment of their remains by the luminous rays they emitted. They then took the[ir remains] and laid them in tombs.

Արեգի Բ

Մարտի Ժ

Վկայաբանութիւն սրբուհւոյն Թէոդոսիայ

1. *Երանելին Թէոդոսիա աղախինն Քրիստոսի էր ի քաղաքէն Տիւրոսի, քրիստոնեայ հաւատով, եւ էր ամաց ութ եւ տասնից: Եւ կացեալ առաջի Ուրվիկիոյ իշխանին՝ խոստովանեցաւ զՔրիստոս, եւ դից ոչ եպագ երկիր, եւ ոչ զոհեաց: Տանջեցին զնա ուժգին եւ ընկեցին ի հուր, եւ հանգեաւ ի Քրիստոս բարի խոստովանութեամբ:*

Յայսմ աւուր վկայութիւն սրբոյն Մելիտոնի

2. *Ընդ աւուրսն ընդ այնոսիկ հրամայեաց Մաքսիմիանոս կռապաշտ արքայն, զի որք իցեն քրիստոնեայք յիւրում արքայական տանն՝ լուծցեն զգօտիս իւրեանց եւ անկանիցին ի պատուոյն եւ ելցեն յարքունեացն: Եւ բազումք կամաւորութեամբ վասն սիրոյն Քրիստոսի լուծին զգօտիս իւրեանց, թողին զպատիւս եւ ելին արտաքս:*

March 10

Areg 2

The martyrdom of the Saint Theodosia

1. The blessed Theodosia, the handmaid of Christ, was from the city of Tyre. She was a Christian and eighteen years old. When she was brought before the prefect Urbicius, she professed Christ and would neither worship nor sacrifice to the gods. They brutally tortured her and threw her into a fire, and she fell asleep in Christ with a good confession.

On this day is the martyrdom of Saint Hesychius

2. In those days the impious emperor Maximinus commanded that those in his royal palace who were Christians were to remove their belts,[1] to divest themselves of their honors, and to depart from the royal court. Many, impelled by their love of Christ, willingly removed their belts, abandoned their honors, and departed.

---

1. The military-style *belt* (Lat. *cingulum*) was an important *symbol* of imperial service.

3. *Եւ տեսեալ զՍիւքիոս բարկացաւ զի գլուխ էր մեծ իշխանացն, Հրամայեաց մերկացուցանել ի պատուական Հանդերձիցն, եւ զգեցուցանել նմա կանացի անարգ Հանդերձ. եւ նախատինս առնելով առաքեաց զնա առ աղախնայս զի փաստակեսցի խլիկ եւ ոստայն: Եւ բազումք ի սիրելեաց իւրոց գային առ նա ի տեսութիւն: Եւ լուեալ Մաքսիմիանոսի կոչեաց առ ինքն եւ ասէ. Ով մագիստրէ, ընդէ՞ր թողեր զպատիւն քո եւ լսող լինիս քրիստոնէից. մինթէ կարող են զայն պատիւ տալ քեզ զոր ես ետու: Ասէ սուրբն Սիւքիոս. Քո պատիւդ առ ժամանակ մի է՝ բայց խոստովանութիւնն Քրիստոսի յաւիտենական շնորհ է եւ պատիւ:*

4. *Եւ դառնացաւ յոյժ եւ Հրամայեաց եւ կապեցին երկանաքար ծանր ի պարանոց նորա եւ ընկեցին ի գետն որ կոչի Որէնդին. եւ այնպէս կատարեցաւ ի Քրիստոս բարի խոստովանութեամբ Մարտի Ժ:*

Յայսմ աւուր վկայութիւն եւ փոխումն սրբոյ վկային Քրիստոսի Ամենաւագին

5. *Երանելիս այս՝ էր ի գաւառէն Դերջանու, ի գեղջէն Կառնբերդակ, այր աշխարհիկ եւ երկրագործ, գեղեցիկ դիմօք եւ վայելուչ Հասակաւ՝ ուժեղ եւ զօրաւոր մարմնով: Եւ ինքն էր բարեպաշտ եւ երկիւղած յԱստուծոյ եւ բարի ծնողաց զաւակ. անուն Հօր նորա էր Թիմեր, եւ մօրն Ջամենտիկին:*

6. *Սա ունէր այլազգւոյ ումեմն սակաւ ինչ պարտս եւ նա եկեալ նեղէր զսուրբն, եւ զգրաստն բռնութեամբ քարշեալ տանէր իբրեւ գրաւական: Ասէ Ամէնաւագ ցեղբայր իւր. Մի թողուր տանել զգրաստն, քեզ լիցի քան թէ այլազգւոյն: Ասէ եղբայրն. Ոչ է ինձ պիտոյ: Եւ բարկացեալ Ամէնաւագն ասէ. Որպիսի քրիստոնէութիւն է այդ ես ոչ գիտեմ:*

3. When [the emperor] saw Hesychius [departing], he became very angry, for he was the head of the prefects. He commanded that [Hesychius] be stripped of his royal garments and be clothed in the demeaning garments of a woman. Having subjected him to this insult, he then sent him among the maidservants to work at spinning and weaving. Many of his friends came to visit him. When he heard of this, Maximinus summoned him before him and said, "O Captain, why did you abandon your office and become a follower of the Christians? Are they able to give you the honors that I have given you?" The holy Hesychius replied, "Your honors are temporal, whereas profession in Christ is an eternal grace and honor."

4. The [emperor] was greatly offended, and he commanded that they tie a heavy millstone around [Hesychius]'s neck and throw him into the river known as the Orontes. In this fashion he met his end in Christ with a good confession on the tenth of March.

On this day is the martyrdom and feast day of the holy martyr of Christ, Amenavag

5. This holy one was from the region of Derjan, from the village of Karnberdak. He was a layman and a farmer, handsome in form and of proportionate size, strong and vigorous in body. And he was pious and a fearer of God and a child of good parents. His father's name was Timer and his mother's was Zamentikin.

6. He had accumulated a little debt with a certain Muslim, and that one came to press the holy one [into paying on it], and he forcibly took his horse away as collateral. Amenavag said to his brother, "Do not let him take away my horse; let it rather belong to you than to that Muslim." But his brother responded, "I have no need of it." Amenavag became annoyed and said, "Whatever kind of Christianity that is, I don't recognize it."

7. *Յայնժամ ասէ այլազգին ցԱմէնաւագն. Ահա ոչ հաճեցար դու ընդ քրիստոնէութիւն, ապա ընկալար զայլզգութիւն. եւ կացին վկայք եթէ ուրացաւ զՔրիստոս։ Զայս լուեալ երկեաւ, եւ փախուցեալ թաքեաւ ժամանակս ինչ, եւ դարձեալ եկն ի գիւղն իւր Կառնբերդակ, եւ եկաց անդ աւուրս ինչ։ Եւ տեսեալ թէ այլազգիք ոչ դադարին ի խնդրելոյ՝ եւ ինքն ոչ կարէ մնալ թաքուն, գնաց առ քահանայն եւ խոստովան եղեւ զմեղս իւր, եւ դաւանեալ զՀայր, եւ զՈրդի եւ զՀոգին սուրբ, հաղորդեցաւ ի մարմնոյ եւ յարենէն Քրիստոսի, եւ զինեալ զինքն հոգեւոր զինով պատրաստ եղեւ ի պատերազմ։*

8. *Ազդ եղեւ իշխանին որոյ անուն էր Ամիր Մահմուտ, եւ դատաւորին որ կոչէր Ամիր Հասան՝ որ ծարաւի էր արեան քրիստոնէից, եւ առաքեալ զօրականս եւ տարան ի գեղաքաղաքն եւ կացուցին յատեան առաջի իշխանին։ Ասէ իշխանն. Դու ընկալեալ ես զայլազգութիւն։ Եւ նա ասէ. Ես քրիստոնեայ եմ։ Եւ վկայքն ասէին թէ. Ուրացաւ զՔրիստոս։*

9. *Յայնժամ իշխանն առաքեաց առ դատաւորն, եւ նա ասէ. Հաստատո՞ւն իցես ի խոստման քում։ Ասէ սուրբն. Ոչ գիտեմ զինչ իցէ խոստումն իմ։ Ասէ դատաւորն. Յանձն առեալ ես ընդունիլ զայլազգութիւն։ Եւ նա ասէ. Հայ եմ ազգաւ եւ հաւատով քրիստոնեայ։*

10. *Եւ հրամայեաց եւ արկին ի բանդ եւ զաւուրս երկուս ոչ ետուն նմա հաց եւ ջուր. եւ կայր անդադար յաղօթս։ Եւ դարձեալ յետ երկուց աւուրց կոչեաց զնա դատաւորն եւ ասէ. Ուրացիր զՔրիստոս, ապա թէ ոչ՝ սպանանել տամ զքեզ եւ քարկոծել։ Եւ նա ասէ. Ամենայն ազգն իմ քրիստոնեայ է, եւ ես զիմ հօրն եւ զմօրն հաւատն ունիմ եւ քրիստոնեայ եմ։ Ասէ դատաւորն. Դու դարձեալ ես յայլազգութիւն եւ ընդէ՞ր քրիստոնեայ կեաս։ Ասէ վկայն Քրիստոսի. Ես հայ եմ, զՀայրն հաւատամ եւ զՈրդին խոստովանեմ։ Յայնժամ ասէ դատաւորն. Հայհոյեաց. ընդէ՞ր լսէք, խցէք զականջս ձեր եւ հարէք։ Եւ ամբոխն աղաղակէր. Հրաման է իշխանին զի մահու մեռանիցի։ Եւ այլք ասէին թէ. Ուրացաւ զՔրիստոս առաջի իշխանին. եւ ջանային խախտել ի հաւատոցն Քրիստոսի։*

7. Then that Muslim said to Amenavag, "You are not pleased with Christianity, so then embrace Islam!" And witnesses rose up [to say] that he had renounced Christ. When [Amenavag] heard this, he panicked and fled, hiding himself for a time. But he turned back and reentered his village Karnberdak, and he stayed there for a short while. When he saw that the Muslims had not ceased searching for him and that he could not remain hidden there, he went to the priest, confessed his sins, and professed the Father, the Son, and the Holy Spirit. He then partook of the flesh and blood of Christ, and having thus armed himself with spiritual weapons, he was ready for battle.

8. Report of [Amenavag] came to the prince, whose name was Amir Mahmut, and to the judge, who was called Amir Hasan and who thirsted for the blood of Christians. They both sent out soldiers, who brought him to a small village and stood him before the tribunal of the prince. The prince said, "Have you accepted Islam?" And he responded, "I am a Christian." And witnesses said, "He renounced Christ."

9. The prince then sent him over to the judge, who asked him, "Are you steadfast in your profession?" The holy one responded, "I do not know. What might my profession be?" The judge said, "You had committed yourself to accept Islam." And [Amenavag] retorted, "I am Armenian by race and a Christian by faith."

10. [The judge] gave the order, and they threw [Amenavag] into prison. For two days they gave him neither food nor drink, but he remained continually in prayer. After another two days the judge summoned him and said, "Renounce Christ; if not, I will hand you over to be stoned and killed." [Amenavag] responded, "My entire nation is Christian. I have the faith of my father and of my mother; I am Christian." The judge shot back, "You converted to Islam, so why do you live as a Christian?" The martyr of Christ responded, "I am Armenian. I believe in the Father, and I profess the Son." Then the judge shouted, "He has blasphemed! How can you listen to him? Stop up your ears and beat him." The crowd was crying out, "It is the command of the prince that he be put to death." Others, on the other hand, kept saying, "He denounced Christ in the presence of the prince." And they tried to turn him away from his faith in Christ.

11. Եւ դարձեալ ասէ դատաւորն. Ուրացիր զՔրիստոս զի ապրեսցիս. եւ բազում պարգեւս խոստանայր, երիվար, արծաթ եւ ոսկի եւ հանդերձս։ Եւ այլազգիքն յամենայն կողմանէ խթէին եւ ասէին. Միանգամ ասա դառնամ եւ ապրեաց, եւ յետոյ զքո հաւատն պաշտեսջիր։ Եւ բազում քաղցր եւ պատրողական բանիւք ջանային մոլորեցուցանել ի հաւատոցն Քրիստոսի։

12. Ասէ Ամէնաւագ. զՔրիստոս Աստուած պաշտեմ, զԵրրորդութիւնն եւ զմի աստուածութիւնն հաւատամ։ Եւ յորժամ լուան զանունն Քրիստոսի՝ ամենեքեան վկայէին թէ. Մահու արժանի է զի հայհոյեաց։ Եւ յորժամ դատաւորն վճռեաց թէ մահապարտ է, յարուցեալ Ամէնաւագն համբուրեաց զվկայսն եւ ասէ. Սպանէք։ Եւ պատեալ ամբոխն շուրջանակի՝ կալեալք զհերացն եւ զհանդերձիցն հարկանէին մեղմագոյն բռամբ, եւ տանէին ի տեղի սպանմանն, զի յերկիւղէն զարհուրեալ ուրասցի. եւ զհանդերձն իւր զգլխովն արկանէին, եւ դարձեալ աղաղակէին առ դատաւորն եւ առ մեծամեծսն եւ ասէին. Դարձաւ յայլազգութիւն մի հարկանէք։

13. Եւ ընթացեալ դատաւորն մերձ՝ ասէ. Հաւատա՞ս եւ դառնաս յայլազգութիւն։ Եւ ծառայն Քրիստոսի աղաղակեաց. Քրիստոնեայ եմ եւ զՔրիստոս Աստուած հաւատամ։ Եւ բարկացեալ դատաւորն խնդրեաց քար, եւ եհար ուժգին զգլուխն. եւ ասէ ամենեցուն. Քարկոծեցէք։ Եւ սկսան քարկոծել, եւ ոմանք դաշնակաւ խոցեցին զկողսն, եւ այլ ոմն եհար ուժգին զգլուխն երկաթի ուռամբ եւ եհեղ զուղեղ գլխոյն. եւ ամենայն բազմութիւնն քարաձիգ լինէին մինչեւ ծածկեցաւ մարմինն ի քարանցն։ Եւ այսպէս ճշմարիտ խոստովանութեամբ աւանդեաց զհոգին իւր առ Աստուած՝ Մարտի Ժ. յուրբաթի օր ի ժամ խաչելութեանն Քրիստոսի եւ մինչեւ յիններորդ ժամն քարկոծեալ եղեւ։

14. Եւ հանեալ անտի մերկացուցին զհանդերձն եւ կապեալ պարան յոտս՝ քարշել տային քրիստոնէիցն բռնութեամբ յերկիր ի վերայ երեսաց, եւ ամբոխն զկնի ընթանային եւ ամենեքեան հարկանէին զմեռեալ մարմինն. Եւ մեզ մասն լիցի, ասէին։ Որպէս ասէ Տէրն. Եկեսցէ ժամանակ որ սպանանիցեն զձեզ՝ համարիցին պաշտօն մատուցանել Աստուծոյ։ Որ եւ կատարեցաւ այս առ սուրբ վկայն Քրիստոսի Ամէնաւագ։

11. The judge said again, "Renounce Christ so that you might live." And he promised [Amenavag] many gifts: horses, silver, gold, and clothing. Muslims on every side began to taunt him and say, "Just once, say 'I convert' and you will be saved; afterwards, you can practice your own faith." With many such sugar-coated, deceitful words, they tried to dissuade him from his faith in Christ.

12. Amenavag responded, "I serve Christ as God; I believe in the Trinity and in one single Godhead." When they heard the name of Christ, they all testified: "He is worthy of death, for he has blasphemed." And when the judge sentenced him to death, Amenavag rose up, embraced those witnesses, and said, "Kill me." The crowd surrounded him, grabbed him by the hair and by his garments, and struck him with rather tempered force. Then they dragged him to the place of execution so that, seized by fear, he would renounce [Christ]. They cast his garments around his head and again cried out to the judge and to the nobles and said, "He has converted to Islam; do not strike him!"

13. The judge ran up to him and said, "Do you believe? Do you convert to Islam?" But the servant of Christ cried out, "I am a Christian, and I believe Christ is God." The judge became angry, demanded a rock, struck him hard on the head, and said to everyone, "Stone him!" And they began to stone him. Some stabbed his sides with daggers, while someone else violently struck his head with an iron hammer and caused his brains to ooze out from his head. The whole multitude kept stoning him until his entire body was covered over by stones. And in this manner he handed his soul over to God by this true confession on the tenth of March; it was a Friday. He was stoned at the very hour of Christ's crucifixion (he was stoned until the ninth hour).

14. They took [his corpse] away from there, stripped off his garments, and tied a rope around his feet. Then they delegated the Christians to drag it about forcefully with his face to the ground. The crowd followed behind, and they all kept striking the dead body and saying, "Let this be our portion." As the Lord once said, "The time is coming when whoever kills you will think he is offering service to God" (John 16:2), which is exactly what came to pass in the case of Amenavag, the holy martyr of Christ.

15. *Եւ զերիս աւուրս կացեալ անթաղ՝ գազանք կամ թռչունք ոչ մերձեցան առ սուրբ մարմինն։ Եւ այլազգիք կալեալ զշունսն տանէին ի վերայ մարմնոյն, եւ տեսեալ զսուրբ մարմինն յետս վազէին։ Եւ ոչ բնաւ նեխեցաւ այլ բուրէր զանուշահոտութիւն։ Եւ լոյս պայծառ ծագեցաւ ի գիշերին, եւ իբրեւ ղամբար վառէր ի վերայ մարմնոյն, եւ ձայն երգոց եւ պաշտամանց լսէին իբրեւ զքահանայից։ Եւ տեսեալ այլազգեացն կարծելով թէ քահանայք երթեալ գիշերի զի գաղտաբար գողասցին եւ թաղեսցեն, ընթացան առ մարմինն զի կալցեն զքահանայսն, եւ ոչ զոք տեսին։*

16. *Եւ յետ երից աւուրց՝ յաւուր կիւրակէի երթեալ հաւատացեալքն առին հրաման յիշխանէն եւ ի դատաւորէն եւ եդին պատուով գերեզմանի։ Եւ այս եղեւ ի թուին Հայոց եօթն հարիւր եւ ութսուն եւ չորս. յորում ժամանակի Յովհաննէս վարդապետ այր բարեկրօն գտեալ ի գաւառն Դերջան՝ ականատես եւ ականջալուր լինելով գրեալ է զհանդէս վկայութեան սուրբ նահատակին։ Եւ Կարապետ գրիչ անցուցեալ է ի կարգս գրչագիր այսմաւուրաց այնր ժամանակի, յորմէ բաց ի յառաջաբանութենէն որ սկսանի. Հուր է սէրն Քրիստոսի եւ յոգիս մաքուրս բորբոքի, զայլն ամենայն գրեթէ բառ առ բառ արձանագրեցաք աստ ի փառս Քրիստոսի։*

15. Although [Amenavag's] sacred corpse remained unburied for three more days, neither wild animal nor bird drew near to it. The Muslims appropriated some dogs and dragged them over his sacred corpse, but as soon as they saw that sacred corpse, they ran off. [The corpse] had not only not decayed, but it began to issue a sweet smell. A brilliant light shone in the night, and like a torch it burned over the corpse. And the sounds of hymns and of worship were heard as if from priests. When the Muslims saw this, they thought that priests had come in the night secretly to steal the corpse and bury it, so they ran to the corpse so that they might arrest the priests but saw no one.

16. Three days later, on Sunday, the faithful came, and having received permission from both the prince and the judge, they deposited the corpse with honor in a tomb. This took place in the Armenian year 784,[2] at which time Yovhannēs Vardapet,[3] a devout man, was flourishing in the region of Derjan. As he had been a witness—both by eye and by ear—it was he who wrote the account of the martyrdom of this saintly hero. The scribe Karapet added it into the entries of the *Yaysmawurk*ᶜ copied out during that time period. Apart from the preface, which begins "The love of Christ is a fire and it burns in pure souls," we have written down everything else here almost word for word for the glory of Christ.[4]

---

2. The Armenian year 784 is equivalent to AD 1295.

3. This Yovhannēs is a bit difficult to identify. We know of two prominent vardapets named Yovhannēs Erznkatsᶜi from this period but the first, Yovhannēs Erznkatsᶜi Pluz, died in 1293, and the other, perhaps better known as Yovhannēs Tsortsoretsᶜi, was still a relatively young man in 1295; he lived until around 1335. No martyrdom of Amenavag has survived, and the attribution of the works of these two authors are often confused.

4. This bit of information is an extremely rare and important glance into one moment of the history of the compilation of the *Yaysmawurk*ᶜ; from the dates it seems that it concerns the revisions associated with Grigor Anavarzetsᶜi. See Mathews, *On This Day: The Armenian Church Synaxarion—January*, xviii.

Արեգի Գ

Մարտի ԺԱ

Վկայութիւն սրբոցն Կոդրատիոսի, Դիոգինոսի, Կիպրիանոսի, Անեկտոսի եւ Կրիսկենտոսի

1. Այս հինգ վկայքս Քրիստոսի էին ի Կորնթացւոց քաղաքէն՝ յամս Դեկոսի եւ Վաղենտիանոսի ամպարիշտ արքայիցն:

2. Սուրբն Կոդրատիոսի մինչդեռ տղայն էր մեռան ծնօղքն, եւ Աստուծոյ հրամանաւն ամպ իջանէր ի վերայ նորա, եւ իբրեւ ստին ջամբէր եւ արբուցանէր: Եւ յորժամ աճեաց ժողովէին առ նա այլ սուրբք եւ զքրիստոնէութիւնն հաստատէին յանձինս իւրեանց:

3. Եւ կացեալ առաջի Ասոնայ իշխանին՝ խոստովանեցաւ զՔրիստոս եւ ոչ ուրացաւ զանբիծ հաւատսն, այլ աստուածային բանիւք յանդիմանէր զիշխանն: Եւ մերկացուցին զսուրբն, եւ գանեցին ուժգին: Տարան եւ զայլ սուրբսն առաջի, եւ նոքա նոյնպէս խոստովանեցան զանուն եւ զհաւատն Քրիստոսի Աստուծոյ մերոյ:

4. Եւ բարկացեալ իշխանին հրամայեաց եւ հատին զգլուխս հինգ սուրբ վկայիցն Արեգի Գ եւ Մարտի ԺԱ: Եւ բղխեաց ի տեղւոջէն յայնմիկ աղբիւր յստակ եւ ցուրտ. եւ երթեալ քրիստոնէիցն թաղեցին զնոսա ի նշանաւոր տեղւոջ:

March 11

Areg 3

The martyrdom of Saints Quadratus, Diogenes, Cyprian, Anectos, and Kriskindos

1. These five martyrs of Christ were from the city of Corinth and lived in the time of the impious emperors Decius and Valentinian.[1]

2. When the holy Quadratus was still a child, his parents died, and at the command of God, a cloud descended over him and like a breast nourished him with food and drink. When he was older, other holy ones would gather around him, and they would encourage each other in their Christian faith.

3. He once stood before the governor Jason, and he professed Christ and did not renounce the immaculate faith; rather, with godlike speech he rebuked the governor. They stripped the holy one, and they whipped him severely. They also brought the other holy ones before [the governor], but they too professed the name and the faith of Christ our God.

4. The governor became very angry and he gave the command to cut off the heads of the five holy martyrs on the third of Areg—that is, the eleventh of March. From that place there burst forth a pure and cool spring. And the Christians came and buried them in a prominent place.

---

1. As Valentinian and Decius lived over a century apart, there is a chronological problem here; it is perhaps most easily resolved by assuming a scribal error in writing Valentinian in place of Valerian, who ruled from 253 to 260, shortly after Decius.

5. *Յայսմ աւուր Սաբաս ստրատելատն երիտասարդ երեսուն եւ ութ ամաց՝ կատարեցաւ ի Հռոմ քաղաքի հրով եւ սրով վասն հաւատոցն Քրիստոսի. ընկեցին եւ յեռացեալ կաթսայ, եւ ապա ընդ այլ եօթանասուն զօրականսն որ նովաւ հաւատացին ի Քրիստոս՝ կատարեցան յԱւրելիանոսէ արքայէն։*

5. On this day, the commander Sabas, a young man thirty-eight years of age, was put to death in Rome by fire and by the sword because of his faith in Christ. Then they threw him into a boiling cauldron. Then he, along with seventy other soldiers who with him had professed their faith in Christ, was put to death by the emperor Aurelian.[2]

---

2. Aurelian was Roman emperor from 270 to 275.

Արեգի Դ

Մարտի ԺԲ

Վկայաբանութիւն սրբոյն Պիոնի քահանայի Զմիւռնիոյ եկեղեցւոյն

1. *Աստուածասէր քահանայն Պիոնիոս էր յաւուրս կռապաշտ արքային Դեկոսի: Եւ կալան զնա վեց արք, բարձին ի Թիկունս իւրեանց եւ տանէին առ դատաւորն Կինդելիանոս, եւ երանելին Պիոնիոս ոտիւքն հարկանէր զկողս նոցա, եւ աղաղակէր. Քրիստոնեայ եմ եւ ոչ զոհեմ կռոց ձերոց: Եւ կացեալ առաջի խոստովանեցաւ զանուն Տեառն Աստուծոյ: Եւ եհատ ի վերայ նորա վճիռ եԹէ. ԶՊիոնիոս որ կամաւորուԹեամբ զինքն քրիստոնեայ անուանեաց՝ հրամայեմ կենդանւոյն հրով այրել:*
2. *Եւ յորժամ գնաց ի տեղին սուրբ քահանայն Պիոնիոս՝ ինքնին ելոյծ զգօտին եւ մերկացաւ ի հանդերձիցն, եւ զաչսն յերկինս համբարձեալ աղօԹեաց առ Աստուած մեծաւ գոհուԹեամբ: Եւ դահիճքն բեւեռեցին զձեռս եւ զոտս նորա ի փայտի, եւ բորբոքեցին չուրջ զնովաւ հուր: Եւ նորա խցեալ զաչսն եւ ի միտս իւր աղօԹէր առ Աստուած. եւ կարծեցին ամբոխն եԹէ մեռաւ: Եւ յորժամ կատարեաց զաղօԹսն՝ ձայնեաց մեծաւ բարբառով. Ամէն, Տէր, ընկալ զոգիս իմ: Եւ աւանդեաց զհոգին իւր առ Աստուած՝ Մարտի ԺԲ:*
3. *Եւ յորժամ չիջաւ հուրն, գնացին քրիստոնեայքն գտին զսուրբ վկայն Քրիստոսի ամբողջ մարմնով եւ պայծառ երեսօք, անկէզ մնացեալ հեր գլխոյն եւ մօրուացն, եւ առաւելապէս հաստատեցան ի հաւատս քրիստոնէութեան անխախտելի: Եւ անհաւատքն երկմտեցին ի կռոցն պաշտամանէն:*

March 12

Areg 4

The martyrdom of Pionius, priest of the church of Smyrna

1. The God-loving priest Pionius lived in the time of the idolatrous emperor Decius. Six men arrested him and hurled him up on their shoulders, intending to bring him to the prefect Kyndelianos. The blessed Pionius began to kick them in the ribs and to cry out, "I am a Christian, and I will not sacrifice to your gods." When he stood before [the prefect], he professed the name of the Lord God. [Kyndelianos] then issued this sentence upon him: "I order that Pionius, who has willingly called himself a Christian, be burned alive in fire."

2. When he arrived at the place [of execution], the holy priest Pionius himself removed his belt and stripped off his garments. He raised his eyes up to heaven and prayed to God with heartfelt thanksgiving. The executioners nailed his hands and his feet to a stake and kindled a fire all around him. He closed his eyes and in his mind began to pray to God. The crowd thought that he had died, but when he finished his prayer, he cried out in a loud voice, "Amen, Lord, receive my spirit." And he handed his spirit over to God on the twelfth of March.

3. When the fire had gone out, the Christians came and found the holy martyr of Christ with his whole body intact and his face resplendent. The hair of his head and that of his beard both remained unsinged. While they were even further strengthened in their own unshakable Christian faith, those unbelievers began to have doubts about their worship of idols.

Արեգի Ե

Մարտի ԺԳ

Տօն է սրբոյ մարգարէին Եզեկիէլի Ե– Եղբ

1. *Մարգարէն Եզեկիէլ գնաց ընդ ժողովրդեանն ի Բաբելոն զոր տարաւ Նաբուգոդոնոսոր արքայն Բաբելացւոց, եւ անդ առ ափն Քոբրայ գետոյ ետես զտեսիլն՝ զքերոբէսն լծեալ ի կառս եւ զԱստուած ի վերայ աթոռոցն, որք ասէին. Օրհնեալ են փառք Տեառն ի տեղւոջ իւրում: Մարգարէանայր ժողովրդեանն որ ինչ անցք անցանելոց էին ժողոբրդեան ընդ նոսա: Յանդիմանէր զժողովուրդսն որք կռապաշտ էին յերկրին Քաղդէացւոց, եւ մանաւանդ զցեղն Դանայ:*
2. *Եւ Քաղդէացիքն կամէին սպանանել զԵզեկիէլ եւ զամենայն օրինապահսն որ ընդ նմա շրջէին: Եւ նորա բաժանեալ զգետն մեծ՝ անց յայնկոյս ամենայն օրինապահօքն, եւ ի Քաղդէացւոցն որք յանդգնեցան մտանել ի գետն խեղդեցան:*
3. *Եւ առաջնորդն ցեղին Դանայ սպան զնա, եւ անդէն թաղեցաւ:*
4. *Իսկ Եզր մարգարէ էր անդէն ի Բաբելոն, եւ եկն զկնի Զօրաբաբելի յԵրուսաղէմ, եւ ետես զչինուած տաճարին եւ զամենայն բարութիւնսն զոր արար Աստուած ժողոբրդեանն: Եւ գրեաց գիրս Զօրաբաբելի եւ Դարեհի եւ ժողովոյն Գովգայ եւ վախճանեցաւ յԵրուսաղէմ եւ թաղեցաւ անդ:*

March 13

Areg 5

The feast of the prophets Ezekiel and Ezra

1. The prophet Ezekiel went with the people to Babylon where Nebuchadnezzar, the king of Babylon, had taken them. And there on the bank of the Chebar River he had a vision of cherubim yoked to a chariot with God above the throne,[1] and they were saying, "Blessed is the glory of the Lord in its place." [Ezekiel] then prophesied about all that was about to befall the people among them. And he rebuked those people who had become idol worshippers in the land of the Chaldeans, especially the tribe of Dan.

2. The Chaldeans wished to kill Ezekiel and all those who kept the observance of the laws and who maintained fellowship with him. But he divided that great river and crossed over to the other side along with all those who were keeping the observance of the laws. All those Chaldeans who dared to enter into the river were drowned.

3. The head of the tribe of Dan killed [Ezekiel], and he was buried there.

4. The prophet Ezra was also there in Babylon, but he followed Zerubbabel to Jerusalem; and he saw the reconstruction of the temple and all the good things that God did for the people. And he wrote letters to Zerubbabel, to Darius, and to the congregation of Gog.[2] He died in Jerusalem and was buried there.

---

1. See Ezekiel 1:1-28.
2. See Ezra 7:1-10:17.

5. *Իսկ միւս Եզրն որ եւ Սաղաթիէլն անուանեցաւ՝ եւ սա էր ի Բաբելոն, եւ սուգ ունէր վասն աւերածին Սիովնի, որ առաքեաց Տէր զհրեշտակ իւր եւ մխիթարեաց զնա: Եւ սա հոգւով Աստուծոյ գրեաց զօրէնս եւ զմարգարէս, եւ արար նոր գիրս եւ ուսոյց զժողովուրդսն, եւ ետես զդարձ գերոյն, եւ վախճանեցաւ եւ թաղեցաւ անդէն:*

Յայսմ աւուր վարք երանելոյն Գրիգորի Հռոմայ Հայրապետին

6. *Այս երանելի այրս Գրիգորիոս էր ի Հռոմ քաղաքէն, յաւուրս բարեպաշտ թագաւորին Յուստինիանոսի. եւ էր կրօնաւոր եւ գրագիր եւ հայր վանացն որ կոչի Կլէոսկորի:*

7. *Եւ ի միում աւուր փորձեաց զնա Աստուած, եւ առաքեաց հրեշտակ ի կերպս աղքատի եւ մերկ նաւավարի, եւ անկեալ յոտս նորա խնդրէր ողորմութիւն, եթէ. Ի ծովուն ընկղմեցաւ նաւն իմ եւ կորուսի զամենայն բեռն նաւին եւ զիմն եւ զօտարաց, եւ ոչ ունիմ ինչ տալ նոցա: Եւ երանելին Գրիգորիոս ետ նմա վեց դահեկան: Եւ դարձեալ երկրորդ անգամ աղքատն խնդրէր. եւ նա նոյնպէս ետ նմա վեց դահեկան: Եւ դարձեալ երրորդ անգամ աղքատն երթեալ խնդրէր, եւ նա դահեկան ոչ ունէր ետ նմա արծաթի սկտեղ:*

8. *Եւ եղեւ ընդ աւուրսն ընդ այնոսիկ եղեւ մեռանել Հռոմայ հայրապետին, եւ աստուածային ընտրութեամբն ձեռնադրեցաւ Գրիգորիոս յառաքելական աթոռն: Եւ հրամայեաց ըստ սովորութեանն իւրում կոչել ի սեղանն իւր երկոտասան աղքատս հացակից լինել նմա:*

5. As for the other Ezra, who was also called Salathiel, he too was in Babylon.[3] He was in mourning there over the destruction of Zion, so the Lord sent his angel to him to comfort him. Then he, by the spirit of God, wrote down the laws and the prophets, and published new books and taught the people. He saw the return of the captivity, and he died and was buried there.

On this day [is celebrated] the life of the blessed Gregory, patriarch of Rome

6. This blessed man, Gregory, was from the city of Rome in the days of the pious emperor Justinian;[4] he was a monk, a scribe, and the head of a monastery known as Clivus Scauri.[5]

7. One day God tested him and sent to him an angel in the form of a poor, naked sailor who fell at his feet and begged him for alms, [saying], "My ship has sunk in the sea, and I have lost all the ship's cargo, both mine and of others. I have nothing to reimburse them." The blessed Gregory gave him six dahekans. The poor man came and begged him a second time, and the blessed one again gave him six dahekans. The poor man came and begged him a third time, and because he had no more dahekans, he gave him a silver dish.

8. It came to pass in those days that the patriarch of Rome died, and by divine election, Gregory was consecrated to the apostolic throne.[6] He gave the command, as was his custom, to invite twelve poor people to his table to share his meal with him.

---

3. See 2 Esdras 3:1.
4. Justinian was Roman emperor from 527 to 565.
5. The Armenian scribe was evidently unfamiliar with this name; Clivus Scauri was the name of the family estate that Gregory turned into a monastery after the death of his father, c. 575.
6. Gregory was elected patriarch of Rome, or pope, in 590.

9. Եւ ի միւսում աւուր յորժամ նստան՝ տեսանէ սուրբ հայրապետն երեքտասան աղքատս նստեալս ի սեղանին. եւ հարցանէր ցսեղանապետն. Երեքտասան աղքատս կոչեցեր այսօր։ Եւ նա ասէ. Ոչ, այլ երկոտասան. եւ ոչ տեսանէր զմինն՝ բայց միայն երանելին Գրիգորիոս, եւ երեւէր նմա երբեմն երիտասարդ՝ երբեմն ծեր։ Բուռն եհար երանելին Գրիգորիոս յերեքտասաներորդ աղքատն, եւ մտին ի միասին ի սենեակ իւր, եւ հարցանէր. Ուստի՞ իցես եւ զի՞նչ անուն է քո։ Եւ նա ասէր. Ընդէ՞ր հարցանես զանուն իմ։ Իմ անունս սքանչելի է, եւ այն աղքատն եմ որոյ ետուր զգանձն եւ զսկտեղն։ Եւ յայնժամ հրամայեաց Աստուած լինել քեզ յաթոռն Պետրոսի՝ Հռոմայ հայրապետ։ Ասէ Գրիգորիոս. Ուստի՞ գիտացեր եւ ո՞վ պատմեաց քեզ։ Եւ նա ասէ. Ես հրեշտակ եմ Աստուծոյ ամենակալին, եւ հրաման առի յայնմ օրէն որ ընդ քեզ լինիմ հանապազ՝ եւ զամենայն խնդիրս քո ես վերաբերեմ առ Աստուած։ Եւ յարուցեալ Գրիգորիոս երկիր եպագ նմա, եւ նա անյայտ եղեւ։

10. Այս երանելւոյս՝ շնորհս գիտութեան տուաւ յԱստուծոյ. եւ մեկնեաց զաստուածաշունչ գիրս զհին եւ զնոր կտակարանս. գրեաց եւ ի Յոբ ճառս քառասուն, եւ այլ գիրս գրեաց հռոմայեցերէն, զոր ի յունական լեզուն Դիալոգոս կոչեն գրոցն։ Գրեաց եւ այլ գիրս ի վարս եւ ի ճգնութիւն սրբոց հարանց եւ եպիսկոպոսաց։ Եւ յորժամ գրէր զճառսն՝ տեսանէր Պետրոս աշակերտն իւր եւ նախասարկաւագն սպիտակ աղաւնի ի վերայ շրթանցն։

11. Այս մեծ հայրապետս Գրիգորիոս տեսանէր զսքանչելի շէնս զոր շինեալ էր Տրայիանոս կռապաշտ արքայն, զկամուրջս յանհուն եւ ի մեծամեծ գետսն, եւ սալարկս ի ձորս եւ ի բազմամօր եւ ի տղմային տեղիս պողոտայիցն, եւ զարմանայր յոյժ, եւ խնդրէր յԱստուծոյ ներումն Տրայանոսի, եւ ասէր եթէ. Առանց Աստուծոյ հրամանի այսպիսի անպատմելի գործս ոչ կարէր առնել։ Եւ ի բազում ժամանակս արտասուօք խնդրէր փրկութիւն Տրայիանոսի։ Եւ եկեալ առ նա հրեշտակ Տեառն ասէ. Վասն քո խնդրոյն Աստուած ներումն շնորհեաց նմա, բայց վասն այլ կռապաշտ մարդոյ զԱստուած մի աղաչեսցես՝ զի ոչ լսէ քեզ։

9. But on one day when they were reclining, the holy patriarch saw thirteen poor people sitting at the table. He asked his chef, "Did you invite thirteen poor people today?" And [the chef] responded, "No, only twelve." For he could not see the one that only the blessed Gregory saw, the one who appeared to him at times young and at other times old. The blessed Gregory grabbed hold of the thirteenth poor person, and they went together into his room, and [Gregory] asked him, "Where do you come from? And what is your name?" And he responded, "Why do you ask my name? My name is wondrous. I am that poor man to whom you gave the money and the dish. At that time God commanded that you become the patriarch of Rome, on the throne of Peter." Gregory said, "How do you know this? Who told you?" And he said, "I am an angel of the all-powerful God, and I have received the command that from this day I am to be constantly with you and am to take all your requests to God." Gregory rose up and prostrated himself before [the angel], but he disappeared.

0. This blessed man was given the grace of knowledge by God, and he commented on the Holy Scriptures, both the Old and New Testaments. He wrote forty homilies on Job, and he composed many other writings in the Latin language that are known in the Greek language as the *Dialogues*.[7] He also wrote other works on the lives and the ascetic labors of the holy fathers and bishops. When he was composing his homilies, his disciple and archdeacon Peter would see a white dove on his lips.

1. This great patriarch Gregory used to gaze upon the stately buildings that the impious emperor Trajan had built, bridges over very deep and wide rivers, paved streets through valleys, and roads through wild and muddy terrain, and he admired them greatly. He begged God that He would forgive Trajan, for he said that had God not allowed it, [Trajan] would not have been able to construct such unimaginable edifices. For a long time he used to pray for Trajan's salvation. Then an angel of the Lord came to him and said, "Because of your prayer, God has granted him forgiveness, but do not entreat God on behalf of any other idolatrous person, for He will not listen to you."

---

7. These books were so popular in many eastern traditions that Gregory was known simply as Gregory Dialogos.

12. *Եւ յետ մահուան երիցս երանեալ Հայրապետին Գրիգորի՝ Պետրոս նախասարկաւագն որ էր աշակերտ իւր՝ գնաց յարեւմուտս եւ մկրտեաց բազում անհաւատ ազգս, զոր կոչեն Սաքսոն եւ Փրանկս: Այս Պետրոս հրամայեաց կանոնօք որ յաւուրս քառասներորդ պահոցն՝ յամենայն աւուր կատարեալ պատարագ մատուցանեն, եւ աւետարան ընթեռնուն. եւ շաբաթ օրն ընդ ծոմութեան պահօք առնիցեն որպէս եւ զայլ հինգ աւուրսն: Եւ մինչեւ ցայսօր արեւմուտք զնոյն կարգ պահեն. բայց Կոստանդինուպօլիս եւ այլ երեք աթոռքն ոչ ընկալան այնպէս:*

13. *Եւ հանգեաւ խաղաղութեամբ ի Հռոմ: Եւ յետ նորա մահուան գնացին Սաքսոնք, եւ Փրանկք զորս մկրտեաց նա եւ արարին զտապանն արծաթի եւ զարդարեցին ոսկի պատկերօք:*

14. *Եւ ձեռնադրեաց նոցա Հռոմայ հայրապետն եւ ամենայն ազգի եւ գաւառի եպիսկոպոսս. եւ լինի մինչեւ ցայսօր:*

2. After the death of the thrice-blessed patriarch Gregory, Peter the archdeacon, who was his disciple, traveled west and baptized many pagan peoples who were called Saxons and Franks. This Peter ordered it put into the canons that on each of the forty days of Lent a full liturgy be celebrated on each day and the gospel be read and that Saturday be made a fast day just like the other five days. Even until today the West observes this rule, but Constantinople and the three other patriarchates do not accept it.

3. [Peter] fell asleep peacefully in Rome, and after his death the Saxons and the Franks whom he baptized came and made for him a sarcophagus of silver and decorated it with golden images.

4. The patriarch of Rome ordained bishops for them and for every nation and region, and this continues until today.

Արեգի Զ

Մարտի ԺԴ

Վկայաբանութիւն սրբոյն Սաբինոսի

1. *Ի ժամանակս կրապաշտ արքային Դիոկղետիանոսի էր սուրբն Սաբինոս յԵրապօլսեայ յԵգիպտացւոց երկրէն, նախարար ի մեծ ազգէ, եւ վասն դժնդակ ժամանակաց հալածանացն ելեալ արտաքոյ քաղաքին ի փոքր եւ ի նեղ տան բնակէր ի Թագստի ընդ այլ քրիստոնեայս, եւ պահօք, եւ աղօթիւք աղաչէին զԱստուած: Եւ բազում քրիստոնեայք ըմբռնեցան ի ձեռս անօրինաց, եւ համբաւեցաւ յոյժ անուն Սաբինոսի, եւ յուզմամբ մեծաւ խնդրէին զնա եւ ոչ գտանէին:*

2. *Եւ մի ոմն աղքատ սովոր էր երթալ առ սուրբն եւ մուրանայր. եւ նա յոյժ ողորմէր նմա եւ կերակրէր եւ սիրէր զնա. եւ նորա երթեալ առ զօրականսն ասէ. Զի՞նչ տայք ինձ եւ ես ցուցից զնա ձեզ: Եւ ետուն նմա երկու դահեկան, եւ գնացին զկնի նորա մինչեւ ի տեղին. եւ մտեալ ի տունն հանին զամենեսեան արտաքս եւ հարցանէին. Ով է ի ձէնջ Սաբինոս: Եւ նա ասէ. Ես եմ: Կապեցին զնա միայն ծանր շղթայիւք եւ տարան առ Արիանոս դատաւորն. եւ հարցանէր զանունն եւ զշնորհսն: Եւ նա ասէ. Քրիստոնեայ եմ եւ կոչիմ Սաբինոս:*

3. *Ասէ դատաւորն. Ծառա՞յ ես թէ ազատ: Սուրբն ասէ. Ազատ եմ եւ բարի մանկութեանս իմոյ զօրական եմ ի գունդս դքսին: Ասէ դատաւորն. Եւ զի՞նչ եղեւ քեզ որ թողեր զզօրականութիւնդ: Ասէ Սաբինոս. Տեսի զանօրէն գործս թագաւորին ձերոյ եւ զանիրաւ չարչարանս ի ծառայս Աստուծոյ, եւ լաւ համարեցայ բնակել ի տան Աստուծոյ քան ի յարկս մեղաւորաց:*

March 14

Areg 6

The martyrdom of Saint Sabinus

1. During the time of the impious emperor Diocletian, the holy Sabinus lived in Hieropolis in the land of Egypt. He was a prefect from a noble family. Because it was a time of extreme persecution, he lived hidden in a small and cramped house outside the city along with other Christians, where they entreated God with prayer and fasting. Many Christians were taken by the lawless, and the name of Sabinus was spread about everywhere. They frantically sought for him far and wide, but they were unable to find him.

2. A certain poor man was in the habit of going to beg from the holy Sabinus. He took great pity on this poor man, and he nourished him and loved him. [One day this poor man] came before some soldiers and said, "What will you give to me if I show you where he is?" They gave him two dahekans and then followed him to the place. Upon entering the house, they dragged them all outside and asked, "Who among you is Sabinus?" And [Sabinus] said, "I am." They bound him alone in heavy chains, and they took him to the judge Arianos, who inquired of him his name and his religion. He responded, "I am a Christian, and I am called Sabinus."

3. The judge then said, "Are you a servant or a free man? The holy one responded, "I am a free man, and since the fullness of my youth I have been a soldier in the general's army." The judge retorted, "And what happened to you that you abandoned your military position?" Sabinus replied, "I witnessed the unjust deeds of your emperor and the criminal tortures of the servants of God, and I deemed it better to dwell in the house of God rather than in the homes of sinners."

4. *Եւ բարկացեալ դատաւորն հրամայեաց կախել զնա եւ տանջել, եւ այնչափ տանջեցին զնա մինչեւ գզեցաւ մարմինն. եւ անտի բարձեալ զսուրբն տարան ի քաղաքն Անտոնինու զկնի դատաւորին՝ զի եւ անդ չարչարեսցէ զնա եթէ ոչ դառնայցէ ի կուռսն:*

5. *Եւ յորժամ գնացին բազում հնարիւք ջանաց դատաւորն, եւ ոչ կարաց փոխել զնա յաստուածապաշտ հաւատոցն: Ղամբարօք այրեցին զկողսն եւ զորովայնն. եւ սուրբն լռեալ ոչ ինչ բարբառէր, եւ որպէս զայլոյ մարմին տանջեալ համարէր: Եհատ ի վերայ նորա վճիռ զի խեղդեսցեն ի գետն:*

6. *Եւ յորժամ տանէին՝ գնացին զկնի նորա բազումք ի հաւատացելոցն. եւ պատուիրէր նոցա սուրբն հաստատուն կալ ի հաւատն Քրիստոսի, եւ յօժարութեամբ մեռանել վասն անուան նորա: Եւ զայս ասաց եթէ. Յիշեցէք յաղօթս ձեր զօր կատարման իմոյ, եւ յերրորդ աւուրն եկեսջիք ի հիւսիսոյ կողմանէ գետոյն եւ գտանիցէք զմարմինս իմ, առջիք եւ թաղեսջիք զիս վիմովն որ յոտս իմ կապեալն է:*

7. *Եւ յորժամ տարան առ գետոյն կապեցին վէմ մեծ յոտսն, արկին ի փոքր նաւակ մի: Եւ սուրբն հայեցաւ յերկինս, գոհացաւ զԱստուծոյ եւ փառաւորեաց զանուն նորա՝ որ արժանաւորեցոյց զնա այնպիսի վկայութեամբ մեռանել: Եւ յաղօթելն նորա ընկեցին ի գետն, եւ աւանդեաց զհոգին իւր առ Քրիստոս Մարտի ԺԴ:*

8. *Եւ յետ երից աւուրց գնացին եղբարքն գաղտ ի գիշերի՝ ի տեղին յորում հրամայեաց սուրբն Սաբինոս, գտին զպատուական մարմին նորա, տարան եւ թաղեցին ի նոր տապանի վիմովն մերձ ի քաղաքն Անդինոյ:*

4. The judge became furious and ordered [Sabinus] to be suspended and tortured, and they tortured him so much that his flesh was torn to shreds. From there they picked him up and brought him to the city of Antinoë, following the judge, so that there too they might torture him if he did not convert to the [worship of] idols.

5. When they arrived, the judge tried by numerous means, but he was unable to turn [Sabinus] away from his God-fearing faith. They burned his sides and his abdominal region with torches, but the holy one remained silent and did not cry out; rather, he reckoned it as if they were torturing someone else's body. [The judge] then decreed that [Sabinus] be drowned in the river.

6. And while they were taking [Sabinus] away, many of the faithful followed after him, and the holy one commanded them to remain steadfast in the faith of Christ, and to die willingly on behalf of His name. And he added this: "Remember the day of my death in your prayers, and on the third day you will go along the north bank of the river, and there you will find my body; take it up and bury me along with the stone that will be bound to my feet."

7. When the [soldiers] brought him to the river, they tied a large stone to his feet and threw him into a small boat. The holy one looked up to heaven, gave praise to God, and glorified the name of Him who had deemed [Sabinus] worthy to die by such a martyrdom. While he was praying, they threw him into the river, and he handed his spirit over to Christ on the fourteenth of March.

8. Three days later the brothers secretly went during the night to the place that Sabinus had commanded them. There they found his venerable body, carried it away and buried him in a new stone tomb near to the city of Antinoë.

Յայսմ աւուր վկայութիւն սրբոց եւ անարծաթ բժշկացն Կոզմայի եւ Դամիանոսի երկու եղբարցն, եւ այլ երից վկայիցն. Անթիմոսի, Ղեւոնդեայ եւ Պապիոսի

9. *Սուրբ եւ անարծաթ բժիշկքն եւ Քրիստոսի մարտիրոսքն Կոզմաս եւ Դամիանոս եղբարք էին Հարազատք յԱրաբացւոց երկրէն, յաւուրս կռապաշտ արքայիցն Մաքսիմիանոսի եւ Դիոկղետիանոսի: Եւ ըստ աւետարանական բանին՝ ձրի բժշկէին զամենայն ցաւս եւ զհիւանդութիւնս, ոչ միայն զմարդկան այլ եւ զանասնոցն: Եւ մատնեցին զնոսա առ Լիսիաս Եգիպտացւոց դատաւորն, եւ կացուցին առաջի նորա, եհարց. Ուստի՞ էք եւ ո՞ր Հաւատով էք եւ զի՞նչ են անուանք ձեր:*

10. *Ասեն սուրբքն. Մեք յԱրաբացւոց եմք եւ քրիստոնեայ Հաւատով. եւ ես անուանիմ Կոզմաս եւ եղբայրս իմ Դամիանոս. եւ եմք ի մեծ ազգէ եւ արուեստիւ բժիշկք: Ունիմք եւ այլ ընկերս՝ եթէ Հրամայես ասասցուք եւ զնոցա անուանսն:*

11. *Ասէ դատաւորն. Ասացէք աներկիւղ: Եւ նոքա ասեն. Անթիմոս, Ղեւոնդիոս եւ Պապիոս: Տարան եւ զնոսա առաջի, եւ նոքա խոստովանեցան զՔրիստոս յամենայն սրտէ: Ասէ դատաւորն. Զոհեցէք կռոցն: Եւ սուրբքն ամենեւին ոչ ետուն պատասխանի: Կապեցին զձեռս եւ զոտս նոցա եւ գանեցին ուժգին եւ ընկեցին ի ծովն: Եւ Հրամանաւ Տեառն լուծան կապանքն եւ ելին ի ցամաքն անվնաս:*

12. *Եւ տեսեալ զնոսա դատաւորն յոյժ զարմացաւ եւ ասէ ցնոսա. Ուսուցէք զիս մոգութիւն առնել: Ասեն սուրբքն Կոզմաս եւ Դամիանոս. Եկեսջիր զկնի մեր յանուն Աստուծոյն մերոյ: Ասէ դատաւորն. Եկից անուամբ աստուծոյն իմոյ Ադրիանոսի: Եւ նոյնժամայն Թիւրեցան երեսք նորա: Եւ սուրբքն եղին ձեռս եւ ողջացուցին:*

On this day is the martyrdom of the two holy, poor brother healers, Cosmas and Damian, and of three other martyrs Anthimos, Leontios, and Papios

9. These holy, poor healers and martyrs of Christ, Cosmas and Damian, were blood brothers from the land of Arabia, in the time of the impious emperors Maximian and Diocletian. According to the word of the gospel, they freely healed every illness and disease, not only those of people but even those of animals. They were denounced to Lysias, an Egyptian judge, and when they were brought into his presence, he asked them, "Where are you from? Of what faith are you? What are your names?"

10. The holy ones answered, "We are Arabs, and we are Christians. I am called Cosmas, and my brother is Damian; we are from a noble family and are healers by profession. We also have other brothers; if you order us we will also tell you their names."

11. The judge responded, "Tell me, without fear." And they said, "Anthimos, Leontios, and Papios." They too were then brought in, and they too professed Christ with all their heart. The judge then said, "Sacrifice to the idols." But the holy ones made no response whatever. So they were bound hand and foot, and they scourged them violently and then threw them into the sea. But at the command of the Lord their bonds loosened, and they emerged unharmed onto dry land.

12. When the judge saw them, he was amazed; and he said to them, "Teach me to do this magic." The holy Cosmas and Damian responded, "Follow us in the name of our God." The judge said, "I will follow in the name of my god, Adrian."[1] And in that instance his face became disfigured. The holy ones laid their hands on him and healed him.

---

1. This is the common reading here, but I find no attempt to identify just who this deity is supposed to be.

13. *Եւ Հրամայեաց եւ ընկեցին ի բորբոքեալ Հուր, եւ պատառեցաւ երկիր եւ եկուլ զսուրբսն ի ներքս, եւ յորժամ չիջաւ Հուրն դարձեալ եՀան զնոսա ամբողջս: Եւ բարկութեամբ լցեալ դատաւորն Հրամայեաց եւ խաչեցին զնոսա եւ քարկոծեցին, եւ քարինքն անդրէն դառնային, եւ բազումք մեռան ի նոցանէ: Եւ ապա նետս ձգէին ի նոսա, եւ ամենեւին սուրբքն ոչ խոցեցան ի նետիցն, այլ մանաւանդ սկսան ի միմեանս ձգել զնետսն, եւ բազումք ի նետաձգողացն եւ ի զօրականացն խոցեցան եւ մեռան:*

14. *Եւ երկուցեալ դատաւորն Հրամայեաց եւ սրով սպանին զսուրբսն յԵգիպտացւոց քաղաքին Մարտի ԺԴ:*

13. [Lysias] then gave the order, and they threw them into a raging fire, but the earth split open and swallowed them inside. When the fire had gone out, it threw them back out completely unscathed. The judge, now full of rage, again gave the order, and they crucified them and stoned them; but the stones turned back, and many of [the judge's men] died. Then they shot arrows at them, but the holy ones were not even wounded by the arrows; rather, they began to shoot the arrows at each other, and many of those bowmen and of the soldiers were pierced and died.

14. Thus, the judge out of fear gave the command, and they slew these holy ones by the sword in this city of the Egyptians on the fourteenth of March.

Արեգի Է

Մարտի ԺԵ

Տօն է ո-Ը մարտիրոսաց. Ագապիոսի եւ երկու Աղեքսանդրոսաց եւ երկու Դիոնէսիոսաց եւ Տիմողայի, Ռոմէլոսի, Պղիսիոնի

1. *Այս ութ վկայքս Քրիստոսի էին յաւուրս Դիոկղիտիանոսի կռապաշտ արքային: Ագապիոս էր ի Գազայ քաղաքէն, Տիմողայոս ի Պոնտոսէ, երկոքին Դիոնէսիոսքն ի Տրապօլսէ, Ռոմէլոս կիսասարկաւագ էր Դիոսպօղու եկեղեցւոյն, Պղիսիոն եւ երկու Աղէկսանդրոսքն յեգիպտոսէ:*
2. *Սոքա միաբանեցան եւ ինքեանք զձեռս իւրեանց կապեցին եւ կամաւորութեամբ կացին առաջի Ուրվանոսի դատաւորին Կեսարու քաղաքին: Եւ համարձակութեամբ եւ պայծառ երեսօք որպէս ի միոյ բերանոյ աղաղակէին. Քրիստոնեայք եմք եւ Քրիստոսի ծառայք, եւ զՔրիստոս Աստուած պաշտեմք, եւ վասն Քրիստոսի պատրաստ եմք ի մեռանել:*
3. *Եւ դատաւորն քաղցրութեամբ եւ ողոքանօք խրատ տայր ուրանալ զՔրիստոս եւ պաշտել զկուռսն, եւ խոստանայր բազում պարգեւս եւ պատիւս եւ իշխանութիւն. եւ յորժամ ոչ կարաց հաւանեցուցանել զնոսա ողոքանօք, ապա սպառնայր բազում տանջանօք, սրով եւ հրով սպանանել. եւ ոչ այնպէս կարաց զսուրբսն խոտորեցուցանել ի հաւատոցն Քրիստոսի: Հրամայեաց դահճացն եւ հատին զգլուխս նոցա Մարտի ԺԵ:*

March 15

Areg 7

The feast of eight martyrs: Agapios, two Alexanders, two by the name of Dionysius, Timolaus, Romulus, and Plisios

1. These eight martyrs of Christ lived during the time of the impious emperor Diocletian. Agapios was from the city of Gaza, Timolaus was from Pontus, the two named Dionysius were from Tripoli, Romulus was a subdeacon from the church of Diospolis, Plisios and the two Alexanders were from Egypt.

2. These were all of one mind, and they themselves bound their hands and willingly presented themselves before Urbanus, the judge of the city of Caesarea. They cried out boldly and unabashedly as if with one voice, "We are Christians and servants of Christ. We worship Christ as God, and for the sake of Christ we are ready to die."

3. The judge counseled them with gentle appeals to renounce Christ and to worship idols. He promised them many gifts, honors, and privileges. But when he was unable to persuade them with these appeals, he threatened them with many tortures and threatened to kill them by the sword and with fire, but even by these means he was unable to turn them away from their faith in Christ. He then gave the order to his executioners, and they cut off their heads on the fifteenth of March.

Յիշատակ է սրբոյ առաքելոյն եւ ընտրելոյ աշակերտին Քրիստոսի Արիստարքոսի

4. *Սուրբ եւ երանելի առաքեալն Քրիստոսի Արիստարքոս էր յաշակերտացն Պօղոսի եւ էր եղբայր Բառնաբայ առաքելոյ: Եւ Հետեւեալ աւետարանին բազում աշխատեալ եւ նշանս առնէր ի Հիւանդս եւ յախտաժէտս անուամբն Քրիստոսի: Եւ յոլով զանազան վշտաց եւ նեղութեանց եւ բանդից Համբերէր ի Հակառակորդ Հրէիցն եւ ի Հեթանոսաց: Աշխատեցաւ եւ ի ճանապարՀորդութիւնս եւ ի ճգնութիւնս Հանապազօր քարոզութեամբն, եւ զբազումս դարձոյց ի Քրիստոս եւ աշակերտեաց ճշմարտութեանն:*

5. *Սա զտուն իւր եկեղեցի արար եւ ընդունէր եւ Հանգուցանէր զեղբարս, եւ ուսուցանէր եւ վարդապետէր միշտ խրատելով զտկարսն, եւ սպասաւորեաց Պօղոսի եւ այլ առաքելոց յաւետարանն:*

Ի նմին աւուր մարտիրոսութիւն սրբոյ ծերոյն Նիկանդրոսի

6. *Զսա ըմբռնեալ ազգի ազգի յեղանակօք չարչարանաց նեղեցին զոՀել կռոցն, եւ յորժամ պինդ եկաց ի խոստովանութեանն Քրիստոսի, սրով Հատին զգլուխ նորա:*

The memorial of Aristobulos, the blessed apostle and elect disciple of Christ

4. The holy and blessed apostle of Christ, Aristobulos, was one of the disciples of Paul, and he was the brother of the apostle Barnabas. He followed the gospel and performed many signs and miracles on the sick and infirm in the name of Christ. He endured many afflictions, sufferings, and imprisonments from his adversaries, both Jews and pagans. He wore himself out both in his missionary journeys and in his asceticism with his continuous preaching, and he converted many to Christ and made them disciples of the truth.

5. He made his own home into a church, where he received and comforted the brothers. He taught and instructed them, always encouraging the weaker ones, and he served Paul and the other apostles in [the service of] the gospel.

On this same day the holy witness Nikander was martyred

6. They seized him and compelled him, by all manner of torture, to sacrifice to the idols. But when he stood firm in his profession of Christ, they cut off his head with the sword.

Արեգի Ը

Մարտի ԺԶ

Նահատակութիւն սուրբ վկայիցն որ ի Գաւթացւոց կոտորեցան

1. *Բինքուրիկոս կռապաշտ արքայն Գաւթացւոց գնաց զինուորօք ի մայրի եւ Հատին փայտ յոյժ, եւ բարձեալ տարան յեկեղեցին ուր քրիստոնեայք զաղօթս իւրեանց կատարէին: Եւ ժողովեաց զամենայն Հաւատացեալսն որք ոչ ուրացան զՔրիստոս՝ եմոյծ զնոսա յեկեղեցին, եւ զփայտն կուտեցին ի մէջ եկեղեցւոյն, եւ բորբոքեցին Հրով, եւ այրեցաւ եկեղեցին եւ սուրբքն, Մարտի ԺԶ:*
2. *Էին վկայքն Քրիստոսի երկու քաՀանայք Բաթոյի եւ Վիրկոս, եւ երկու որդիք եւ երկու դստերք, եւ Արպիւլան կրօնաւոր եւ երկոտասան աշխարՀականք՝ Արիպաս, Կոնատոս, Ագէաս, Ովիաս, Իգաթրաս, Իսկոյիս, Սիլաս, Սիգիսաս, Սուիրիլոս, Սուինպլաս, Թերթաս, Փիլիգաս: Եւ եօթն կանայք՝ Աննա, Աղաս, Վարկա, Անեմայի, Մայիկոյ, Մովիկլիոյ: Էին ամենեքեան որք Հրով այրեցան յեկեղեցին անձինք քսան եւ վեց:*
3. *Եւ այր մի քրիստոնեայ առեալ նշխար եւ ձէթ եւ խունկ եւ բաժակ՝ երիվարովն յայլ տեղի յեկեղեցին յաղօթս կալ, եւ զնա ընկեցին ի Հուրն եւ մարտիրոսացաւ ընդ այլ սրբոցն, եւ եղեւ մարմինն իւր եւ արիւնն փոխանակ նշխարին եւ բաժակին պատարագ ընդունելի Աստուծոյ:*

March 16

Areg 8

The martyrdom of the holy martyrs who were killed by the Goths

1. Wingurich,[1] the impious king of the Goths, went with his soldiers into a forest, cut down a great number of trees, and carried them to the church, where Christians were offering up their prayers. He assembled together all those faithful who would not renounce Christ, sent them into the church, heaped up the wood in the middle of the church, and set it on fire. The church and these holy ones were burned down on the sixteenth of March.

2. These martyrs of Christ were two priests, Bathoy and Vircos; two sons and two daughters; the monk Arpilon; and twelve laypeople: Abipas, Conatus, Ageas, Ovias, Igatras, Iskois, Silas, Sigisas, Suirilos, Suinplas, Tertas, and Piligas. There were also seven women: Anna, Adas, Varca, Anema, Maiko, Marnica, and Vico.[2] Altogether there were twenty-six souls that were burned in the fire in that church.

3. A certain Christian male who had gone by horse to another church to pray—and who was bringing them consecrated bread, oils, incense, and a chalice—was also thrown into the fire and martyred along with those other holy ones. His body and his blood became an acceptable sacrifice to God in the place of the consecrated bread and the chalice.

---

1. Wingurich was an early Visigothic subking, who sometime around the year 375 burned numerous Christians to death in a church in the Crimea.

2. I have followed Bayan, *Le Synaxaire armenien,* 169n1, where on the basis of the Latin text he divides the last name in the list of women into two separate names; the Armenian text he used reads the names of only six women, which would result in only twenty-five souls being burned.

4. *Եւ կին մի այրի քրիստոնեայ Թագուհի լեալ այլազգեաց, որոյ անուն էր Գայիադի, գնաց յայրեցեալ եկեղեցին ժողովեաց զնշխարս սրբոց վկայիցն եւ պատուով Թաղեաց:*

Յայսմ աւուր վկայութիւն սրբոյն Երմոսի, Սարապիոնի եւ Պաւլինոսի

5. *Սոքա էին ի քաղաքէն Հռոմայ Քրիստոսի հաւատովն: Կալան զնոսա եւ տարան առ եպարքոս քաղաքին, եհարց զնոսա եւ նոքա խոստովանեցան զինքեանս քրիստոնեայս եւ Քրիստոսի ծառայս:*
6. *Արկին զնոսա ի մԹին եւ ի ժահահոտ բանդ, եւ նոքա ուրախանային եւ խնդային ընդ ճշմարիտ խոստովանուԹիւն իւրեանց: Եւ հանին ի բանդէն եւ կացուցին առաջի եպարքոսին, եւ ողոքանօք եւ սպառնալեօք խրատ տայր ուրանալ զՔրիստոս եւ զոհել կռոցն: Եւ սուրբքն ոչ հաւանեցան խրատու նորա, այլ մանաւանդ քարոզէին մեծաւ բարբառով զՀայր եւ զՈրդի եւ զսուրբ Հոգի, եւ նզովեցին զկուռսն եւ անէծս արկին ի վերայ կռապաշտիցն:*
7. *Եւ բարկացեալ եպարքոսին հրամայեաց պարան կապել յոտս նոցա, եւ քարշեցին զնոսա ընդ քարս եւ ընդ վէմս եւ ընդ ծառս. եւ կոտորեցան ամենայն մարմինք նոցա, եւ լցան արեամբ տեղին յորժամ քարշէին, եւ ոչ Թողին զնոսա ի քարշելոյ մինչեւ աւանդեցին զհոգիս իւրեանց:*
8. *Եւ ոմանք բարեպաշտք եդին զմարմինս նոցա ի նշանաւոր տեղւոջ:*
9. *Կատարեցան սուրբ վկայքս Քրիստոսի՝ Երմիոս, Սարապիոն եւ Պաւլինիոս Մարտի ԺԶ:*

4. A certain Christian widow, who was queen to those foreign pagans and whose name was Gaiadi, went into the church after it was burned down and collected all the remains of those holy martyrs and buried them with honor.

On this day was the martyrdom of the holy Hermas, Sarapion, and Paulinus

5. These men were from the city of Rome and were of the Christian faith. They were seized and taken to the eparch of the city; he interrogated them, and they professed that they were Christians and servants of Christ.

6. They were cast into a dank and foul-smelling prison, but they exulted and rejoiced in their true profession. They were taken out of the prison and stood again before the eparch, who both by gentle persuasion and with threats counseled them to renounce Christ and to sacrifice to the idols. But these holy ones were not afraid, and they did not acquiesce to his counsels, but rather in a loud voice began to proclaim the Father, the Son, and the Holy Spirit. They also condemned the idols and heaped curses upon those idolaters.

7. The eparch became very angry and commanded that they bind their feet with rope, and drag them across rocks, stones, and trees. Their bodies were shredded, and the places where they were dragged were inundated with blood, but they did not leave off dragging them around until they had given up their spirits.

8. Certain pious persons placed their bodies in a distinguished place.

9. These holy martyrs of Christ—Hermas, Sarapion and Paulinus—were martyred on the sixteenth of March.

Արեգի Թ

Մարտի ԺԷ

Վարք երանելոյն Աղեքսիոսի մարդոյն Աստուծոյ համառօտ ամփոփին

1. *Ալեքսիոս Աստուծոյ մարդն՝ որդի էր միամօր մեծատան առն փառաւորեալ պատրկի, որոյ անուն էր Եփեմիանոս, ի մեծ քաղաքէն Հռոմայ, յաւուրս բարեպաշտ արքայիցն Արկադէոսի եւ Ոնորիոսի:*
2. *Ուսուցին նմա զփիլիսոփայական եւ զհռետորական համճարս արտաքին իմաստութեան, եւ զնոր աստուածաշունչ գիրս պատուիրանացն Աստուծոյ: Եւ յորժամ եղեւ ի չափ հասակի Ալեքսիոս՝ խօսեցան նմա կին ի թագաւորական տոհմէ, եւ արարին զհարսանիսն:*
3. *Եւ յորժամ եղեւ երեկոյ եմուտ յառագաստ հարսինն, եւ նախ քան զմերձենալ ի կինն՝ ծագեաց լոյս մարդասիրութեանն Աստուծոյ ի սիրտ Ալէքսիոսի, եհան զմատանին ի ձեռացն՝ պատեաց ի ծիրանի չուշտակ, ետ հարսինն եւ ասէ. Առ պահեա զայս առ քեզ, եւ Աստուած լիցի ի միջի մերում ընդ իս եւ ընդ քեզ:*
4. *Եւ զայս ասացեալ ել ի սենեկէն. եւ էին ամենեքեան որ ի տանն ի քուն: Եւ դիմեաց միայն յարեւելս կոյս, գնաց յԵդեսիա քաղաք յորում էր անձեռագործ պատկերն Քրիստոսի ի սուրբ դաստառակին, որում մեծաւ փափաքանօք երկիր եպագ: Եւ երթեալ յեկեղեցին սրբուհւոյ Աստուածածնին, փոխեաց զհանդերձս իւր ընդ աղքատի, եւ զգեցաւ պատառատուն մազեղէն եւ մուրայր ի քաղաքին:*

March 17

Areg 9

The life of the blessed Alexius, the Man of God, the voluntary poor man

1. Alexius, the Man of God, was the only son of a wealthy man, a renowned patrician, whose name was Ephemianus. He lived in the great city of Rome in the days of the pious emperors Arcadius and Honorius.

2. He was taught the philosophical and rhetorical sciences according to the profane curriculum, as well as the new divine scriptures of the commandments of God. And when Alexius came of age, he was betrothed to a girl from a royal family, and they celebrated the wedding ceremony.

3. When it was evening he entered into the chamber of his new bride, but before he could draw near to his wife, the light of God's love for mankind shone into the heart of Alexius. He removed the ring from his finger, wrapped it in a purple handkerchief, gave it to his bride, and said, "Take this and keep it with you, and God will be in our midst—both with me and with you."

4. After he said this, he went out from the room. All those who were in the house were sleeping. He hastened alone into the eastern regions, and he went to the city of Edessa, where there was an image of Christ not made by hands upon a linen cloth.[1] He venerated this cloth with much ardor. He then went to the Church of the Holy Mother of God, changed his garments with those of a poor man, put on a shabby hair shirt, and began to beg around the city.

---

1. This image, also known as the *mandylion*, was widely venerated throughout the Christian East; see Cameron, "History of the Image of Edessa."

5. Իսկ Հայր նորա առաքեաց յամենայն կողմանս զծառայս իւր ի քննել եւ ի գտանել զորդին իւր, զի երեք Հազար ծառայս ունէր արծաթակազմ երիվարօք եւ դիպակազգեստս: Գնացին յուզող ծառայքն եւ յԵդեսիա քաղաքն, եւ տեսեալ զԱլեքսիոս ոչ ծանեան, այլ որպէս աղքատի տային նմա ողորմութիւն. եւ դարձան ունայն ի տուն իւրեանց:

6. Եւ երանելին Ալեքսիոս արարեալ յայնմ քաղաքի օտարաբար մեծ եւ առաքինի ճգնութեամբ, պաՀօք եւ արտասուալից աչօք զամս տասն եւ ութ: Եւ ի շաբաթօջն էր նորա կերակուր երկու նուկի Հաց որ է տասն եւ ութ դրամակշեռ, եւ նոյն չափովն ջուր:

7. Եւ ի միում գիշերի երեւեցաւ յերազի ամենասրբուՀի աստուածածնին եկեղեցպանին Հրեշտակ Տեառն եւ ասէ. Մոյծ զմարդն Աստուծոյ յեկեղեցին, վասն զի արժանաւոր է արքայութեանն Աստուծոյ: Եւ բանս այս յայտնի եղեւ ամենայն քաղաքացեացն, եւ երթային ի տեսութիւն. եւ յայնմ օրէ անուանեցաւ Աստուծոյ մարդ:

8. Եւ ետես երանելին զի յոյժ փառաւորեցաւ ի մարդկանէ՝ փախեաւ ի քաղաքէն եւ ի բազում աւուրս գնաց ի ծովեզրն, եւ մտեալ ի նաւ կամէր երթալ ի Տարսոն քաղաքն յեկեղեցի սուրբ առաքելոյն Պօղոսի: Եւ ելեալ Հողմն ընդդիմակաց եւ մրրիկ յոյժ, եւ տարաւ զնաւն ի Հռոմ ուր ոչն կամէր վասն ծնողացն եւ տանն իւրոյ:

6. Եւ ելեալ Հայրն ետես զնա եւ ոչ ծանեաւ, յանձնեաց զնա միում ի ծառայից իւրոց, զի որպէս աղքատի Աստուծոյ արասցէ նմա ողորմութիւն: Եւ բազում նեղութիւնս անցուցին այլ ծառայքն Հօր նորա ընդ նա, այպն եւ ծաղր առնելով եւ ապտակելով, որ եւ խորտկարարքն լուանային զսկաւառակսն եւ զպտուկսն եւ զջուր լուացմանն Հեղուին ի վերայ գլխոյ եւ անձին նորա:

10. Եւ յետ ժամանակաց գիտաց զմաՀն իւր, խնդրեաց քարտէս եւ գրեաց զամենայն գործս վարուց իւրոց, գրեաց եւ զանուանս Հօրն եւ զմօրն եւ զՀարսինն եւ զիւրն, եւ ունելով զքարտէսն ի ձեռին իւրում աւանդեաց զՀոգին իւր առ որ ցանկացաւն Քրիստոս Մարտի ԺԷ:

11. Եւ ձայն եղեւ յերկնից յապարանս Թագաւորին եւ ասէ. Խնդրեցէք տունն Եփեմիանոսի զԱստուծոյ մարդն որ աղօթեսցէ վասն Հռոմայ եւ վասն ամենայն երկրի: Եւ առժամայն գնաց Թագաւորն Ոնորիոս փութապէս ի տուն Եփեմիանոսի՝ ամենայն իշխանօքն եւ գտին զերանելին մեռեալ. կամեցան ի ձեռանէն առնուլ զքարտէսն, եւ ամենեւին ոչ կարացին Հանել ի ձեռացն:

5. His father sent his servants out into every region to search for and to find his son, for he had three thousand servants on horses with silver harnesses embroidered in brocade. This search party of soldiers went also to the city of Edessa, and although they saw Alexius, they did not recognize him. They even gave him alms as to a poor man, and they returned empty-handed to their own homes.

6. The blessed Alexius conducted himself like a stranger in that city with great and virtuous asceticism, with fasting and tears, for eighteen years. For an entire week his diet consisted of two ounces of bread (which is eighteen pennies' worth) and the same amount of water.

7. One night an angel of the Lord appeared in a dream to the sacristan of the Church of the Holy Mother of God, and he said, "Bring that Man of God into the church for he is worthy of the kingdom of God." These words were made known to all the residents of the city and they went out to see him. And from that day he was called "the Man of God."

8. The blessed one saw that he was being greatly honored by men, so he fled from the city. Several days later he arrived at the seashore and embarked on a ship, intending to go to the city of Tarsus to the Church of Saint Paul the Apostle. But there rose up an opposing wind and a severe storm, and it brought the ship to Rome, where he did not want to go because of his parents and his household.

9. His father came out and saw him but did not recognize him. He then entrusted [Alexius] to one of his servants in order to give him alms as to a poor man of God. The other servants of his father brought many humiliations upon him, mocking him and slapping him around. The kitchen crew would wash the plates and the pots and then pour the dirty dishwater over the head and body of Alexius.

10. Sometime later, Alexius knew that his death was at hand, and he asked for some paper. He wrote down all the deeds of his life; and he also wrote down the name of his father, his mother, and his bride, as well as his own. Grasping the paper in his hand, he handed his spirit over to Christ, for whom he longed, on the seventeenth of March.

11. A voice came down from heaven into the imperial palace and said, "Search the house of Ephemianus for the Man of God, who will pray for Rome and for all the earth." Immediately the emperor Honorius went in haste to the house of Ephemianus with all his princes, but they found that the blessed one had died. They wanted to take the paper from his hand, but they were utterly unable to remove it from his hand.

12. *Եւ Թագաւորն անկաւ ի վերայ ոտից երանելոյն եւ մեծաւ արտասուօք խնդրէր զքարտէսն, եւ դեռ եւս ոչ գիտէին թէ Ալեքսիոս իցէ, եւ առժամայն եբաց զձեռն իւր, եւ ետ զքարտէսն ի Թագաւորն: Եւ հրամայեաց Այխտի դպրին իւրոյ ընթեռնուլ զԹուղթն մեծաձայն ի լուր ամենայն ժողովրդեանն: Եւ իբրեւ լուան ահ մեծ եւ զարմացումն կալաւ զամենեսեան:*

13. *Իսկ հայրն եւ մայրն իբրեւ տեսին եթէ Ալեքսիանոս է որդին իւրեանց, անկան ի վերայ մարմնոյ նորա, եւ զողբսն եւ զկոծս նոցա ընդ գրով ոչ կարեմ արկանել:*

14. *Եւ բարձեալ տարան յեկեղեցին սրբոյ առաքելոյն Պետրոսի, եդին ի տապանի մեծաւ օրհնութեամբ եւ փառաբանութեամբ: Եւ յետոյ փոխեցին զնշխարսն յարծաթի տապան՝ զուգեալ ոսկւով եւ ակամբք. եւ մինչեւ ցայսօր անուշահոտ ձէթ բղխէ ի մարմնոյն, եւ մեծ սքանչելիք լինին ի հիւանդս եւ յամենայն նեղեալս:*

12. Then the emperor fell at the feet of the blessed one, and with many tears he began to plead for the paper (for they did not yet know that it was Alexius), and suddenly he opened his hand and gave the paper to the emperor. He then commanded his scribe Aëtius to read the letter aloud in the hearing of all those people. And when they heard it, great fear and wonder seized all of them.

13. When his father and mother saw that it was their son Alexius, they fell upon his body, but I am unable to express in writing their sorrow and their grief.

14. They took him up and brought him to the Church of the Holy Apostle Peter and laid him in a coffin with many words of blessing and honor. Afterwards they transferred his remains into a silver ark embellished with gold and precious stones. Even to this day a sweet-smelling oil pours forth from his body, and great miracles take place for the sick and for all the afflicted.

Արեգի Ժ

Մարտի ԺԸ

Վարք Կիւրղի Երուսաղեմայ Հայրապետին

1. *Ի յաւուրս Կոստանդեայ Հերձուածող արքային որդւոյ սրբոյն Կոստանդիանոսի մեծի Թագաւորին, էր Կիւրեղ ի սուրբ քաղաքէն Երուսաղեմի, ուղղափառ Հաւատով, եւ էր յոյժ ուսեալ զաստուածային հին եւ նոր կտակարանս, նոյնպէս եւ զամենայն Հանճարս արտաքին փիլիսոփայութեանն: Եւ Թագաւորն Կոստանդեա յարիոսական Հերձուածն եւ ի դաւանութիւնն խոտորեցաւ, եւ ի բաց ընկէց զհօրն իւրոյ զուղղափառ Հաւատն:*
2. *Իսկ երանելին Կիւրեղ աստուածիմաստ վարդապետութեամբն իւրով յոյժ սանձէր եւ պապանձեցուցանէր զամենայն լեզու Հերձուածողացն: Եւ յորժամ ոչ կարացին ընդդիմանալ կամ տալ պատասխանի ըստ արժանեաց, Հնարս իմացան բայց ոչ ի կամաց իւրեանց՝ այլ Աստուծոյ Հրամանաւն: Եւ նստուցին զնա յաթոռ Հայրապետութեան, եւ ձեռնադրեցին զնա Երուսաղեմայ պատրիարք, կարծէին ունայնախորհուրդքն՝ որ եթէ Հանցեն զնա յառաքելական յաթոռն՝ Հաւանի բանից նոցա, եւ լինիցի իբրեւ զնոսա Արիոսի եւ Մանենդոսի խոստովանութեամբն, եւ յակնկալութենէն իւրեանց վրիպեցան:*
3. *Քանզի երանելի Հայրապետն Կիւրեղ աստուածային զօրութեամբն առաւելապէս յանդիմանէր եւ կշտամբէր զնոսա, եւ յայտնապէս նզովէր եւ ընդ անիծիւք արկանէր, եւ զբազումս ի նոցանէ դարձուցանէր յուղղափառութիւն: Եւ նախանձեալ չարին խորհրդակիցն Ակակիոս Կեսարիոյ Պաղեստինացւոց եպիսկոպոսն՝ Հրամանաւ արքային ժողովեաց զամենայն Հերձուածող ժողովուրդն, եւ բռնութեամբ զսուրբն Կիւրեղ իջոյց յաթոռոյն, եւ Հալածեաց ի քաղաքէն եւ ի սահմանացն եւ ի Հայրապետական աթոռոյն եւ ի ժառանգութենէ, եւ նստաւ ինքն յաթոռ պատրիարքութեանն:*

March 18

Areg 10

The life of Cyril, the patriarch of Jerusalem

1. In the days of Constantius, the schismatic ruler and son of the great emperor Saint Constantine,[1] Cyril lived in the holy city of Jerusalem. Orthodox in his faith, he was very learned in the divine Old and New Testaments, as well as in all the wisdom of secular philosophy. The emperor Constantius went astray into the Arian heresy and their confession of faith, and he rejected the orthodox faith of his father.

2. Then the blessed Cyril, with his divinely inspired teaching, forcefully bridled and silenced every discourse of the heretics. When they were unable to stand against him or to make any worthy response to him, they devised a ruse, not by their own volition, but by the command of God. They elected him to the patriarchal throne, and they consecrated him as the patriarch of Jerusalem. These empty-headed fools thought that if they raised Cyril up to the apostolic throne, he would acquiesce to their wishes and become like them in their confession of Arius and Mani. But they were deluded in their expectations.

3. In fact, the blessed patriarch Cyril with divine power began all the more to rebuke and to censure them. He openly anathematized them and heaped curses upon them, and he converted many of them to orthodoxy. Acacius, the bishop of Caesarea in Palestine, driven to jealousy by his evil confidants, gathered together all those heretical people at the command of the emperor and forcefully removed Cyril from the throne and exiled him from the city, its environs, and from the patriarchal throne and from his diocese. Then he himself sat on the patriarchal throne.

---

1. Flavius Julius Constantius (Constantius II), second son of Constantine the Great and Fausta, was emperor from 337 to 361.

4. *Իսկ երանելին Կիւրղոս ելեալ յԵրուսաղեմէ փախստական գնաց ի Տարսոն քաղաքն, եւ ընկալաւ զնա Սիղուանոս սքանչելի եպիսկոպոսն Տարսոնայ մեծաւ խնդութեամբ, եւ նստոյց զնա յաթոռ եպիսկոպոսութեանն իւրոյ, զի ուսուսցէ եւ հաւատացուսցէ զուղղափառ ժողովուրդն եւ դարձուսցէ զմոլորեալսն յԱրիոսի եւ ի Մանենդոսի ժանգոյն: Եւ նա ոչ դադարէր ի լուսաւորելոյ զամենեսեան:*

5. *Եւ յորժամ լուաւ ժանգահաւատն Ակակիոս՝ բորբոքեցաւ նախանձու, դիմեաց բազում ամբոխիւ եւ իբրեւ զայսահար գնաց ի Տարսոն քաղաքն, եւ յոյժ մեղադրէր սպառնալեօք Սիղուանոսի վասն ընդունելոյն զԿիւրղոս: Եւ նա զբանս նորա չաղփաղփութիւն եւ առասպելս համարեցաւ եւ ամենեւին ոչ կամեցաւ լսել նմա: Եւ ժանտն Ակակիոս հրապուրեաց զիշխանս քաղաքին եւ բռնութեամբ զԿիւրեղ եւ զՍիղուանոս եւ զամենայն ժողովուրդն յաքսորս առաքեցին: Եւ Թագաւորն զանարժանն Եւդոքսիոս նստոյց յաթոռ Կոստանդինուպօլսի, եւ զչարալեզուն Եւնոմիոս զեպիսկոպոսն Գերմանիկոյ փոխեաց յաթոռն Կիլիկիոյ:*

6. *Իսկ սուրբն Կիւրղոս յաքսորս եւ ի բանդս եւ ի հալածանս բազում ժամանակս ի չարչարանս կեցեալ՝ ոչ յուսահատեցաւ եւ ոչ ետ անձին իւրում տրտմութեամբ իջանել ի դժոխս, այլ յարաժամ ի բերան ունէր զմարգարէական բանն եթէ. Համբերելով համբերէի Տեառն եւ նայեցաւ առ իս: Եւ ի քարոզելոյ եւ յուսուցանելոյ ոչ դադարէր, եւ ոչ ետ քուն աչացն եւ ոչ հանգիստ մարմնոյն իւրոյ մինչեւ այց արար Աստուած ժողովրդեան իւրոյ:*

7. *Մեռաւ Կոստանդիոս եւ Թագաւորեաց ուրացողն Քրիստոսի Յուլիանոս, եւ յետ նորա պիղծն Վաղէս, եւ յաւուրս նորա այլ դառնութիւն հասուցանէին ճշմարտութեան վկայիցն. այլ թէպէտ եւ իբրեւ զմայրսն Լիբանանու բազմացան եւ բարձրացան՝ այլ իբրեւ զփոշի անցին եւ կորեան ունայնութեամբ աւուրք նոցա:*

4. The blessed Cyril departed from Jerusalem and went as a fugitive to the city of Tarsus. There Sylvanus, the marvelous bishop of Tarsus, received him with great joy, and he appointed him to his own episcopal seat so that he might teach and convince those people who were orthodox and convert those gone astray from the pestilence of Arius and Mani. And he never ceased enlightening everyone.

5. When that pestilential-thinking Acacius heard this, he became furious with envy and hastened with a large crowd and went like one possessed to the city of Tarsus, where he reproved Sylvanus severely and with threats for having received Cyril. [Sylvanus] considered his words as silliness and idle tales, and he refused to listen to him. The malevolent Acacius then seduced the princes of the city, and they forcibly sent Cyril, Sylvanus, and all the people into exile. The emperor then set the unworthy Eudoxius on the throne of Constantinople, and he transferred the evil-tongued Eunomius, bishop of Germanikē, to the throne of Cilicia.[2]

6. As for the holy Cyril, he then suffered a long time in exile, in prison, and in persecution, but he did not lose hope nor did he allow himself to fall into despair due to sadness. Rather, he kept these prophetic words constantly in his mouth, "I waited patiently for the Lord and He looked upon me" (Psalm 39:1, Arm.). And he did not cease preaching and teaching, and he gave no sleep to his eyes nor rest to his body until God visited His people.

7. Constantius died, and Julian, that apostate from Christ, became emperor, and after him the impious Valens.[3] In his days further bitter sufferings were instigated against the martyrs of truth. But although they increased and rose up like the cedars of Lebanon, nevertheless their days passed like the dust, and they perished into nothingness.

---

2. There is some corruption here; Germanikē, historical Marash (modern Kahramanmaras), is in Cilicia, but Eunomius was bishop of Cyzicus in Mysia on the northwest coast of modern Turkey.

3. Julian reigned from 361 to 363, and Valens from 364 to 378, after having actually succeeded Jovian whose short reign is not mentioned here.

8. *Եւ յորժամ հաճեցաւ Աստուած առաքեաց փրկիչ ժողովրդեան իւրոյ զաստուածապարգեւ տուրսն զմեծն Թէոդոս Թագաւոր քրիստոնէից. եւ նա կանգնեաց եւ սրբեաց զամենայն եկեղեցիս ուղղափառաց եւ դարձոյց զհալածեալսն յաքսորանաց եւ առաքեաց յիւրաքանչիւր յաթոռս իւրեանց. զԿիւրեղ յԵրուսաղէմ, զՄելիտոս յԱնտիոք, զԵւսեբիոս ի Սամուստիա: Կացոյց զնոսա գլխաւորս հարիւր եւ յիսուն սուինհոդոսին զոր արար ընդդէմ հոգէմարտ հերձուածոյն, յորում էր Գրիգոր աստուածաբանն եւ սուրբն Ներսէս Հայոց հայրապետն, եւ այլք:*

9. *Իսկ սուրբն Կիւրեղ յետ այնչափ նեղութեանց եւ հալածանօք աքսորանաց եւ աշխատանաց՝ դարձեալ ընկալաւ զաթոռն իւր, յոր անարժանքն ըստ արժանեացն Աստուծոյ ընտրութեամբն նստուցին: Եւ ի բարի եւ ի խորին ծերութիւն հասեալ հանգեաւ յերկնից յարքայութիւնն՝ Մարտի ԺԸ, թողեալ մեզ յիշատակ յաւիտենական զվարդապետական գիրս իւր ի լուսաւորութիւն ամենայն ուղղափառ ժողովրդեանն:*

10. *Կալաւ զաթոռն Երուսաղեմի յառաջ եւ յետոյ սուրբն Կիւրեղ ամս քառասուն եւ երեք, եւ ի հալածանսն յորժամ ընկեցին յաթոռոյն ամս երեսուն եւ չորս:*

8. When God deigned, He sent a savior to His people, a divine gift, Theodosius the Great, as emperor for the Christians.[4] He reestablished and purified all the churches of the orthodox, and he brought back all those who had been sent off into exile; and he sent them back to their own sees: Cyril to Jerusalem, Melitus to Antioch, and Eusebius to Samosata. He also appointed them as heads for a council that he convoked against the heresy of the Pneumatomachians with one hundred and fifty [bishops],[5] among whom were Gregory the Theologian,[6] the holy Armenian patriarch Nersēs,[7] and others.

9. The holy Cyril, after innumerable tribulations, persecutions, exiles, and toils, once again took over his diocese, where unworthy men had elected him from among the worthy ones by the will of God. And in a goodly advanced old age, he came to his rest in the kingdom of heaven on the eighteenth of March, having left for us as an eternal memorial his magisterial writings for the enlightenment of all the orthodox people.[8]

10. The holy Cyril occupied the throne of Jerusalem, before and after [his exile], for forty-three years, and from the persecution when they deposed him from the throne, thirty-four years.

---

4. Theodosius I the Great, the first of the truly orthodox emperors, reigned from 378 to 395. He is remembered in the *Yaysmawurkʿ* on January 19; see Mathews, *On This Day: The Armenian Church Synaxarion—January,* 168-71.

5. The Council of Constantinople, the second ecumenical council, often referred to as the Council of the One Hundred and Fifty, was convoked in 381.

6. Gregory the Theologian (Arm. *Astouadzaban*) was one of the Cappadocian fathers, along with Basil and Gregory of Nyssa and, for a short time, patriarch of Constantinople. He is remembered in the *Yaysmawurkʿ* on January 25; see Mathews, *On This Day: The Armenian Church Synaxarion—January,* 208-15.

7. The story of Nersēs and his exile was already recounted with other details of his life on his feast day, February 19; see Mathews, *On This Day: The Armenian Church Synaxarion—February,* 124-31.

8. The compiler here is almost certainly referring to Cyril's *Catechetical Lectures,* which were very popular and were very quickly translated into other languages, including Armenian.

Յաղագս սուրբ վկայութեան սրբոյն Որէնդի եւ վեց եղբարցն իւրոց

11. *Յետ մահուանն Դիոկղետիանոսի արքային թագաւորեաց Մաքսիմիանոս անօրէնն. եւ ելին ազգ բարբարոսաց յարեւմտից ի սահմանս Հռոմոց՝ որք էին Մավրիտանիք եւ Սկլաւք, եւ յոյժ աւերէին եւ ջնջէին զԹիրաք եւ զՄակեդոնիա եւ զայլ արեւմտից գաւառսն:*

12. *Եւ գրեաց Մարմարովթ բարբարոսաց արքայն առ Մաքսիմիանոս զի ելանիցէ մենամարտիլ ընդ նմա միայն ինքն եւ կամ զայլ ոք տացէ, եւ որ յաղթէ՝ հնազանդեսցի նմա միւս կողմն: Եւ ի տարակուսի լեալ Մաքսիմիանոս քանզի յոյժ երկնչէր ի Մարմարովթայ վասն զօրաւոր եւ հզօր զօրութեան նորա, զի անձամբն որպէս հսկայ էր եւ քաջ պատերազմող: Եւ Մաքսիմիանոս յիշխանացն կամ ի զօրականացն իւրոց զոք ոչ կարաց գտանել որ ելանիցէ մենամարտիլ ընդ Մարմարովթայ:*

13. *Եւ ազդեցուցին նմա վասն սրբոյն Որէնդի՝ եթէ զօրեղ զօրական է եւ հզօր պատերազմող. կոչեաց զնա առաջի իւր՝ եւ տեսանէ զի էր երիտասարդ եւ գեղեցիկ տեսլեամբ, հաճոյ թուեցաւ նմա եւ առաքեաց ընդդէմ թշնամւոյն: Եւ սուրբն Որէնդիոս վեց եղբարբքն աղօթեցին առ Աստուած, եւ մտեալ ի մարտն՝ յաղթեաց ինքն միայն սկայազօր պատերազմողին եւ սպան զնա, եւ հատեալ զգլուխն տարաւ առ Մաքսիմիանոս արքայն: Եւ հնազանդեցան նմա անթիւ զօրքն բարբարոսաց, եւ աղաղակեաց մեծաւ բարբառով Մաքսիմիանոս արքայն, գոհութիւն մատուցանէր զովասանութեամբ կռոցն եթէ ի նոցանէ տուաւ յաղթութիւնն, եւ նոքա զօրացուցին զՈրէնդիոս եւ ետուն նմա զքաջութիւնն:*

14. *Իսկ սուրբ վկայն աղաղակեաց համարձակութեամբ. Քրիստոս զօրացոյց զիս եւ ետ զյաղթութիւն եւ օգնեաց ինձ եւ ոչ աստուածքն քո: Եւ թագաւորն ամաչեաց ի նմանէ զի յոյժ ուրախացոյց զնա, եւ առժամայն ոչ արար նմա չար, այլ մանաւանդ վերափոխեաց ի վեհագոյն պատիւ, եւ բազում տուրս պարգեւեաց նմա, եւ սուրբն ոչինչ կամեցաւ առնուլ ի նմանէ, բայց միայն խնդրեաց զգօտին Մարմարովթայ արքային, զի յոյժ պատուական եւ մեծագին էր. եւ շնորհեաց նմա:*

On this day is the martyrdom of the holy Orentius and his six brothers

1. After the death of the emperor Diocletian, Maximinus[9] came to the throne. A nation of barbarians came forth from the west to the outskirts of Rome; these were the Mauretanians and the Scythians, who severely ravaged and destroyed Thrace and Macedonia as well as other western provinces.

2. Marmaroth, the king of the barbarians, wrote to Maximinus to come out and fight against him, either himself alone or to provide someone else. And to the one who was victorious, the other would be subservient. Maximinus was filled with anguish, for he was exceedingly afraid of Marmaroth because of the great power and might of his strength, for in stature he was like a giant, and he was a powerful combatant. Maximinus was unable to find anyone from among his princes or his soldiers to go out to fight against Marmaroth.

3. Then they made [Maximinus] aware of the holy Orentius, who was a strong soldier and a powerful combatant. [Maximinus] then summoned him into his presence, and he saw that he was young and handsome to look upon. He approved of him and sent him out against the enemy. The holy Orentius, together with his six brothers, prayed to God. He then entered the contest and was victorious over that gigantic combatant. He killed him, cut off his head, and brought it to the emperor Maximinus. And that vast army of barbarians then became subject to him. The emperor Maximinus then cried out in a loud voice and offered praise and acclamation to the idols as if it were by them that the victory had been given and that they had strengthened Orentius and given him courage.

4. Then the holy martyr Orentius cried out boldly, "Christ has strengthened me. He has given me the victory and helped me, not your gods!" The emperor was put to shame by him who had just made him very joyful, so at that moment he did him no harm but even bore him up with the greatest honors and granted him many gifts. But the holy one refused to accept anything from him. He asked only for the belt of King Marmaroth, for it was quite exquisite and of great value, and he granted him this.

---

9. I.e., Maximinus Daia; see p. 17n1 above.

15. *Եւ յետ աւուրց խոչեաց առ ինքն եւ բազում աղաչանօք եւ խոստմամբ ողոքէր եւ խրատ տայր ուրանալ զՔրիստոս եւ զոհել կռոցն, եւ ոչ կարաց դարձուցանել: Եւ հրամայեաց զօրականացն զի զսուրբն Որէնդիոս եւ զվեց եղբարսն իւր աքսորեսցեն ի հեռաւոր երկիր: Եւ ըստ հրամանի նորա տարան զնա ի քաղաքն Տրապիզոնդի եւ զվեց եղբարսն ցրուեցին յԱփխազս եւ ի Ճքերս եւ ի Ջալիկի, եւ անդ ի սովոյ եւ ի մերկութենէ հանդեան բարի խոստովանութեամբ ի Քրիստոս:*

16. *Եւ ի սրբոյն Որենդիոսի կապեցին վէմ մի ի պարանոցն մեծ յոյժ, եւ ընկեցին ի ծովն: Եւ հրեշտակապետն Ռափայէլ եհան զնա ի ցամաքն, եւ կացոյց ի վերայ վիմի եւ անդ աղօթելով առ Աստուած աւանդեաց զհոգին Մարտի ԺԸ: Եւ երեւեցաւ սուրբն քրիստոնէից, եւ երթեալ առին զմարմին եւ թաղեցին պատուով:*

15. Some time later, [Maximinus] summoned [Orentius] to him, and with many entreaties and promises he began to persuade and to counsel him to renounce Christ and to sacrifice to the idols, but he refused to convert. So [Maximinus] ordered his soldiers to exile Orentius and his six brothers into a far-off country. At the command [of the emperor] they brought [Orentius] to the city of Trebizond, and they split up his six brothers in Abkhazia, Djorokh, and Lazikē. And in these places they fell asleep from famine and exposure with a good confession in Christ.

16. As for the holy Orentius, they tied a very huge stone around his neck and then threw him into the sea. The archangel Raphael pulled him out onto dry land and set him upon a rock; while praying there, he committed his spirit to God on the eighteenth of March. This holy one appeared to the Christians, and they came, took up his corpse, and buried him with honor.

Արեգի ԺԱ

Մարտի ԺԹ

Վկայութիւն սրբուհւոյն Կոպրիլայ

1. *Յաւուրս Դիոկղետիանոսի եւ Մաքսիմիանոսի ամբարիշտ*
թագաւորացն՝ էր սրբուհին Կոպրիլա, ի քաղաքէն Կիւրենայ,
քրիստոնեայ եւ քրիստոնէից զաւակ: Եւ յորժամ եղեւ չորեքտասան
ամաց՝ ետուն զնա առն, եւ կեցեալք ի միասին ամս երկու եւ
ամիսս վեց, եղեւ գլխացաւ եւ ի բժշկաց նմա օգուտ ոչ եղեւ:
2. *Եւ ընդ աւուրսն ընդ այնոսիկ էր ի բանդին սուրբն Թէոդորոս*
Կիւրենոյ եպիսկոպոսն վասն Հաւատոյն Քրիստոսի: Գնաց ի
բանդին առ նա երանելին Կոպրիլա, վասն դնելոյ ձեռն ի վերայ
գլխոյն զի ողջասցի, որպէս եւ եղեւ իսկ: Եւ յորժամ գնաց առ
նա՝ եգիտ զերանելի երկու կուսանսն զԼուկիա եւ զԱրուաս, որք
երթեալ էին առ նա եւ լսէին զվարդապետութիւն նորա:
3. *Եւ եղեւ մարտիրոսանալ սրբոյն Թէոդորոսի Կիւրենոյ*
եպիսկոպոսին, եւ դատաւորն սպառնալեօք պատուիրէր նոցա
ուրանալ զՔրիստոս, եւ նոքա ամենեւին ոչ Հաւանեցան եւ ոչ
երկեան ի սպառնալեացն: Եւ էր Կոպրիլա յոյժ գեղեցիկ տեսլեամբ,
եւ դատաւորն տռփացաւ ի նա ցանկութեամբ, եւ պշուցեալ Հայէր
յերեսն: Հրամայեաց եւ եդին ի ձեռս նորա կայծակունս եւ
կնդրուկ զի խնկեսցէ կռոցն, եւ երանելի կինն զմատունսն փակեաց
ի վերայ Հրոյն մինչեւ այրեցան ձեռքն, եւ գեղ երեսաց Թարշամեցաւ:

March 19

Areg 11

The martyrdom of Saint Cyprilla

1. In the days of the impious emperors Diocletian and Maximianus,[1] the holy Cyprilla lived in the city of Cyrene. She was a Christian and from a Christian family. When she was fourteen years old, [her parents] gave her in marriage. She and [her husband] had been living together for two and a half years when she contracted a head ailment for which the doctors had no cure.

2. At that time the holy Theodore, the bishop of Cyrene, was in prison because of his faith in Christ. The blessed Cyprilla went to him in prison so that he might place his hand on her head and she might be healed; and so it happened. And when she went to him, she found two blessed virgins, Lucia and Aroa, who had come to him and were listening to his teaching.

3. It came to pass that the blessed Theodore, bishop of Cyrene, was martyred, and the judge demanded with threats that the [three women] renounce Christ. But they adamantly refused and had no fear of his threats. Now Cyprilla was very beautiful, and the judge burned with desire for her and began to rivet his gaze upon her. He then gave the command that they put into her hands burning coals and incense so that she might offer the incense to the idols, but that blessed woman closed her fingers around the fire until her hands burned and the beauty of her face was marred.

---

1. Maximianus Herculius was coemperor with Diocletian; he reigned from 286 to 305.

4. *Կախեցին զնա մերկ զփայտէ եւ երկաթի քերչօք քերեցին զմարմինն, եւ ընդ արեանն ելանէին քրտունք եւ ի ստեանցն բղխէր կաթն: Եւ տեսեալ դատաւորին զարմացաւ յոյժ, իջուցին ի փայտէն, եւ աղօթեալ առ Աստուած՝ աւանդեաց զհոգին Մարտի ԺԹ: Եւ բուրեաց ի մարմնոյն անուշահոտութիւն:*

5. *Իսկ երանելի կուսանքն Լուկիա եւ Արուաս հրամանաւ դատաւորին թաղեցին զսրբուհին Կոպրիա մեծաւ պատուով: Եւ կաթն ի ստեանց բղխելոյ ոչ դադարէր, եւ աղաչեցին կուսանքն զԱստուած եւ արգելաւ կաթն ի ստեանցն:*

Յայսմ աւուր տօն սրբոյն Յովհաննու Երուսաղէմայ Հայրապետին

6. *Յովհաննէս Նստաւ յաթոռ Հայրապետութեան յետ սրբոյն Կիւրղի Երուսաղեմացւոյ, որ եւ վասն ոսկեսիրութեան յանդիմանեցաւ ի սրբոյն Եպիփանէ, զի այլ ամենայն առաքինութեամբ գերազանցեալ էր յոյժ: Որ յետ բազում վաստակոց եւ արդեանց վասն եկեղեցւոյ հանգեաւ խաղաղութեամբ ի Քրիստոս:*

4. They hanged her naked from a tree, and they scraped her body with iron nails; along with the blood there came forth sweat and from her breasts there poured forth milk. When the judge saw this, he marveled greatly and had her taken down from the tree. She prayed to God and handed her soul over to God on the nineteenth of March, and a sweet odor poured out from her body.

5. Then at the command of the judge, the blessed virgins, Lucia and Aroa, buried the holy Cyprilla with great honor. As the milk had not ceased pouring out from her breasts, the virgins prayed to God, and the milk ceased [flowing] from her breasts.

On this day is the feast of John, the patriarch of Jerusalem

6. John sat on the patriarchal throne after the holy Cyril of Jerusalem. Because of his love for gold, he was reprimanded by the holy Epiphanius, for he was preeminent in all the other virtues. After much labor and exertion on behalf of the church, he fell peacefully asleep in Christ.

Արեգի ԺԲ

Մարտի Ի

Վկայաբանութիւն սրբոց Յունանու եւ Բարաքիսի եւ ինն մարտիրոսաց Զանիթեայ, Ղազարոսի, Մարութայի, Ներսեհի, Եղիայի, Մարինի, Աբիբոսի, Սիմբեթեայի եւ Սաբայի

1. *Քրիստոսի մարտիրոսքն Յունան եւ Բարաքիոս՝ էին ի Պարսիկս առ Սաբուռիոսիւ Հրապաշտ արքային Պարսից: Եւ յաւուրս մեծի Թագաւորին Կոստանդիանոսի էին կրօնաւորք աբեղայք, եւ ելեալ ի վանաց իւրեանց գնացին ի գեօղն որ կոչի Մարդաբոք, յորում էին ի բանդի ինն խոստովանող վկայքն Քրիստոսի: Եւ մտեալ ի բանդս ողջունեցին եւ քաջալերէին զնոսա Հաստատուն կալ ի սէրն Քրիստոսի, եւ մեռանել վասն անուան նորա եւ ժառանգել զանստուեր լոյսն եւ զանապառ կեանսն յարքայութեանն Աստուծոյ:*

2. *Եւ տեսեալ զնոսա ոմանք ի Պարսիցն երթեալ մատնեցին զնոսա երեք մոգպետացն որք էին իշխանք, Մաադրաթ, Շիրա, Մախառնիս. եւ առաքեցին զօրականս եւ տարան առաջի՝ զՅունան եւ զԲարաքիոն: Եւ ողորմանօք խրատ տային եւ նեղէին զնոսա պաշտել զարեգակն եւ զհուր. եւ ոչ կարացին դարձուցանել զնոսա ի լուսոյն Քրիստոսի:*

March 20

Areg 12

The martyrdom of Saints Jonas and Barachisias, and of the nine martyrs Xanthos, Lazaros, Maroutha, Nersēs, Elijah, Mari, Habib, Simberdes, and Sabas

1. These martyrs of Christ lived in Persia during the time of Shapur,[1] the fire-worshipping king of the Persians. In the days of the great emperor Constantine,[2] they were solitary monks who left their monastic dwellings and went to a village called Mardabok, where there were nine witnesses who had been imprisoned for professing Christ. When they entered the prison, they greeted them and encouraged them to remain steadfast in their love for Christ, to die on behalf of His name, and thus to inherit that light without shadow and that life without end in the kingdom of God.

2. Some of the Persians saw them and went and denounced them to three of the chief magi who were also princes: Masdrath, Shira, and Makharnis. These sent soldiers, and they brought Jonas and Barachisias into their presence. With persuasive words, they counseled them and then pressed them to worship the sun and the fire, but they were unable to turn them away from their hope in Christ.

---

1. Shapur II, also known as "The Great," was ruler of the Sasanian Empire from 309 to 379; during much of his reign he was involved in invading Armenia or Mesopotamia.
2. Constantine the Great was emperor from 306 to 337.

3. Հրամայեցին եւ զՅունան միայն կապեցին պարսկօրէն, զերկու ոտսն ի մի եւ զերկու ձեռսն ի մի, եւ անցուցին փայտ ընդ ձեռսն եւ ընդ ոտսն, եւ ընկեցին որպէս կոճղ յերկիր: Եւ արք զօրաւորք Հարկանէին զնա ուժգին որպէս զվէմ դալար բրօք, եւ քարշէին արտաքս յաւուրս սաստիկ ցրտոյ. եւ թողին զնա մերկ նոյն կապանօք զգիշերն ամենայն: Եւ առաւօտուն Հարցանէին եթէ. Որպէս եղեր ի գիշերիս: Եւ նա ասէ. Մինչեւ ծնեալ է մայրն իմ զիս յերկիր՝ այսպիսի անուշ քուն եւ Հանգիստ ոչ եմ լեալ:

4. Տարան առաջի եւ զսուրբն Բարաքիոս, եւ նոքա նոյնպէս եւ զնա պատրողական բանիւք ջանային խաբել, եւ ամենեւին ոչ կարացին խախտել ի Հաւատոցն Քրիստոսի: Կախեցին զերանելին գլխիվայր, եւ Հատին զմատունս ձեռացն եւ ոտիցն, եւ արկին զերկոսեանն ի բանդ:

5. Իսկ զինն սուրբ վկայսն ի ցերեկի ոչ իշխէին Հարցանել եւ քննել վասն վարդապետութեանն Յունանու եւ Բարաքիոսի. այլ ի գիշերի Հարցաքննութիւն առնէին, եւ բռնադատէին զնոսա ուրանալ զՔրիստոս եւ լինել պարսկական Հաւատովն: Եւ նոքա որպէս ի միոջէ բերանոյ մեծաւ անարգանօք նզովեցին զուրացողսն Քրիստոսի աստուածութեանն եւ զպաշտօղս արեգականն եւ Հրոյ: Այրեցին Հրով զկողս եւ զկուշտս նոցա, եւ Հալեալ կապար Հեղին յարտեւանունսն եւ յունչս եւ յականջս նոցա, եւ ապա քարշեցին արտաքս եւ Հատին զինն մարտիրոսացն զգլուխն, եւ ընկեցին զմարմինսն ի խոր գուբ:

6. Եւ զսրբոյն Յունանու շուրջ զգլխովն քերթեցին եւ Հանին փող, Հատին եւ զլեզուն, եւ զմարմինն պնդեցին ի մամուլս, մինչեւ ամենայն ոսկերքն ջախջախեցան:

7. Եւ զսրբոյն Բարաքիոս գլորեցին մերկ ի վերայ փշոց, եւ Հերձեալ եղեգունս եւ պնդեցին բարակ չուանօք ընդ մարմինն մինչեւ թաղեցաւ յանձնն: Եւ ապա մի մի բռնութեամբ քարշէին զՀերձեալ եղեգունս, եւ յոյժ կտրատեցաւ անձնն՝ եւ արիւնն որպէս առու Հեղոյր ի մարմնոյն: Եւ ապա ընկեցին զերկոսեանն ի խոր գուբն կիսամահ, ուր եւ զայլ ինն սուրբսն ընկեցին, եւ այնպէս աւանդեցին զՀոգիս իւրեանց առ Աստուած Մարտի Ի:

3. [The three chief magi] commanded that they bind Jonas alone in the Persian style with the two feet together and the two hands together, and then insert a large branch through the hands and the feet and throw him down on the ground like a log. And the soldiers struck him viciously with green branches as if on a rock, then dragged him outside during a time of extreme cold. They left him there naked in those same bonds throughout the entire night. In the morning they asked him, "How did you pass the night?" And he responded, "Since my mother brought me into the world, I have never had such a pleasant and restful sleep."

4. They then brought in the holy Barachisias, and in the same fashion they also tried to deceive him with seductive words, but they were completely unable to turn him away from his faith in Christ. They then hanged the blessed one up upside down, and they cut off the fingers from his hands and [the toes] from his feet and then threw both of them into prison.

5. They did not dare to interrogate or to examine those nine holy witnesses during the day concerning the teaching of Jonas and Barachisias, so they began their interrogation during the night. They pressed them to renounce Christ and to come over to the Persian belief. But they, as if with one mouth, cursed with many insults those who denied the divinity of Christ and worshipped the sun and the fire. The [interrogators] then burned their flanks and their midriffs with fire, melted down lead, and poured it over their eyelids and into both their noses and their ears. And then they dragged these nine martyrs outside, cut off their heads, and then threw their corpses into a deep pit.

6. They peeled the skin from around the head of the holy Jonas, pulled out his larynx, cut out his tongue, and then they bound his body onto a winepress until every one of his bones was crushed.

7. As for the holy Barachisias, they rolled [his body] naked over thorns; then they cut down some reeds and tied them with thin cords around him until his entire body was covered. Then with great force they pulled those cut reeds out one by one, and his entire body was completely torn to pieces, and his blood poured out like a river from his body. They then threw both [Jonas and Barachisias] half dead into that deep pit where they had thrown the other nine holy ones, and in this way they handed their souls over to God on the twentieth of March.

8. *Եւ ոմն մի պարսիկ քրիստոնեայ որոյ անուն էր Աբդիշոյ տուեալ հինգ հարիւր դրամ գնեաց զմետասան մարմին սրբոց վկայիցն, եդիր պատուով ի տեղի նշանաւոր:*

Յայսմ աւուր վկայութիւն սրբոյն Եմելիանոսին

9. *Քրիստոսի վկայն Եմելիանոս էր ծառայ առն հեթանոսի, ի քաղաքէն Դորոսթոլեայ, յաւուրս յանցող արքային Յուլիանոսի, ուրացողին Քրիստոսի. եւ ինքն էր քրիստոնեայ:*

10. *Եւ ի միում աւուր գտեալ զդուրս տաճարի կռոցն ի բաց եւ ի ներքս ի մարդկանէ ոչ զոք ետես, էառ ծանր կռան եւ մտեալ խորտակեաց զամենայն բագինսն մանր, եւ զզոհսն ցրուեաց: Եւ յորժամ տեսին քուրմքն կալան զոմն հողագործ, տանջէին եւ քարշէին առաջի Բիկանիրի: Եւ տեսեալ Եմելիանոս զայրն ի նեղութեան, եկաց առաջի եւ խոստովանեցաւ զմեղսն զոր արար, եւ ասէ. Ես եմ քրիստոնեայ, եւ արժան էր ինձ որ զայն առնէի: Մերկացուցին զնա եւ հարին ուժգին արջառաջլօք, ապա ընկեցին ի հուր եւ ոչ այրեցաւ, եւ գոհանալով եւ փառաւորելով զԱստուած՝ աւանդեաց զհոգին իւր առ Աստուած: Եւ շնորհս տուաւ յԱստուծոյ սրբոյն Եմելիանոսի արագահաս օգնական լինել ամենայն նաւակոծելոց ի մրրկեալ ալեաց ծովու:*

8. One of those Persians, a Christian whose name was Abidîšô, paid five hundred drachmas and purchased the eleven bodies of the holy martyrs; he then placed them with honor in a distinguished place.

On this day is the martyrdom of the holy Emilianus

9. Emilianus, the martyr for Christ, was a servant of a certain pagan in the city of Dorostorum, in the days of Julian, the apostate emperor who renounced Christ. He was himself a Christian.

10. One day he found the gates to the temple of the idols open, and he saw no other person inside. He picked up a heavy hammer, entered, and smashed all the altars into little pieces. When the priests of the idols saw what had happened, they seized a certain farmer, tortured him, and brought him before [the judge] Bikanir. When Emilianus saw the man in such torment, he presented himself and confessed the sins he had committed and said, "I am a Christian, and it was necessary to do what I did." They then stripped him and beat him severely with bullwhips. They then threw him into a fire, but he was not burned. Rather, he gave praise and glory to God while he handed his spirit over to God. Grace was given by God to the holy Emilianus to come swiftly to all those who suffer shipwreck from the stormy waves of the sea.

Արեգի ԺԳ

Մարտի ԻԱ

Վարք սուրբ Հօրն Բենեդիկտոսի

1. Սուրբ Հայրն Բենեդիկտոս էր ի Կամպանիոյ երկրէն, յոյժ տեղեակ աստուածային կտակարանաց, եւ ի տղայութենէ սիրեաց զվարս միայնակեցութեան, եւ բնակէր յայրի միում անգիտելի ի մարդկանէ:

2. Եւ ի տօնի սուրբ զատկին երեւեցաւ Աստուած երիցու միոջ՝ որ պատրաստեալ էր իւր բազում խորտիկս եւ կամէր ճաշակել ընտանեօք իւրովք, եւ ասէ ցնա. Երէց՝ դու ազգի ազգի խորտիկս պատրաստեցեր քեզ, եւ ծառայն իմ Բենեդիկտոս յայս նիչ այրի քաղցեալ է, տար նմա ի խորտկաց այտի: Եւ առժամայն առեալ երիցուն յամենայն խորտկացն տարաւ նմա ի ցուցեալ այրն: Եւ ասէ ցնա երէցն. Արի Հայր եւ ճաշակեսցուք ի միասին ի պարգեւացս զոր առաքեաց քեզ Աստուած՝ զի Զատիկ Տեառն է: Եւ ասէ սուրբն. Արդարեւ Զատիկ է, որովհետեւ տեսի զքեզ եւ ոչ գիտէր եթէ Յարութիւն Փրկչին էր: Եւ ասէ երէցն. Ստուգապէս Յարութիւն Տեառն է, եւ գոհացեալք զԱստուծոյ ճաշակեցին ի միասին:

3. Եւ կին մի փայտեղէն ամանով ցորեան բերէր նմա, եւ սատանայ ընկէց զամանն եւ ջարդեաց, եւ սկսաւ կինն լալ: Եւ առեալ սրբոյն զանօթն ի ձեռս իւր եւ խաչակնքեալ ի վերայ ողջացոյց եւ ետ ցկինն, եւ գնաց ուրախութեամբ:

March 21

Areg 13

The life of our holy father Benedict

1. Our holy father Benedict, deeply versed in the divine testaments, was from the region of Campania.[1] From his childhood he loved the solitary life and began to live in a cave unknown to anyone else.

2. On the holy feast of Easter, God appeared to a certain priest while he was preparing a number of roasted dishes, wishing to eat them with his family, and said to him, "O priest, you have prepared for yourself these various roasted dishes, but my servant Benedict is suffering hunger in a certain cave; take some of your roasted dishes to him." The priest immediately took a portion from all his roasted dishes and brought them to the cave that [God] had indicated. The priest said to [Benedict], "Come, father, let us eat together from the gifts that God has sent to you, for it is the paschal feast of the Lord." And the holy one responded, "Truly it is a paschal feast since I have seen you," for he did not know that it was the [day of the] resurrection of the Savior. And the priest said, "It is truly the [day of the] resurrection of the Lord, so let us give praise to God and eat together."

3. A woman once brought him some grain in a bowl, but Satan knocked the bowl [out of her hands] and broke it, and the woman began to cry. The holy one picked up the vessel in his hand, made the sign of the cross over it, and thus repaired it. He then gave it to the woman, and she went away full of joy.

---

1. This region in southeastern Italy is actually where Benedict spent the end of his life. He grew up in Nursia (modern Norcia), which is in the region of Perugia, north of Campania.

4. *Եւ եկեալ եղբարք ի վանաց մի աղաչէին զնա լինել նոցա առաջնորդ, եւ գնաց առ նոսա. եւ նոքա տաղտկացեալ ի սքանչելի վարուց նորա եւ ի խրատուէ խառնեցին ի կերակուր նորա մահադեղ, եւ խաչակնքնեալ սրբոյն ի վերայ ամանոյն՝ առժամայն հերձաւ: Եւ հրաման ետ սուրբն ագռաւու միոյ եւ առեալ զխարդախ կերակուրն ընկէց արտաքոյ վանաց, եւ ինքն եկեալ ընկալաւ ի ձեռաց հօրն զանխարդախ կերակուրն:*

5. *Եւ գնաց սուրբն ի նոցանէ, եւ շինեաց երկու վանս եւ ժողովեաց ովեաց աշակերտս բազումս, եւ ուսոյց նոցա զկարգ եւ զկրօն ճգնաւորաց եւ կրօնաւորաց: Գրեաց ինքն գիրս եւ կանոնս վարուց կրօնաւորաց եւ քաղաքականաց զոր մինչեւ ցայսօր ունին ամենայն ազգք Հռովմայեցւոց, եւ առնեն անպակաս վանականք եւ աշխարհականք:*

6. *Եւ հասեալ ի խորին ծերութիւն հանգեաւ ի Քրիստոս Մարտի ԻԱ:*

Յայսմ աւուր վկայութիւն սրբուհւոյն Մատրոնայ Թեսաղոնիկեցւոյ

7. *Կինս այս էր աղախին հրէի միոյ կնոջ որոյ անուն էր Պաւլիտեա, սանտրէր եւ հիւսէր զհերս տիկնոջ իւրոյ: Եւ ի ժամ աղօթիցն յուղարկէր զտիկինն իւր ի ժողովարանն հրէից եւ ինքն երթայր յեկեղեցին քրիստոնէից եւ յաղօթս կայր:*

4. Some brothers came from one of the monasteries to beg him to become their abbot. He went with them, but they became annoyed with his astonishing way of life and of his counsel, so they mixed some poison into his food. When the holy one made the sign of the cross over the bowl, it immediately broke. The holy one then commanded a crow, and it took up that contaminated food and threw it outside the monastery and returned to receive from the hand of the father some uncontaminated food.

5. The holy one then took his leave of them, built two monasteries, and gathered together some brothers there. Because they had no water, he caused a spring of water to come forth. He gathered together numerous disciples and taught them the rule and the conduct of monastic and ascetical life. He composed books and regulations for the lifestyles of both ascetics and laypeople, which even to this day all the nations of the Romans possess, and the monks and laypeople both practice unfailingly.[2]

6. He attained to a ripe old age and fell asleep in Christ on the twenty-first of March.

On this day is the martyrdom of Saint Matrona of Thessalonica

7. This woman was the maidservant of a certain Jewish woman whose name was Politeia; she brushed and braided the hair of her mistress. At the hour of prayer she would accompany her mistress to the Jewish synagogue, and then she would go to the Christian church and pray.

---

2. *The Rule of Benedict* quickly became the standard guide for much of western monastic life, and is even still used by many laypeople as a guide for their own Christian life. It was translated into Classical Armenian by Saint Nersēs Lambronatsʿi. It has been translated many times into English.

8. *Եւ մատնեցին զնա առ տիկինն իւր եթէ քրիստոնեայ է, եւ նա դարձեալ պատմեաց Հրէիցն։ Եւ ժողովեցան առ նա եւ գանեցին զՄատրոնա ուժգին չորք արք, եւ արկին ի բանդ կապանօք, եւ թողին զնա զաւուրս չորս անսուաղ։ Եւ ապա հանին ի բանդէն եւ այնչափ գանեցին զնա միւսանգամ՝ մինչեւ ամենայն մարմինն քերթեցաւ, եւ դարձեալ արկին ի բանտ եւ անտես արարին զնա բազում աւուրս, եւ ի սովոյն եւ ի ցաւագին վշտացն վիրաւորեալ անձինն՝ աղօթելով եւ բարի խոստովանութեամբ աւանդեաց զհոգին իւր առ Աստուած Մարտի ԻԱ։*

9. *Եւ հրամայեաց տիկինն իւր հանել ի բանդէն զմարմին նորա եւ ձգել արտաքոյ քաղաքին, զոր առեալ քրիստոնէիցն թաղեցին ի պողոտայն։*

10. *Եւ յետ հալածանացն Աղեկսանդրոս Թեսաղոնիկոյ եպիսկոպոսն ի ներքս ի քաղաքին շինեաց մատուռն, եւ անդ հանգոյց զնշխարս սրբուհւոյն Մատրոնայ։*

11. *Իսկ Պաւլիտեա տիկինն իւր յոյժ աղքատացաւ եւ մուրանայր. եւ ի սովոյն եմուտ ի հնձան զի ժողովեսցէ զճմլեալ խաղողոյն զկուտսն, անկաւ գերան հնձանին ի վերայ նորա եւ չար մահուամբ սատակեցաւ։*

12. *Եւ նշխարք սրբոյն Մատրոնայի զամենայն ախտս եւ զհիւանդութիւնս փարատէ որք հաւատով ապաւինին ի տապանի։*

8. Some betrayed her to her mistress, [informing her] that [Matrona] was a Christian, and she went and repeated this to the other Jews. Four men surrounded Matrona and beat her severely. They then threw her bound into prison, and they left her there for four days without any food. They brought her back out from prison and beat her again so badly that her entire body was lacerated. They then threw her back into prison and abandoned her there for many days. As a result of her hunger and her painfully wounded body, she gave up her spirit to God, while praying and with a good confession, on the twenty-first of March.

9. Her mistress commanded that they take her corpse out from the prison and cast it outside the city. Christians took it up and buried her along the road.

10. After the persecutions, Alexander, the bishop of Thessalonica, had a chapel built in the center of the city, and he had the remains of the holy Matrona reposed there.

11. As for Politeia, her mistress, she became very poor and had to turn to begging. Due to her hunger, she went into a winepress in order to collect the seeds from the pressed grapes, when a beam from the winepress fell on her, and thus she perished by an awful death.

12. The relics of the holy Matrona remove all sorts of infirmities and illnesses of those who faithfully place their trust in her tomb.

Արեգի ԺԴ

Մարտի ԻԲ

Վարք Ակակիոսի խոստովանող եպիսկոպոսին

1. *Յաւուրս Դէկոսի ամբարիշտ արքային՝ խոստովանողն Քրիստոսի սուրբ եպիսկոպոսն Ակակիոս, համարձակութեամբ քարոզէր զՔրիստոս ի մէջ ժողովրդեան կռապաշտիցն, ի գաւառս եւ ի քաղաքս եւ ի գեօղս: Եւ կալեալ զնա անօրինացն կացուցին առաջի հիւպատոսին Մարկիանոսի, եւ հարցանէր վասն քարոզութեանն եւ վարդապետութեանն իւրոյ: Իսկ երանելի քահանայապետն Քրիստոսի բացեալ զբերան իւր՝ պայծառ բանիւք քարոզեաց զՔրիստոսի աստուածութիւնն եւ զկամաւոր մարդեղութիւնն, եւ զփրկական չարչարանսն, եւ զերեքօրեայ յարութիւնն, զվերանալն յերկինս, եւ զմիւսանգամ գալուստն եւ զհատուցումն գործոց ամենայն մարդկան: Եւ յանդիմանեաց զչաղփաղփութիւն առասպելագրաց հեթանոսաց:*
2. *Եհարց Մարկիանոս եւ վասն սէրովբէից եւ քերովբէից: Եւ նա պատմեաց նմա մի ըստ միոջէ զորպիսութիւն եւ զկերպս ամենայն անմարմին զուարթնոցն յորոց վերայ նստեալ է Աստուած եւ հանգչի ի սուրբս իւր: Եւ բռնաւորն ոչ հաւատաց եւ ոչ ընդունեցաւ, այլ մանաւանդ հրամայեաց եւ ձաղկեցին զերանելի եպիսկոպոսն ուժգին եւ արկին ի բանդ:*
3. *Եւ գրեաց Մարկիանոս զամենայն բանսն առ Դեկոս արքայն: Եւ նա առաքեաց հրաման զի առանց անարգանաց եւ գանից արձակեսցեն զսուրբն Ակակիոս: Եւ առժամայն հանին ի բանդէն եւ արձակեցին խաղաղութեամբ: Եւ գնաց ի տուն իւր ունելով յանձին իւրում զչարչարանս Քրիստոսի: Եւ զբազումս լուսաւորեաց վարդապետութեամբ իւրով եւ խառնեաց ի հաւատն Քրիստոսի. եւ կատարեաց մեծ սքանչելագործութեամբ զկեանս իւր եւ ըստ հաճոյիցն Աստուծոյ հանգեաւ ի Քրիստոս Մարտի ԻԲ:*

March 22

Areg 14

The life of Acacius, bishop and confessor

1. In the days of the impious emperor Decius, the holy bishop and confessor of Christ Acacius was courageously proclaiming Christ among idol-worshipping people in the provinces, in the cities, and in the villages. Those wicked ones seized him and brought him before Marcianos, the consul, who questioned him about his preaching and his teaching. Then that blessed hierarch of Christ opened his mouth, and with brilliant eloquence he proclaimed the divinity of Christ, his voluntary incarnation, his salvific passion, his resurrection on the third day, his ascension into heaven, his coming back in the future, and his recompensing everyone for their works. And he condemned the absurd nonsense in their pagan mythology.

2. Marcianos also asked him about the seraphim and the cherubim. [Acacius] described for him in detail the types and the forms of all the incorporeal angels along with whom God sits and reposes among his holy ones. That tyrant was not persuaded nor did he accept this, but rather he commanded that the holy bishop be severely flogged and thrown into prison.

3. Marcianos wrote down all these things for the emperor Decius. And [Decius] ordered that they release the blessed Acacius without any insults or any beatings. They immediately released him from prison and sent him off in peace. He then went home bearing in his body the sufferings of Christ. He enlightened many by his teaching and brought them into the faith of Christ. He completed his life with great miracles, and according to the will of God, he fell asleep in Christ on the twenty-second of March.

Արեգի ԺԵ

Մարտի ԻԳ

Վկայութիւն Մարկոսի Արեթուսայ եպիսկոպոսի եւ Կիւրղի սարկաւագին եւ այլոց մարտիրոսաց

1. *Յորժամ Աստուած ներողութեամբն իւրով թոյլ տուեալ՝ թագաւորեաց գազանաբնութիւնն Յուլիանոս, ուրացողն եւ հայհոյիչն Քրիստոսի, թագուցեալ եւ գաղտակեաց կռապաշտքն համարձակեցան, եւ յայտնապէս զթոյնս իւրեանց հեղին եւ սփռեցին: Եւ շինեցին տաճար կռոցն եւ բագինս կանգնեցին, եւ շաղախեցին զերկիր յարենէ եւ ի ճենճերաց զոհիցն, եւ զդաւանողս ճշմարտութեանն անարգէին եւ թշնամանէին, այպն առնէին եւ անգոսնէին:*
2. *Եւ ոչ ժուժկալեալ քրիստոնէիցն նոցա՝ զնոյն եւ նոքա առնէին, եւ անօրէնքն վստահանալով ի պիղծ արքայն իւրեանց՝ սկսան գանել ձաղկել եւ կոփահարել զբարեպաշտսն: Կամեցան ըմբռնել եւ զերանելին Մարկոս զԱրեթուսայ եպիսկոպոսն, վասն զի նա յաւուրս Կոստանդիանոսի թագաւորին բազում տաճարս կռոց եւ բագինս խորտակեաց եւ եկեղեցի շինեաց:*
3. *Եւ լուեալ զչար խորհուրդս նոցա՝ փախեաւ ըստ տէրունական հրամանին, եւ անօրէնքն փոխանակ նորա զայլ ոք կալան: Եւ գիտացեալ երանելին գնաց առ նոսա. եւ նոքա որպէս կատաղի շունք՝ ոչ ի ծերութիւնն խնայելով, եւ ոչ յալեացն պատկառելով, մերկացուցին զնա եւ չարչար գանիւք վիրաւորեցին զամենայն մարմին նորա:*
4. *Ժողովեցին մանկունս ի դպրոցաց, եւ երկաթի գրչօք ծակոտեցին զգագաթն նորա. եւ օճին զմարմինն մեղու՝ եւ ի խորշակի աւուր կախեցին ի բարձրաւանդակի. եւ պիծակք եւ գոռեղք եւ մեղուք եւ մժեխք կրծեցին զմարմինն եւ զոսկերսն:*

March 23

Areg 15

The martyrdom of Mark, the bishop of Arethusa, the deacon Cyril, and other martyrs

1. While God in his mercy was allowing it, the beastly natured Julian, who rejected and blasphemed Christ, had become emperor. Idol worshippers, who had been hiding and concealing themselves, were now emboldened and they now openly poured forth and disseminated their venom. They built a temple for their idols, erected altars, and saturated the earth with the blood and the burnt meat of their sacrifices. They also began to contemn and insult those who were professing the truth, and they even began to mock and ridicule them.

2. The Christians did not endure this patiently, and they did the same back; but those criminal ones, banking on the support of their detestable emperor, began to flog, to scourge, and to beat the faithful. They even wished to apprehend the blessed Mark, bishop of Arethusa, for in the days of the emperor Constantine he had destroyed numerous temples and altars to the idols and had built churches [in their places].

3. Hearing of their evil intentions, [Mark] fled at the command of the Lord, and those criminal ones installed someone else in his place. When the blessed one learned of this, he went to them, but they, like rabid dogs, showed no respect for his old age or for his venerable gray hairs. They stripped him naked, and with vicious beatings they crippled his entire body.

4. They gathered up children from the schools, and these punctured his skull with iron quills and covered his body in honey. Then, during the hottest part of the day, they propped him up on a high place where wasps, horseflies, bees, and mosquitoes bit away at his flesh and his bones.

5. *Եւ յորժամ իջուցին՝ պահանջէին ի նմանէ եւ խնդրէին գանձս զի չինեսցեն զտաճար կռոցն զոր կործանեաց, եւ նորա ոչ ինչ ունելով տալ ասէր. Զանձն իմ ետու փոխանակ եւ այլ ոչ ինչ պարտիմ ձեզ: Եւ առժամայն արձակեցին զնա եւ զարմանային ընդ համբերութիւնն: Այլ զոր յաւուրսն յայնոսիկ ի ծովու եւ ի ցամաքի չարչարէին զքրիստոնեայսն հրամանաւ բռնաւորին՝ ընդ գրով ոչ ոք կարէ արկանել:*

6. *Իսկ զերանելին Կիւրեղ սարկաւագն որ յաւուրս Կոստանդիանոսի յերկիրն Փիւնիկեայ աստուածանախանձ ջանիւք բազում տաճարս կռոց կործանեաց, եւ զբագինս խորտակեաց, զայն յիշեցին ամբարիշտքն եւ կալեալ սպանին զնա: Պատառեցին զորովայնն եւ հանեալ զլեարդն հաղորդեցան ամենեքեան, եւ նոյնժամայն ատամունքն իւրեանց անկան, եւ լեզուքն նեխեալ տրորեցան, եւ յաչացն կուրացան, եւ սկսան աղաղակել եւ յայտնել զքրիստոնէից զօրութիւնն:*

7. *Եւ յԱսկաղոն եւ ի Գազա եւ ի Պաղեստինեայ քաղաքսն բազում բարեպաշտ քահանայք եւ կրօնաւորք եւ կուսան կանայք եւ աշխարհականք կալեալ պատառէին զորովայնսն եւ արկանէին ի ներքս գարի եւ տային կերակուր խոզից:*

8. *Եւ ի Սեւաստիա բացին զտապան սրբոյն Յովհաննու Մկրտչին եւ զմնացեալ անդ պատուական մարմինսն այրեցին հրով եւ զփոշին հողմով ցրուեցին:*

9. *Եւ մի ոմն Արտեմիանոս անուն առ սրբով Կոստանդիանոսիւ զօրավար եւ դուքս լեալ Եգիպտոսի, այր իմաստուն եւ ընտրեալ հաւատով, բազում կուռս եւ բագինս խորտակեաց, եւ զտաճարս պղծագոհացն կործանեաց, զնա ընկեցին ի պատուոյն եւ յիշխանութենէն եւ հատին զգլուխ նորա: Եւ զԵմէլիանոս քաջ զօրականն հրով այրեցին:*

10. *Եւ զայս եւս հրամայեաց անօրէն բռնաւորն, զի քրիստոնեայ ոք՝ ոչ իշխան եւ ոչ զօրական լիցի, եւ որք իցեն՝ անկցին: Եւ դարձեալ օրինադրութիւն գրեաց հրամանաբար, որպէս զի քրիստոնէից որդիք ոչ ուսանիցին զարտաքին գրոց համարողական, զհռետորական, զփիլիսոփայական, զհոմերոսական ստորոգութեան հանճարս. Զի, ասէր, ուսանին զմերս, զիտեն եւ զիւրեանցն, եւ երկոքումբք սպառազինին, եւ զինու բանիւք մարտնչին եւ յաղթեն մեզ:*

5. After they brought Mark down, they pressed him and demanded from him money so that they might rebuild their idol temple that he had destroyed, but he, having no money to give them, said, "I have given you my person instead; I have no other obligation to you." Immediately they released him as they were amazed at his endurance. But as for what the Christians suffered in those days at the command of that tyrant, both on land and on sea, no one is able to put it down in writing.

6. As for the blessed Cyril, he was a deacon in the region of Phoenicia in the days of Constantine. With divine zeal he had destroyed many temples to the idols and laid waste their altars. The impious remembered him, seized him, and killed him. They slashed open his belly and removed his liver, which they all ate together. Immediately, their teeth fell out, their tongues rotted and became putrid, their eyes lost their sight, and they began to shout out and to proclaim the power of the Christians.

7. In Ascalon, in Gaza, and in the cities of Palestine, many orthodox priests, monks, consecrated virgins, and laypeople were seized. They had their bellies ripped out, grain stalks shoved inside them, and they were then fed to pigs.

8. In Sebaste, they opened up the tomb of Saint John the Baptist, and they burned in fire all that remained of his precious corpse, and they scattered the ashes in the wind.

9. A certain man, Artemianos by name, in the time of the holy Constantine, was a general and commander in Egypt, a man wise and tested in his faith, and one who had smashed numerous idols and their altars and destroyed the temples of their filthy sacrifices. They deposed this man from his office and from his authority, and then they cut off his head. They also burned the brave soldier Emilianus in fire.

10. That lawless tyrant [Julian] also issued an order that no Christian could become a leader or a soldier, and those that already were would have to step down. He also promulgated an authoritative written edict that no children of Christians would be allowed to learn secular letters: mathematics, rhetoric, philosophy, and the wisdom of the Homeric compositions. "For," he said, "they learn ours, they know already their own; so they arm themselves with both, and with their words as armor, they fight against us and are victorious."

11. *Եւ ոմն երիտասարդ քրիստոնեայ եւ զօրական Թէոդորոս անուն՝ երթայր ընդ մէջ Հրապարակին եւ երգէր զերգս մարգարէին Դաւթի եւ յամենայն տան սաղմոսին ասէր. Յամօթ լիցին ամենեքեան ոյք պաշտեն զկուռս Հեթանոսաց, ալէլուիա: Եւ կալեալ զնա ի մէջ Հրապարակին կախեցին, եւ արջառաջլօք զթիկունս Հարին, եւ զկողսն երկաթի ճանկօք քերեցին, եւ զամենայն օրն թողին ի կախաղանին, եւ երեկոյին իջուցին եւ կապեցին շղթայիւք եւ արկին ի բանդ:*

12. *Եւ ընդ առաւօտն ասէ Յուլիանոս. Զարմանալի է Համբերութիւն քրիստոնէից, զի մեծաւ ուրախութեամբ եւ յօժարութեամբ ընդունին զչարչարանս եւ պարծին ի տանջանս: Հրամայեաց եւ արձակեցին զվկայն Քրիստոսի ի կապանաց եւ ի բանդէն: Եւ Հարցանէին ընդ արիական եւ քաջ զօրականն Քրիստոսի եթէ. Զգայի՞ր զսաստիկ եւ զդառն տանջանսն: Եւ նա ասէ. Յառաջագոյն ի սկիզբն չարչարանացն զգայի սակաւ ինչ վշտացն, եւ ապա ընդարմանայր անձնս եւ որպէս ի քուն թմրեալ կայի:*

13. *Զայսպիսի չարիս գործեաց Յուլիանոս եւ այլ բազում խստագոյն քան զայսոսիկ եւ գնացեալ ի պատերազմ ի Պարսս, չար կորստեամբ սատակեցաւ:*

14. *Կատարի տօն այս սրբոց վկայիցս Քրիստոսի՝ Մարտի ԻԳ:*

11. There was a certain young Christian soldier, whose name was Theodoros, who would go around through the public places and sing the songs of the prophet David. After every stanza of each psalm, he would say, "Let all those who worship the pagan idols be put to shame. Alleluia." They seized him and hung him up in the middle of the public place, lashed his back with bullwhips, lacerated his sides with iron hooks, and left him on the gallows for the entire day. In the evening, they took him down, bound him in chains, and threw him into prison.

12. In the morning, Julian said, "The endurance of these Christians is amazing, for they accept our tortures with great joy and willingness; they even boast of their sufferings." He then ordered that they release the martyr of Christ from his chains and from prison. They asked of the valiant and courageous soldier of Christ, "Were you aware of such violent and bitter tortures?" And he replied, "In the very beginning I felt a little discomfort from the tortures, but then my body became numb, and it seemed as if I were asleep."

13. Julian accomplished such evil deeds and many more even worse than these. He went off to wage war against the Persians, where he was killed in a violent death.

14. The feast of these holy martyrs of Christ is the twenty-third of March.

Արեգի ԺԶ

Մարտի ԻԴ

Վկայաբանութիւն Աբդայի եպիսկոպոսին եւ Որմզդանայ եւ Սայենի եւ Բենիամինի սարկաւագին

1. *Ի ժամանակս բարեպաշտ Թագաւորին Թէոդոսի Փոքու՝ Եազկերտ Հրապաշտ արքայն Պարսից շարժեաց պատերազմ քրիստոնէից եւ եկեղեցւոյ Աստուծոյ: Եւ իբրեւ լուաւ Աբդա եպիսկոպոսն վառեցաւ աստուածային նախանձու եւ Հրով այրեաց զպիւռիոնն պարսից, պիւռիոն՝ զտաճարն անուանէին յորում զՀուրն բորբոքէին եւ երկիր պագանէին Հրապաշտքն:*

March 24

Areg 16

The martyrdom of the bishop Abda, of Hormizd, of Sayeni, and of the deacon Benjamin

1. At the time of the pious emperor Theodosius the Younger,[1] Yazdgird, the fire-worshipping ruler of the Persians,[2] embarked on a war against the Christians and the churches of God. When he learned of this, the bishop Abda burned with divine zeal, and he burned in fire the *pyrheum* of the Persians (the *pyrheum* is what they call the temple wherein the fire worshippers burn the fire and worship it).

1. That is, Theodosius II; see p. 37n4 above.

2. Yazdgird II was ruler of Sasanian empire from 438 to 457. It was he who led the Persian forces against Armenia in the famous battle of Avarayr in 451, recorded by Ghazar Pʿarpetsʿi and, most famously, by Eghishē Vardapet.

2. Եւ լուեալ ի մոգուցն արքայն Պարսից, կոչեաց զերանելի եպիսկոպոսն առ ինքն, եւ նախ հանդարտութեամբ ընդ գործն մեղադրեաց նմա եւ հրամայեաց չինել զպիւռիոնն զոր այրեաց: Իսկ սուրբ եպիսկոպոսն հակառակաբանէր եթէ անհնար է այլ զնա չինել: Եւ նա հրամայեաց եւ առաջի իւր զսուրբ եպիսկոպոսն սպանին, եւ զամենայն եկեղեցիսն աւերեցին, եւ երեսուն ամ զմրրիկ հալածանացն ի քրիստոնէիցն ոչ վերացոյց: Եւ հրամայեաց մոգուցն զբարեպաշտութեան դաւանողսն ըմբռնել, եւ հատանել զոմանց զձեռս եւ զոտս, եւ զոմանց զականջս եւ զունչսն, եւ զոմանց զերկուս աչս խաւարեցուցանել: Եւ զայլոց զգլուխս ի ճակատէն մինչեւ ի մօրուսն քերթել, եւ զոմանս ճեղքեալ եղեգամբ զմարմինսն քերթէին. եւ զոմանց կապէին զձեռս յետս՝ եւ չաղախէին զանձինս ճարպով եւ ընկենուին ի խոր գուբ, եւ արկանէին բազում մկունս եւ աքիսս, եւ այնչափ զգուշանային որ ոչ կարէին զեռունքն փախչել, եւ ի քաղցոյն կրծէին զմարմինս սրբոցն: Եւ զայս առնելով անօրինացն ոչ կարացին ահացուցանել զճշմարիտ ծառայսն Աստուծոյ, եւ մանաւանդ յորժամ տեսանէին յայսպիսի խիստ տանջանս՝ ինքնակամ ընթանային փափաքմամբ ի մահ:

3. Եւ ոմն մի մեծ իշխան Թագաւորին՝ մեծատուն յոյժ եւ քրիստոնեայ որոյ անուն էր Որմզդան, զնմանէ լուաւ արքայն եթէ քրիստոնեայ է, կոչեաց առաջի եւ պատուիրեաց նմա զի մի անուանեսցի քրիստոնեայ՝ այլ ուրանալ զՔրիստոս: Ասէ Որմզդան. Եթէ ոք ի քո ծառայիցդ ուրասցի զքեզ՝ դու որ մահկանացուդ ես՝ զնա մեծ տանջանաց արժանի առնես, ո՞րչափ մանաւանդ որ զԱստուած երկնի եւ երկրի՝ զանմահ Թագաւորն ուրանան ի յաւիտենական եւ յանշէջ հուրն մատնին:

4. Եւ զայն լուեալ արքային ընկէց զնա ի փառաց եւ ի պատուոյն, եւ եհան ի տանէն եւ ի ստացուածոցն, եւ հրամայեաց որ մերկ արածէր զուղտսն: Եւ յետ բազում աւուրց ետես զնա մերկ աշխատութեամբ յուղտսն, առաքեաց նմա շապիկ եւ ասէ. Յիշեա զքո առաջին մեծութիւնն եւ զքաղցր կեանսն եւ զփափկութիւնն, եւ ուրացիր զքրիստոնէութիւնդ, եւ հաւատա ի պաշտամունս մեր: Եւ նորա լուեալ զդառն զբանս Թագաւորին՝ առեալ զշապիկն պատառեաց: Եւ նա բարկութեամբ հրամայեաց եւ ի տեղւոջն սպանին զնա վասն Քրիստոսի հաւատոցն:

2. When the ruler of the Persians heard this from the magi, he summoned the blessed bishop. At first, he reproached him without irritation for what he had done and requested that he rebuild the *pyrheum* that he had burned down. But the holy bishop contended that it would be impossible for him to rebuild another [*pyrheum*]. [Yazdgird] ordered that [Bishop Abda] be killed in his presence. They then demolished all the churches and for the next thirty years never lifted his storm of persecution against the Christians. He ordered the magi to seize those who professed the true faith and to cut off the hands and feet of some of them, of others their ears and their noses, and of yet others to put out both their eyes. To some they would peel the skin off their faces from the forehead down to the beard, while to others they would strip off their flesh with shredded reeds. To some they would bind their hands behind them, and they would smear their bodies with fat and cast them into a deep pit; then they would throw down hordes of mice and weasels. And they took every precaution to ensure that these rodents could not escape and that due to their hunger they would consume the flesh of these holy ones. But even after having done all these things, those impious ones were unable to put any fear into true servants of God, especially because when they would see such cruel tortures, they would hasten willingly, desirous of death.

3. There was a certain great prince of the king, who was very wealthy. He was also a Christian, and his name was Hormizd. When the ruler heard that he was a Christian, he summoned him before him and ordered him no longer to call himself a Christian but rather to renounce Christ. Hormizd said, "If any of your servants were to renounce you, you who are mortal, you would account him as deserving of great tortures; how much more would those who renounce the God of heaven and earth, the immortal King, be delivered into the eternal and unending fire?"

4. When he heard this, the ruler stripped him of his ranks and his privileges, divested him of his house and his properties, and ordered him to go out naked and pasture the camels. Some time later he saw him naked at his task with the camels; so he had a tunic sent to him, and he said, "Remember your prior magnificence, your luxurious life, and your pleasures; so renounce your Christianity and believe in our religion." When [Hormizd] heard these stinging words of the king, he took the tunic and tore it up. Then [Yazdgird] angrily commanded that they kill him on the spot for his faith in Christ.

5. *Եւ զայլ ոմն պարսիկ քրիստոնեայ մեծատուն յոյժ, Հազար ծառայից տէր, որում անուն էր Սայենի, բազում անգամ ջանաց Թագաւորն դարձուցանել ի Քրիստոսի Հաւատոցն: Եւ յորժամ ոչ կարաց Հաւանեցուցանել՝ որոշեաց ի ծառայիցն զմինն որ քան զամենեսեան էր անպիտան, եւ աղտեղի եւ գարշելի տեսլեամբ, ետ նմա զտէրն իւր ծառայ եւ զտիկինն նմա կին, եւ Հրամայեաց նոցա ծառայել նմա Հնազանդութեամբ: Եւ այն ամենայն եղեւ առ նա, եւ ոչ ի բաց եկաց ի յուսոյն Քրիստոսի:*

6. *Կալան եւ զսարկաւագ ոմն որում անուն էր Բենիամին եւ արկին ի բանդ զերկու ամ: Եւ ընդ աւուրսն ընդ այնոսիկ առաքեցան դեսպանք ի Հոռոմոց Թագաւորէն ի Պարսիկս, եւ լուան զԲենիամինէ սարկաւագէն եթէ վասն Քրիստոսի արգելաւ ի բանդի, խնդրեցին յեսդեկերտէ արքայէն Հանել զնա ի բանդէն եւ ազատել: Ասէ արքայն. Վստահացուսցէ զմեզ ձեռնագրով որ զպարսիկ մոգ ոչ դարձուսցէ ի Հաւատն իւր, եւ ոչ վարդապետութեամբն իւրով ուսուցանէ զօք յերկրիս մերում, եւ ապա վասն խնդրոյ ձերոյ ազատեցից զնա ի կապանացն:*

7. *Եւ լուեալ Բենիամինի ոչ առ յանձն առնել զՀրամանս Թագաւորին ասելով. ԱնՀնարին է ինձ զշնորՀսն Աստուծոյ իմոյ արգելուլ ի մարդկանէ, այլ որչափ կարող եմ լուսաւորեմ զխաւարեալսն ի մոլորութենէ, զի մի պատիժ կրեցից ընդ Թագուցանողին զտաղանդ տեառն իւրոյ: Եւ արքայն վասն աղերսանաց եւ խնդրոյ դեսպանացն՝ ազատեաց զսարկաւագն ի բանդէն:*

8. *Եւ նորա ելեալ ոչ դադարէր յուսուցանելոյ եւ ի մկրտելոյ զկրակապաշտ ժողովուրդն Պարսից: Եւ յետ տարւոյ միոյ յորժամ դարձան դեսպանքն Հոռոմոց՝ ազդեցուցին վասն նորա արքային որ առնէր: Տարան զնա առաջի, եւ նա աստուածիմաստ բանիւք յոյժ յանդիմանեաց զյիմարութիւն գազանամիտ ազգին Պարսից: Եւ Հրամայեաց ընդ եղընգունսն Հարկանել սրեալ եղէգն, եւ արիւնն իբրեւ առու Հեղոյր ի ձեռացն եւ յոտիցն: Եւ դարձեալ սրեցին երկայնագոյն եղէգն՝ եւ արկին ի ծածուկ ջրաՀեղ մարմինն՝ եւ ստէպ արկանէին եւ Հանէին. եւ յայնչափ դառն կսկծանացն ի գոՀանալոյ եւ ի փառաւորելոյ զԱստուած ոչ դադարէր:*

5. The king also tried many times to turn away from the faith another Persian Christian, a very wealthy man and master of a thousand servants, whose name was Sayeni. But when he was unable to persuade him, he singled out one of his servants, the one who was the most incompetent of them all, both filthy and loathsome to look upon, and gave his master to him as his servant and his mistress to be his wife, and [the king] ordered them to serve him obediently. All these things happened to [Sayeni], but he never abandoned his faith in Christ.

6. They also seized a deacon whose name was Benjamin, and they threw him into prison for two years. During this time envoys were sent from the Byzantine emperor to Persia, and they heard that the deacon Benjamin had been thrown into prison for the sake of Christ. They pleaded with the king Yazdgird to release him from prison and to set him free. The king responded, "Let him give us his word in writing that he will not convert any Persian magus to his faith and that he will not teach his doctrine to anyone in our land. Then, according to your entreaty, I will release that deacon from prison."

7. When he heard this, Benjamin refused to carry out the command of the king, saying, "It is impossible for me to impede the grace of my God for a human being; as a matter of fact, to the degree I am able, I will enlighten those who are in the darkness of error lest I incur punishment along with the one who buried the talent of his master." Then the king, on account of the petitions and entreaties of the envoys, released the deacon from prison.

8. After he set out, [Benjamin] did not cease teaching and baptizing those fire-worshipping people of Persia. A year after those Byzantine envoys returned, the king was informed about what [Benjamin] was doing, and they brought him into the presence [of the king]. [Benjamin], with words filled with the wisdom of God, thoroughly exposed the crazy-minded folly of the Persian nation. The king then commanded that sharpened reeds be thrust underneath his nails, and blood poured out like a stream from his hands and his feet. Then they thrust in even longer reeds; they even shoved one into his private parts and then kept pushing it in and pulling it out. However bitter the pain, he never ceased giving praise and glory to God.

9. *Եւ տեսեալ արքային եԹէ առ ոչինչ Համարի զտանջանսն, Հրամայեաց եւ երկսայրի գաւազան երկաԹի պաքաձեւ արկին ընդ նստոյ տեղին մինչեւ յորովայնն. եւ այնպէս Հզօր եւ զօրեղ զօրականն Քրիստոսի աւանդեաց զՀոգին ի ձեռս Հրեշտակաց։*

10. *Կատարի տօն այս մարտիրոսացս Մարտի ԻԴ։*

9. When the king saw that he accounted these tortures as nothing, he commanded that they rend him with an iron double-edged rod shaped like an arrow from his nether region to his belly. And in this manner the mighty and valorous soldier of Christ rendered up his soul into the hands of the angels.

10. The feast of these martyrs is celebrated on the twenty-fourth of March.

Արեգի ԺԷ

Մարտի ԻԵ

Յիշատակ Մելքիսեդեկի առաջին քահանայի

1. *Թագաւորն Սաղիմ շինէ քաղաք եւ կոչէ ըստ անուան իւրում Սաղիմ: Եւ ծնանի զՄելքին. եւ Մելքի առ իւր կին զՍաղա՝ եւ ծնաւ ի նմանէ որդի, եւ անուանեաց ըստ անուան իւրոյ Մելքի: Եւ դարձեալ ծնաւ որդի, եւ անուանեաց Մելքիսեդեկ. եւ Հայրն սերէր զՄելքի, եւ մայրն սերէր զՄելքիսեդեկ:*

2. *Եւ յաւուր միում ի տօնի աստուածոցն ասէ Հայրն ցՄելքիսեդեկ. Երթ որդեակ ի նախիրն եւ բեր մեզ զուարակս եօթն եւ խոյս տասն զի մատուսցուք ողջակէզ աստուածոցն: Եւ գնաց Մելքիսեդեկ, եւ ի ճանապարՀին, մտախոՀ լեալ ասէ. Զի՞նչ են կուռքն անշունչք որ ումեք օգնել ոչ կարեն. գնացից առ Հայր իմ եւ ասացից նմա Թերեւս լուիցէ ինձ:*

3. *Եւ դարձաւ առ Հայրն եւ ասէ, Հայր, ընդէ՞ր կորուսանեմք զանասունս մեր զոՀելով կռոցն որ ոչ ումեք օգնել կարեն, եւ բարի առնել կամ չար. այլ Աստուծոյ պա՞րտ է զոՀել որ արար զերկինս եւ զերկիր եւ զամենայն որ ի նոսա: Եւ բարկացաւ Հայրն ի վերայ Մելքիսեդեկի, եւ ասէ. Եթէ ոչ երթեալ բերցես զոր ասացի քեզ՝ փոխանակ անասնոցն զքեզ զոՀեցից աստուածոցն: Եւ գնաց Մելքիսեդեկ բերել ըստ Հրամանին:*

4. *Եւ ասէ Թագաւորն Մելքի ցԹագուՀի Սաղա. Եկ եւ զմի յորդւոց մերոց մատուսցուք զոՀ աստուածոց մերոց: Եւ ԹագուՀին սկսաւ լալ, եւ գիտաց եթէ ոխս ունի ընդ Մելքիսեդեկի վասն բանիցն զոր ասաց, եւ ասէ. վայ ինձ զի ցաւօք եւ երկամբք ծնայ եւ աշխատութեամբ սնուցի, եւ աՀա ընդունայն եղեւ ամենայնն:*

March 25

Areg 17

The memorial of Melchizedek, the first priest

1. The king Salem built a city, and he named it Salem, according to his own name. He begot Melchi, and Melchi took Sala as his wife. From her was born a son, and he named him according to his own name, Melchi. She again bore a son, and [Melchi] named him Melchizedek. The father loved Melchi, and the mother loved Melchizedek.

2. One day, on a feast of the gods, his father said to Melchizedek, "Go, my son, to the herd and bring back for us seven oxen and ten rams that we may offer them up as holocausts to the gods." Melchizedek went, but along the way he pondered this and said, "What are these lifeless idols that are unable to help anyone? I will go to my father, and I will tell him this; perhaps he will listen to me."

3. So he returned to his father and said, "Father, why do we put to death our animals by sacrificing them to idols who are incapable of helping anyone or of doing any good or evil? Should we not sacrifice to the God who made heaven and earth and all that is in it?" The father then got very angry with Melchizedek and said, "If you do not go and bring back those animals as I told you, I will sacrifice you to the gods in the place of the animals." So Melchizedek went off to bring them back as he was ordered.

4. King Melchi said to his queen Sala, "Come, let us offer up one of our sons as a sacrifice to our gods." Then the queen began to weep, for she knew that he had a grudge against Melchizedek on account of what he had said, and she said, "Woe is me, for I have given him birth in pain and in labor, and I have raised him with much toil, but now all that is for nought."

5. Եւ թագաւորն կամեցաւ մխիթարել զթագուհին, եւ ասէ․ Մի տրտմիր թագուհի, այլ արկցուք վիճակ, եթէ ինձ ելանէ՝ մատուսցուք զորդին իմ, եւ եթէ քեզ՝ մատուսցուք զորդին քո. զի կարծէր թէ կնոջն ելանէ վիճակն։ Եւ արկին վիճակ եւ ել վիճակն թագաւորին, եւ պատրաստեցին զենուլ զպատանին։ Եւ եկն Մելքիսեդեկ եւ եբեր զզուարակսն եւ զխոյսն եւ զնոխազսն։ Եւ ժողովեցան ամենայն ազգատոհմ թագաւորին եւ թագուհւոյն ի զենումն Մելքեայ, եւ ոչ ոք մնաց յազգէ նոցա որ ոչ եկին անդ։ Ժողովեցին եւ այլ բազում մանկունս, եւ անասնոցն ոչ գոյր թիւ, եւ գնացին ամենեքեան ի տուն կռոցն։

6. Եւ ասէ մայրն ցՄելքիսեդեկ․ Ոչ ինչ ցաւ է քեզ զի զեղբայր քո զենուն, ընդէ՞ր ոչ աղաչես զԱստուածն քո զի թերեւս փրկեսցէ զնա։ Եւ ասէ Մելքիսեդեկ․ Գործ է իմ այսօր երթալ կալ յաղօթս առ Աստուածն իմ։ Եւ ել նա ի գլուխ լերին Թափովրայ, եւ եդեալ զծունկս իւր յերկիր եւ համբարձեալ զձեռս իւր առ Աստուած, եւ յանկարծակի եղեւ մէգ եւ մառախուղ, եւ շարժեալ երկրին՝ ընկղմեցաւ քաղաքն առ հասարակ, եւ ոչ ոք մնաց յազգէ Մելքիսեդեկի ոչ այր եւ ոչ կին։

7. Եւ էջ Մելքիսեդեկ ի լեռնէ անտի, եւ տեսեալ ընկղմեալ զքաղաքն երկեաւ, եւ ել ի լեառն Թափովր, եմուտ յանտառն եւ ուտէր զծայրս ծառոց եւ ըմպէր ի ցօղոյ երկնից։ Եւ ներկաւ մարմին նորա եւ բուսաւ մազ ընդ ամենայն անձն նորա եւ ծածկեաց զնա, եւ աճեցին եղենգունք ձեռացն եւ ոտից նորա իբրեւ թիզ մի, եւ եկաց յանտառին ամս եօթն։

8. Եւ յետ եօթն ամաց երեւեցաւ Աստուած Աբրահամու եւ ասէ․ Առ ընդ քեզ հանդերձ եւ կերակուր եւ ածելի եւ մկրատ, եւ ել ի լեառն Թափովր, եւ ձայնեա երիցս անգամ. Այր դ Աստուծոյ։ Եւ ելցէ առ քեզ յանտառէն այր մի վայրենաձեւ կերպարանօք, եւ դու մի զարհուրիր ի նմանէ։ Այլ ած զհեր գլխոյ նորա եւ հարթեա զեղենգունս ձեռացն եւ ոտից նորա, եւ զգեցո նմա հանդերձ եւ տուր կերակուր, եւ նա օրհնեսցէ զքեզ զի քահանայ Աստուծոյ բարձրելոյ է նա, անհայր, անմայր՝ չհամարեալ յազգս։

5. The king then wished to console his queen and said, "Do not be grieved, my queen—let us cast lots. If it falls to me we will sacrifice my son; if it falls to you we will sacrifice your son." For he thought that the lot would fall to his wife. So they cast the lot, and the lot fell to the king. So they prepared to sacrifice the young man. Melchizedek then came bringing the oxen, the rams, and the goats. The entire household of the king and the queen gathered together for the sacrifice of Melchi; there was no one from their family who did not come. There also gathered there many other young people and a large number of animals; they all made their way to the temple of the idols.

6. The mother said to Melchizedek, "Are you not utterly sad that they are sacrificing your brother? Why don't you pray to your God that He might perhaps save him?" And Melchizedek responded, "My task today will be to go and pray to my God." And he went up to the top of Mount Tabor, set his knees on the ground, and raised his hands up to God. There suddenly rose up a fog and a mist, and the earth shook, and the city was completely swallowed up, and no one remained from the family of Melchizedek, neither man nor woman.

7. Melchizedek descended from that mountain, but on seeing that the city had been swallowed up, he was afraid and went right back up Mount Tabor, entered into a forest, and began to eat from the ends of the tree branches and to drink from the dew of heaven. His flesh turned color, his hair grew out over his entire body and covered it, and the nails of his hands and his feet grew about a palm's length, and he lived in this forest for seven years.

8. After these seven years, God appeared to Abraham and said, "Take with you clothing and food, as well as a razor and a pair of scissors; go up onto Mount Tabor and cry out three times, 'O Man of God.' There will come out of the forest a man looking like a wild man. Do not be alarmed by him. Just cut off the hair of his head, file down the nails of his hands and his feet, put the clothing on him, and give him the food. He will then bless you, for he is a priest of God Most High. He is without mother and without father, unreckoned among his kinfolk.

9. *Եւ արար Աբրահամ զամենայն զոր հրամայեաց նմա Տէր. եւ ել ի լեառն Թափոր եւ ձայնեաց երիցս անգամ. Այրդ Աստուծոյ: Եւ ել յանտառէն այր մի գազանաձեւ, եւ տեսեալ զնա Աբրահամ զարհուրեցաւ, եւ ասէ ցնա. Զի՞նչ խնդրես: Եւ ասէ Աբրահամ. Հրամայեաց ինձ Աստուած ածել զգլուխ քո եւ հարթել զեղենգունս քո եւ զգեցուցանել քեզ հանդերձս, եւ դու օրհնեսցես զիս:*

10. *Եւ ասէ Մելքիսեդեկ. Արա զոր ինչ հրամայեաց քեզ Աստուած: Եւ իբրեւ արար Աբրահամ զոր հրամայեաց նմա Տէր, ասէ Մելքիսեդեկ. Օրհնեալ է Աբրահամ յԱստուծոյ բարձրելոյ. եւ ոչ կոչեսցի անուն քո Աբրամ, այլ Աբրահամ եղիցի անուն քո. եւ կին քո ոչ կոչեսցի Սարա, այլ Սառա եղիցի անուն նորա: Եւ էջ ընդ Աբրահամու եւ բնակեցաւ ընդ նմա: Եւ ասէ Տէր ցԱբրահամ. Զի ոչ ոք մնաց յազգէ Մելքիսեդեկի ի վերայ երկրի, այլ Մելքիսեդեկ կոչեսցի անհայր, անմայր՝ չհամարեալ յազգս նմանեալ որդւոյն Աստուծոյ առանց խորհրդոյ:*

11. *Եւ յորժամ գայր Աբրահամ ի կոտորածէ Թագաւորացն, ել ընդ առաջ նորա Մելքիսեդեկ եւ ետ նմա կոտորակ հացի եւ բաժակ, եւ օրհնեաց զնա: Եւ Աբրահամ տասանորդս ետ նմա յամենայն աւարէն, եւ եկաց մնաց քահանայ Աստուծոյ բարձրելոյ:*

12. *Եւ կատարի տօն քահանայապետին Աստուծոյ Մելքիսեդեկի՝ Արեգի ԺԷ եւ Մարտի ԻԵ:*

13. *Իսկ ըստ հաւաստի աստուածաչունչ գրոց է այսպէս. երանելին Մելքիսեդեկ՝ Թագաւոր էր Սաղիմայ՝ քահանայ Աստուծոյ բարհրելոյ. եւ յորժամ դարձաւ Աբրահամ ի կոտորածէ Թագաւորացն՝ ել ընդ առաջ նորա Մելքիսեդեկ արքայ Սաղիմայ, եւ մատոյց նմա պատարագ հաց եւ գինի քանզի քահանայ էր Աստուծոյ բարձրելոյ. եւ օրհնեաց զԱբրահամ եւ ասէ. Օրհնեալ Աբրահամ յԱստուծոյ բարձրելոյ որ արար զերկինս եւ զերկիր. օրհնեալ Աստուած բարձրեալ որ մատնեաց զԹշնամիս քո ի ձեռս քո: Եւ Աբրահամ տասանորդս ետ յամենայնէ զոր աւարեալ էր ի Թշնամեաց:*

9. Abraham did all that the Lord had commanded him: he went up onto Mount Tabor and called out three times, "O Man of God." There came forth from the forest a man who looked like a wild man. When he saw him, Abraham was alarmed. [That man] said to him, "What are you looking for?" And Abraham responded, "God commanded me to shave your head, to file down your nails, and to put these clothes on you—and that you would then bless me."

10. Melchizedek said, "Do what God has commanded you." And when Abraham finished what the Lord had commanded him, Melchizedek said, "Blessed is Abraham by God Most High, and your name shall not be called Abram, but your name shall be Abraham. And your wife shall not be called Sarai, but her name shall be Sarah."[1] And he went down with Abraham, and he dwelt with him. And the Lord said to Abraham, "Because none of the family of Melchizedek has remained on earth, Melchizedek shall be called fatherless and motherless, not reckoned among the nations like a son of God, but without any mystery.

11. When Abraham returned from the defeat of the kings, Melchizedek came out before him and gave him a morsel of bread and a cup [of wine] and blessed him. Abraham gave to him a tenth of all his plunder. [Melchizedek] continued to be the priest of God Most High.[2]

12. The feast of Melchizedek, the high priest of God, is celebrated on the seventeenth of Areg, or the twenty-fifth of March.

13. But[3] according to the authority of the divine scriptures [the tale] is thus: The blessed Melchizedek was king of Salem and priest of God Most High. When Abraham returned from his defeat of the kings, Melchizedek the king of Salem came out before him and offered up for him a sacrifice of bread and wine because he was a priest of God Most High, and he blessed Abraham and said, "Blessed be Abraham by God Most High, who made heaven and earth. Blessed is God Most High, who handed over your enemies into your hand." Abraham then gave him a tenth of everything that he had plundered from his enemies.

---

1. See Genesis 17:5, 15, where it is God himself who changes their names.
2. See Genesis 14:17-20.
3. The rest of this entry for Melchizedek is marked in Bayan's text as version B, i.e., a separate account that he has inserted from his alternative edition. I have included it here since it is an entirely different account; it can be read rather as theological exposition supplemental to the preceding historical account.

14. *Մելքիսեդեկ օրինակ եղեւ երկնաւոր քահանայապետին մերոյ Քրիստոսի, որ զքահանայութիւնն երդմամբ ընկալաւ յԱստուծոյ Հօրէ՝ ըստ նախաձայնելոյ մարգարէին Դաւթի թէ. Դու ես քահանայ յաւիտեան ըստ կարգին Մելքիսեդեկի, եւ Տէր ընդ աջմէ քումմէ։*

15. *Մելքիսեդեկ թարգմանի թագաւոր արդարութեան. եւ Տէրն մեր ունէր զթագաւորութիւն հօր իւրոյ Դաւթի ըստ մարմնոյ՝ կացեալ թագաւոր յաւիտենից ի վերայ ամենեցուն. Երդուաւ Տէր Դաւթի ճշմարտութեամբ եւ ոչ ստեաց նմա ի պտղոյ յորովայնէ նորա նստուցանել յաթոռ նորա։ Որպէս եւ հրեշտակապետն Գաբրիէլ յառաջագոյն ազդեաց ասելով. Յաթոռն Դաւթի նստցի, եւ թագաւորեսցէ ի վերայ տանն Յակոբու ի յաւիտեան, եւ թագաւորութեան նորա վախճան մի լիցի։*

16. *Ունէր Քրիստոս եւ զարդարութիւն փրկութեան, զի ոչ այնքան կարող զօրութեամբ՝ որքան արդար իրաւամբք դատապարտեաց զթշնամին կենաց եւ փրկութեան մերոյ, մահուամբ խաչի իւրոյ փոխարինելով զպարտիս մեր. եւ եղեւ մեզ յԱստուծոյ արդարութիւն եւ փրկութիւն, եւ արդարութեամբ իւրով արդարացոյց զմեզ, ազատեալ ի ծառայութենէ մահու եւ դժոխոց։*

17. *Մելքիսեդեկ կոչեցաւ թագաւոր խաղաղութեան, եւ փրկիչն մեր արար խաղաղութիւն յերկինս եւ յերկրի. եւ հաշտեցոյց զԱստուած ընդ մարդկայինս ազգի կենսաձիր արեամբ իւրով՝ զոր եհեղ ի վերայ քառաթեւ սուրբ խաչին, որպէս երգէին հրեշտակք ընդ հովուաց յաւուր ծննդեան Փրկչին. Փառք ի բարձունս Աստուծոյ եւ յերկիր խաղաղութիւն։*

18. *Մելքիսեդեկ հաց եւ գինի մատոյց Աբրահամու նահապետին յորժամ դարձաւ ի պատերազմէ թագաւորացն, եւ Տէրն մեր զմարմին եւ զարիւն իւր հացիւ եւ գինեաւ ետ առաքելոցն սրբոց ի խորհրդական ընթրիսն, եւ նոյնպէս կարգեաց նուիրել մինչեւ ի կատարած աշխարհի ասելով. Զայս արարէք առ իմոյ յիշատակի։*

14. Melchizedek has become the image of Christ, our heavenly high priest, who received the high priesthood by oath from God the Father according to that which was foretold by the prophet David: "You are a priest forever according to the order of Melchizedek. The Lord is at your right hand" (Psalm 110:4-5).

15. Melchizedek is translated as "King of Righteousness." And our Lord held the kingdom of David, his father, according to the flesh, as he is the eternal king over all men. The Lord had in truth sworn an oath to David—and He did not lie to him!—that "from the fruit of his loins He would set upon his throne," just as the archangel Gabriel had previously announced, saying "On the throne of David he will sit, and he will reign over the house of Jacob for ever, and of his kingdom there will be no end" (Luke 1:32).

16. Christ also held the righteousness of salvation, for he did not condemn the enemy of our life and our salvation so much by the force of power as by the right of justice, satisfying our debts by his death on the cross. And by the power of God he became for us our righteousness and our salvation, for by his justice he justified us and freed us from the servitude of death and hell.

17. Melchizedek is called the king of peace, and our Savior brought peace to the heavens and to earth. He reconciled God to the human race by his life-giving blood, which he shed upon the four-winged cross, just as the angels were singing with the shepherds on the day of the Savior's birth: "Glory to God in the highest, and on earth peace" (Luke 2:14).

18. Melchizedek offered bread and wine to the patriarch Abraham after he returned from war against the kings, and our Lord gave his flesh and his blood in the bread and the wine to the holy apostles at the mystical supper. Similarly, he arranged to renew it until the end of the world when he said, "Do this in memory of me" (Luke 22:19).

19. *Մելքիսեդեկ անհայր անմայր կոչեցաւ. եւ Քրիստոս ըստ աստուածային յաւիտենական ծննդեանն ի Հօրէ՝ է անմայր, եւ ըստ մարդկային ժամանակաւոր ծննդեանն ի սրբոյ կուսէն՝ անհայր. եւ ինքն է տիրապէս մի Որդի, մի Տէր, մի Քրիստոս, Աստուած ճշմարիտ եւ մարդ ճշմարիտ: Զի այնպիսի վայելէր միջնորդ հաշտարար ի մէջ Աստուծոյ եւ մարդկան, եւ քահանայ յաւիտենական առ ի քաւելոյ զմեղս բազմաց. քանզի լոկոյ մարդոյ փրկել զարարածս անհնարին էր, եւ սոսկ Աստուծոյ չարչարիլ եւ մեռանիլ անկարելի: Զի որպէս առաքեալն ասէ. Բազում են կացեալ քահանայք՝ վասն մահուն արգել լինելոյ, իսկ սա վասն յաւիտեան կալոյ առանց անցանելոյ ունի զքահանայութիւնն: Ուստի եւ կենդանի առնել համօրէն կարող է զմատուցեալս նովաւ առ Աստուած, քանզի միշտ կենդանի է լինել բարեխօս վասն նոցա:*

20. *Եւ կատարի տօն քահանային Աստուծոյ Մելքիսեդեկի Արեգի ԺԷ եւ Մարտի ԻԵ:*

9. Melchizedek is called fatherless and motherless. Christ, according to his divine eternal birth from the father, is motherless, and according to his human temporal birth from the holy virgin, is fatherless. He is truly one son, one Lord, one Christ, true God, and true man. For in this way he is properly an intermediary and conciliator between God and man, an eternal priest to wash away the sins of many, for it is impossible for man alone to save creatures, as it is not possible for God alone to suffer and to die. Just so the apostle says, "Priests were numerous, because they were prevented by death but He, because He is eternal and cannot pass away, holds the priesthood. By this then He is able to make completely alive all those who draw near to God through him, since he always lives to be an intercessor for them" (Hebrews 7:23-25).

0. The feast of Melchizedek, the priest of God, is celebrated on the seventeenth of Areg, or the twenty-fifth of March.

Արեգի ԺԲ

Մարտի ԻԶ

Վկայութիւն սրբոյն Պօղոսի եւ քեռն իւրոյ Յուլիանեայ

1. *Քրիստոսի մարտիրոսքն Պօղոս եւ Յուլիանէ՝ քրիստոնեայք*
էին ի քաղաքէն Պտղոմիդեայ՝ յաւուրս Աւրեղիանոսի անօրէն
արքային. եւ դեռ եւս մանկունք էին:
2. *Եւ յորժամ եկն Թագաւորն ի քաղաքն եւ ետես զնա սուրբն*
Պաւղոս՝ ասէ ցքոյր իւր. Մեծ փորձութիւն եմուտ ի քաղաքս մեր,
բայց զօրութեամբն Քրիստոսի ոչ երկիցուք. եւ սկսաւ զնշան
խաչին կնքել յերեսն: Ետես զնա Թագաւորն եւ կոչեաց առ ինքն
եւ ասէ. Որպէ՞ս իշխեցեր զնշանդ զայդ առնել յերեսդ: Եւ նա
խոստովանեցաւ զքրիստոնէութեան հաւատն իւր:
3. *Կախեցին զսուրբն եւ տանջեցին զնա: Եւ ընթացաւ Յուլիանէ*
քոյրն իւր առ Թագաւորն եւ ասէ. Անիրաւ չարչարես զեղբայրն
իմ ով բռնաւոր: Հրամայեաց եւ զնա կախել եւ քերել զմարմինն:
Եւ յորժամ տանջեցին զնոսա՝ իջուցին ի փայտէն եւ նեղէին
ուրանալ զՔրիստոս. եւ ոչ հաւանեցան բանից նոցա: Եւ արկին
զնոսա յեռացեալ ձիւթով տապակ, եւ առժամայն եղեւ ցուրտ եւ
ոչ այրեցան: Ապա տարածեցին զնոսա ի վերայ հրացեալ երկաթի
մահճաց. հրամայեաց՝ եւ ի վերաց հրոյն հարկանէին զսուրբսն
երկայն բրովք: Եւ դահիճքն Կոդրատոս եւ Ակակիոս խնայէին ի
հարկանել եւ ողորմէին. եւ տեսեալ զայն արքային եհատ զգլուխս
նոցա: Եւ ապա հատին զսրբոցն Պօղոսի եւ զՅուլիանեայ զգլուխսն
Մարտի ԻԶ:

March 26

Areg 18

The martyrdom of Saint Paul and of his sister Juliana

1. The martyrs of Christ, Paul and Juliana, were Christians from the city of Ptolemais in the days of the impious emperor Aurelian, and they were at the time still young people.

2. The emperor came to the city, and when the holy Paul saw him, he said to his sister, "A great trial has come into our city, but by the power of Christ we need have no fear." And he began to make the sign of the cross on his forehead. The emperor saw this, summoned [Paul] before him, and said, "How have you rashly made that sign on your forehead?" And he confessed his Christian faith.

3. They hung up the holy one, and they tortured him. His sister Juliana ran to the emperor and said, "You are punishing my brother unjustly, O tyrant!" He then ordered that she too be hung up and that her skin be flayed. After they had tortured them, they took them down from the pole and constrained them to renounce Christ, but they gave no heed to their words. So they threw them into a cauldron of boiling oil, and it immediately became cold so that they were not burned. Then they stretched them out over a bed of red-hot iron, and [the emperor] commanded that they beat these holy ones over the fire with long clubs. The executioners Quadratus and Acacius took pity on them and refrained from beating them. Upon seeing this, the emperor had their heads cut off. Then he also had the heads of Paul and Juliana cut off on the twenty-sixth of March.

Արեգի ԺԹ
Մարտի ԻԷ

Վկայութիւն կուսին Կատարինեայ սրբուհւոյն

1. *Այս իմաստասէր եւ հանճարեղ կինս էր ի քաղաքէն Աղեկսանդրու, դուստր լեալ Կոստանդեայ թագաւորին, եւ անուն կուսին Կատերինեա: Եւ էր յոյժ գեղեցիկ տեսլեամբ երեսօք եւ անձամբ, եւ քրիստոնեայ հաւատով, յաւուրս անօրէն արքային Մաքսէնդի: Եւ այնչափ էր մտավարժ եւ երագամիտ մինչ գի ուսաւ ի բուն իսկ զամենայն հելլենական եւ զհռետորական եւ զիմաստասիրական հանճարն. զՀոմերոսն եւ զՎիրգիղոն, եւ զԱսկղիպիոս, զԱրիստոտէլ, զՊղատոն, զՓիլիստիոն, զԱնիսի եւ զԱմրիսի զմոգուցն, զՍիբելայն եւ զԴիոնիսիոն. նոյնպէս եւ զնախաբժշկացն՝ զԻպոկրատէս եւ զԳաղիանոս, եւ զամենայն հռետորական եւ զփիլիսոփայական, եւ զաստեղագիտութեան եւ զերկրաչափական եւ զթուելական զամենայն գիրս հելլենական՝ ճարտարմտութեամբն ուսաւ եւ ի բերան ընթեռնոյր: Եւ յոյժ հմուտ եղեւ ամենայն բարբարոսաց լեզուաց, եւ զեօթանասուն եւ զերկու ազգաց զխօսս ուսաւ: Եւ յոյժ զարմանային որք տեսանէին զնա եւ լսէին ի նմանէ, եւ համբաւ իմաստութեան նորա հռչակեցաւ ընդ ամենայն ազգս:*

2. *Եւ ի միում աւուր ետես զթագաւորն Մաքսենտիոս, որ բազում ամբոխիւ զոհս մատուցանէր կռոցն. եւ երթեալ եմուտ ի տաճարն, եւ սկսաւ կշտամբել եւ յանդիմանել զթագաւորն վասն գարշելի կռոցն տօնի ի գրոցն Հոմերոսի հելլենացւոյն եւ ի Վիրգիլիոսի հռովմայեցւոյն. եւ յոյժ զարմացան ընդ սքանչելի բանս իմաստութեան նորա, եւ դարձեալ ընդ բարբառ բազում եւ ազգի ազգի լեզուացն զոր խօսեցաւ զահի հարան:*

March 27

Areg 19

The martyrdom of the holy virgin Catherine

1. This intelligent woman and lover of wisdom was from the city of Alexandria, and she was the daughter of the governor Costus. The name of this virgin was Catherine. She was very beautiful, both in her physical person and in her character. She was a Christian by faith and lived in the days of the emperor Maxentius.[1] She was so quick and skillful of mind that she learned thoroughly all of Greek wisdom, both rhetorical and philosophical: Homer, Virgil, Asclepius, Aristotle, Plato, Philistion, the magicians Jannes and Jambres, the Sibyl, and Dionysius, as well as the ancient medical works of Hippocrates and Galen. And she completely absorbed all the other Greek works of rhetoric, philosophy, astronomy, geometry, and mathematics. She was quite expert in many foreign tongues, for she had learned the languages of seventy-two nations. All those who saw her and listened to her were deeply amazed, and the renown of her wisdom was spread abroad throughout every nation.

2. One day she saw the emperor Maxentius, surrounded by a great crowd, offering up sacrifices to the idols. She went and entered into the temple and from the Greek works of Homer and the Latin works of Virgil began to rebuke and to censure the emperor on the subject of the feast of the idols. They all greatly marveled at the astonishing wisdom of her words, and they were also awestruck at the many foreign languages of various nations that she spoke.

---

1. Marcus Aurelius Valerius Maxentius ruled from 306 to 312.

3. *Եւ ետես երանելի կինն զԹագաւորն եւ զամբոխն շրտուցեալ եւ ոչ կարէին պատասխանի առնել. սկսաւ խօսել պարզ բանիւք եւ ասէ ցԹագաւորն. Ընդէ՞ր ժողովեցեր զբազմութիւն ամբոխիս, եւ ունայնութեամբ կորուսանես զանձինս դոցա ի մոլորութիւն կռոցդ: Այժմ սԹափեցո զխելս մտաց քոց եւ լուր ինձ, եւ ծանիր զայն որ անճառելի բանիւ հաստատեաց զամենայն աշխարհս, զի նա միայն է ճշմարիտ Աստուած որ առաքեաց զմիածին իւր յերկիր, զի կեցուսցէ զանձինս մեր խաչիւն իւրով. նա է Փրկիչ մոլորելոց եւ Աստուած աստուծոց եւ նմա փառք յաւիտեանս:*
4. *Յայնժամ ի տարակուսի լեալ Թագաւորն, տարաւ զնա զկնի իւր յապարանսն, կարծէր Թէ ողոքանօք դարձուսցէ զնա ի կուռսն եւ ուրանայ զՔրիստոս: Իսկ նա առաւել ջանայր աստուածիմաստ բանիւք զԹագաւորն հաւանեցուցանել:*
5. *Եւ հրամայեաց Թագաւորն բերել յիսուն հռետորական վարդապետս, զի խօսեսցին ընդ նմա ի հելլենական հանճարիցն: Եւ յորժամ սկսան խօսել առաջի Թագաւորին, սրբուհի Կատերինեա հրեշտակային օգնականութեամբն՝ զվեհագոյն հռետորական վարդապետսն զարմացոյց եւ յամօԹ արար, եւ երեւեցոյց զնոսա տգէտս եւ անիմաստս: Յայնժամ փիլիսոփայքն յամօԹ եղեն, եւ երկեան խօսել կամ հարցանել ի փիլիսոփայական գրոց:*
6. *Իսկ երանելին Կատերինեա տեսեալ զնոսա ի տարակուսի՝ պատմեաց նոցա զմարգարէութիւն հեԹանոս իմաստասիրացն որ յառաջ քան զՔրիստոսի գալուստն էին. զՎիրգիլիոսի որ ասէ. Յերից միութենէն մինն ի մարմին տեսաւորի եւ յերից աներեւութիցն ոչ պակասի: Եւ Սիբիլա կին էր, եւ գրեաց ի գիրս իւր ի չարս պատճենի վասն խաչին, ասէ. Ով երիցս երանեալ փայտ՝ քանզի օծեալն տարածէ զբազուկս իւր ի վերայ քո: Եւ նախ գուշակեաց մինն զխորհուրդ սրբոյ Երրորդութեանն, եւ միւսն զչարչարանսն Քրիստոսի: Եւ այլ բազում բանիւք յառաքելոյն Պետրոսի եւ ի սաղմոսացն ԴաւԹի ուսուցանէր եւ խրատ տայր հռետորացն եւ փիլիսոփայիցն հաւատալ ի Քրիստոս:*

3. When this blessed woman saw that both the emperor and the crowd were silent and unwilling to respond, she began to speak with simpler words, and she said to the emperor, "Why have you assembled this great crowd and pointlessly destroy all their souls by perverting them with your idols? Now, stir up your mind's wits and listen to me. Acknowledge that one who, by his unspoken word, created this entire world, for he alone is true God who sent his only begotten to earth that he might deliver our souls by his cross. He is the savior of those who have fallen into error, and he is the God of gods and to him is eternal glory."

4. Then the emperor, now full of doubt, made her follow him back to the palace, for he thought that with some gentle persuasion he might convert her to the idols and she might renounce Christ. But she exerted herself all the more to convince the emperor by her divinely inspired words.

5. The emperor then gave the order to bring fifty masters of rhetoric to discourse with her on Greek learning. When they began to speak in the presence of the emperor, the blessed Catherine, with angelic assistance, amazed those eminent masters of rhetoric and put them to shame; she showed them to be ignorant and foolish. At that moment the philosophers were also seized by shame, and they feared to speak or even to ask a question about the philosophical writings.

6. The blessed Catherine, seeing them all now in doubt, recounted to them the prophecies of the pagan philosophers who had come before Christ. Virgil had said, "From the union of three one appears in the flesh, and of the three invisibles there is no imperfection."[2] The Sibyl was a woman, and she wrote in her writings, in that series of her decrees, concerning the cross when she said, "O wood thrice-blessed, because the anointed one stretches out his arms upon you."[3] One had foretold the mystery of the holy Trinity, and the other the sufferings of Christ. And by many other sayings from the apostle Peter to the psalms of David she continued to teach and to admonish the rhetoricians and philosophers to believe in Christ.

---

2. I was unable to track down this quotation; therefore, the translation must remain less precise than I would prefer.
3. *Sibylline Oracles* VI.33–34.

7. Եւ ասէ ցնոսա. Ով կոյրք եւ անիմայք եւ պակասամիտք ծաներուք զՏէրն մեր Յիսուս Քրիստոս որ վասն մեր մարմնացաւ եւ խաչեցաւ եւ թաղեցաւ եւ յարեաւ ի մեռելոց եւ յերկինս համբարձաւ, եւ գալոց է դատել զկենդանիս եւ զմեռեալս որում փառք յաւիտեանս:

8. Իսկ Թագաւորն զհռետորսն իբրեւ ետես յամօթ լեալ եւ ի տարակուսի՝ բարկացաւ յոյժ, եւ հրամայեաց հուր բորբոքել եւ այրել զյիսուն իմաստասէրսն: Եւ յորժամ տանէին զնոսա յայրումն՝ մինն ի նոցանէ խրատ տայր այլոցն զի անկանիցին յոտս սրբուհւոյ կուսին, եւ առցեն զդրոշմն Քրիստոսի. որպէս եւ արարին. եւ հաւատացին ի Քրիստոս: Եւ ասէ ցնոսա. Երանի է ձեզ զի փախեայք ի մոլորութենէն եւ ծանեայք զԱստուած. արդ ընկալարուք զմկրտութիւն հրոյ եւ ուրախասջիք ընդ հրեշտակս յաւիտեան: Եւ կատարեցան հրով յիսուն արքն այնոքիկ խոստովանելով զՏէրն մեր Յիսուս Քրիստոս եւ մազ մի ի գլխոց նոցա ոչ այրեցաւ ի հուրն. եւ բազումք յամբոխէն հաւատացին ի Քրիստոս:

9. Եւ զերանելոյն Կատերինեայ մերկացուցին զծիրանի բեհեզն եւ զոսկի զարդսն ի գլխոյն եւ ի բազկացն եւ ի պարանոցէն, եւ հարկանէին ուժգին ի վերայ հանդերձին եւ արկին ի բանդ:

10. Եւ կին մի այրի՝ Թագուհի լեալ երբեմն Մագսենտիոսի արքային՝ ցանկայր տեսանել զԿատերինեա, եւ լսել ի նմանէ բանս իմաստութեան: Եւ Պորփիւրիոս ստրատելատն տարաւ ի գիշերի զԹագուհին առ նա, եւ նորին վարդապետութեամբն հաւատաց ի Քրիստոս, եւ երթեալ ի տուն իւր մկրտեցաւ ի քրիստոնէից:

11. Եւ դարձեալ տարան զերանելին Կատերինեա ի հարցումն, եւ նա անփոփոխելի բնութեամբ խոստովանէր զՔրիստոս: Կապեցին զնա ի սրալից անիւ, եւ հրեշտակ Տեառն իջեալ յերկնից կորզեաց զնա ի դժնդակ մեքենայից: Յայնժամ հաւատացեալ Թագուհին ընթացաւ հերարձակ առ Թագաւորն, եւ անգոսնելով մեղադրէր նմա ընդ անխիղճ անողորմութիւն նորա. եւ ինքն խոստովանեցաւ համարձակութեամբ զՔրիստոս: Եւ հատին զգլուխ նորա եւ կատարեցաւ մարտիրոսութեամբ:

7. She then said to them, "O you blind, foolish, and senseless people, come to know our Lord Jesus Christ who took on flesh for your sake, was crucified, rose from the dead, and ascended into heaven, and will come again to judge the living and the dead; to Him be eternal glory."

8. When the emperor saw that the rhetoricians had been put to shame and into confusion, he became exceedingly angry and gave the command to light a fire and burn the fifty philosophers. While they were taking them to the blaze, one of [the philosophers] counseled the others to fall at the feet of the holy virgin and to receive the seal of Christ. They all did this and professed belief in Christ. [Catherine] then said to them, "Blessed are you for you have fled from your error and have come to know God. Now accept this baptism by fire, and you will rejoice with the angels forever." Those fifty men then died in the fire, professing our Lord Jesus Christ, and not a single hair from their heads was burned in the fire. Many then from the crowd also came to believe in Christ.

9. They then stripped the blessed Catherine of her purple muslin robe, the golden dressings from her head, her arms, and her neck; they then beat her vigorously, dressed her in other garments, and threw her into prison.

0. A certain widow, who had once been queen to the emperor Maxentius, desired to see Catherine and to hear from her words of wisdom. So Porphyry, an army officer, brought the queen to her in the night, and through the teaching of [Catherine] she came to believe in Christ. When she returned to her house, she was baptized by Christians.

1. They again brought in the blessed Catherine for questioning, but she, with an adamantine disposition, professed Christ. They bound her to a wheel covered with sharp spikes but an angel of the Lord came down from heaven and snatched her from that cruel apparatus. Then the queen, who had just come to the faith, ran up before the king completely disheveled and began to contemn and upbraid him for his unconscionable lack of compassion, and she boldly proclaimed Christ. They then cut off her head, and she died there as a martyr.

12. *Իսկ զսրբուհի կոյսն Կատերինեայ յոյժ աղաչեաց Թագաւորն եւ խրատ տայր ուրանալ զՔրիստոս, եւ տեսեալ եթէ ամենեւին ոչ լսէ, եհատ վճիռ գլխատման նորա: Եւ յորժամ տանէին ի կատարումն՝ բազում ժողովուրդք երթային զկնի լալով: Եւ յորժամ գնացին ի տեղին՝ աղաչեաց զդահիճսն անսալ փոքր մի մինչեւ կացցէ յաղօթս: Եւ համբարձեալ զձեռս իւր եւ զաչս յերկինս ասէ. Տէր Աստուած իմ լուր ինձ եւ կատարեա զխնդրուածս իմ, եւ տուր ամենեցուն որք յիշեն զանուն աղախնոյս քո Կատարինեայ զառատ ողորմութիւն քո, եւ առողջութիւն մարդոյ եւ անասնոյ, եւ որք յիշեն զիս յաւուր ոգեվարի՝ առաքեա զհրեշտակ խաղաղութեան որ ջնջեսցէ զմեղս նոցա եւ խաղաղութեամբ աւանդեսցէ զհոգին: Ընկալ եւ զհոգիս իմ խաղաղութեամբ եւ քեզ փառք յաւիտեանս:*

13. *Եւ ի կատարել զաղօթսն խօսեցաւ Տէր յամպոյն եւ ասէ. Եկեսջիր ի կայանս Հօրն քոյ որ յերկինս է, հրեշտակք պսակս եւ ղամբարս ունելով մնան գալստեան քոյ զի եկեսցեն քեզ ընդ առաջ: Եւ զխնդրուածս քո կատարեցից, եւ տաց ամենեցուն որք կատարեն զյիշատակս քո հարիւրապատիկ զխնդրուածս նոցա: Եւ յաւուր ոգեվարի եթէ ոք յիշեսցէ զանուն քո՝ առաքեցից զհրեշտակ խաղաղութեան, եւ քաղցրութեամբ աւանդեսցի հոգի նորա:*

14. *Եւ յետ աստուածային ձայնին ասէ երանելին ցդահիճսն. Եկայք եւ կատարեցէք զհրամայեալսն ձեզ ի Թագաւորէն ձերմէ: Եւ այնպէս հատին զգլուխ նորա Մարտի Իէ: Եւ փոխանակ արեան կաթն բղխեաց ի պարանոցէն, եւ հրեշտակք Աստուծոյ բարձին զմարմինն եւ տարեալ եդին ի Սինէական լերինն:*

15. *Եւ գրեաց զպատմութիւն վկայութեանն Աթանասիոս դպիր եւ ծառայ սրբուհւոյն Կատարինեայ:*

12. The emperor then vigorously pleaded with the holy virgin Catherine and exhorted her to renounce Christ, but once he saw that she was not listening at all, he decreed her decapitation. While they were taking her to the place of execution, many people were following along weeping. And when they reached the place, she begged the executioner to listen for a moment while she prayed. She raised her hands and her eyes up to heaven and said, "O Lord my God, hear me and fulfill what I ask of You. Grant to all those who remember the name of Your handmaid Catherine Your abundant mercy and health to both man and beast. And to all those who remember me on the day of my death, send Your angel of peace to wipe away their sins and to release their soul in peace. Receive now my soul in peace, and to You be eternal glory."

13. When she had finished her prayer, the Lord spoke from a cloud and said, "Enter into the dwelling of your Father who is in heaven. Angels carrying crowns and lanterns await your coming so that they might go before you. I will fulfill what you ask of me, and I will give to all those who celebrate your memory a hundredfold what you have asked on their behalf. And on the day of your death, I will send my angel of peace to whoever remembers your name, and his soul will be handed over in sweetness."

14. After this divine voice [had spoken], the blessed one said to the executioner, "Come, carry out what you have been commanded to do by your emperor." And so they cut off her head on the twenty-seventh of March. In the place of blood, milk flowed out from her neck, and angels of God raised up her body and bore it up to Mount Sinai.

15. Athanasius, the scribe and servant of the holy Catherine, composed this account of her martyrdom.

Արեգի Ի

Մարտի ԻԸ

Վկայութիւն սրբոյ Վահանայ Գողթնացւոյն

1. *Վկայն Քրիստոսի Վահան՝ որդի էր Խոսրովու իշխանին Գողթն գաւառի: Եւ յորժամ տաճիկք հրամանաւ Աբդլմելիքի այրեցին զիշխանսն Հայոց ի Նախճուան յեկեղեցին ի պատճառս երդման ժողովեալ ածին զնոսա անդ զի միամիտ կացցեն ի ծառայութիւն Իսմայելացւոց: Եւ ապա փակեցին զդուրս եկեղեցւոյն աղխսով, եւ վառեցին հրով զեկեղեցին զի փայտաշէն էր, եւ առ հասարակ այրեցան իշխանքն հրով նահատակեալք. եւ ինքեանք ասպատակ սփռեցան յաշխարհն Հայոց, աւար առեալ զամենայն՝ վարեցին ի գերութիւն զարս եւ զկանայս եւ զմանկտիս. ընդ որս եւ գերեցաւ Վահան մանուկ երից ամաց եւ տարեալ ի Սամառա եդուն ի դպրոց, եւ ուսաւ երագամտութեամբ զամենայն ուսումնս Տաճկաց, եւ եղեւ դիւանադպիր եւ դպրապետ ի դրան արքունի:*
2. *Իսկ յորժամ առ Ոմար զիշխանութիւնն Տաճկաց բարեմիտ եղեւ առ քրիստոնեայս եւ մանաւանդ առ ազգս Հայոց, հրամայեաց եւ զամենայն գերեալսն ազատել:*

March 28

Areg 20

The martyrdom of Saint Vahan of Goghtn

1. Vahan, the martyr for Christ, was a son of Xosrov, the governor of the district of Goghtn.[1] When the Arabs, by the order of Abd al-Malik,[2] incinerated the princes of Armenia in the church of Nakhichevan where they had brought them to assemble and swear an oath to stand united in the service of Islam, they blocked up the doors of the church with bricks, and they set the church on fire, for it was built of wood, and all princes together burned as martyrs in the fire. These [Muslims] then plundered the land of Armenia, pillaging everything and taking into captivity both women and children. Among these the young Vahan—only three years old—was led into exile, taken to Samarra, and handed over to the royal secretaries where he, due to his keen intellect, learned everything that the Arabs taught him, and he became a royal secretary and a chief secretary in the royal palace.

2. Then when the rule of the Arabs fell to Umar,[3] he was more sympathetic toward Christians and especially to the Armenian nation, giving the command for all those in exile to be set free.

1. A fuller account of Vahan's life in English translation can be found in Maksoudian et al., *The Light of the World*, 105–27.
2. Abd al-Malik ibn Marwan, the fifth Umayyad caliph, ruled from 685 to 705.
3. Umar ibn Abd al-Aziz, the nephew of Abd al-Malik, and the eighth Umayyad caliph, ruled from 717 to 720.

3. Արձակեցաւ եւ Վահան, զոր անուանեցին տաճկունքն Վահապ, եւ եկեալ ի գաւառ իւր ի Գողթն՝ առ իւր կին յազգէն Սիւնեաց: Եւ խոստովանէր զՔրիստոս համարձակ զոր ի տղայութենէն ուրացուցին տաճիկք, եւ ցանկայր մեռանել մարտիրոսութեամբ. եւ երթայր յանապատն կրօնաւորէր:

4. Ընդ աւուրսն ընդ այնոսիկ մեռաւ իշխանն Տաճկաց Ոմարն, եւ իշխանացաւ Շամա, որ է Շէհմ: Եւ գնաց Վահան առ նա, զի կամ համարձակ կալցի զքրիստոնէութիւնն կամ մեռցի մարտիրոսութեամբ: Եւ գնացեալ ի դուռն ոչ ոք համարձակէր ասել վասն քրիստոնէութեանն. ապա ինքն իսկ գրեաց զքրիստոնէութիւնն իւր եւ եցոյց յարքունիս: Եւ իսկոյն կոչեցին առաջի Շամայ, եւ նա հարցանէր զնա եթէ քրիստոնեայ իցէ: Եւ նա համարձակութեամբ խոստովանեցաւ զՔրիստոս Աստուած եւ Որդի Աստուծոյ: Եւ նա խոստանայր նմա պարգեւս եւ պատիւս եթէ լսէ նմա, եւ նա ոչ առ յանձն ամենեւին: Եւ նա հրամայեաց սրով սպանանել զնա:

5. Եւ հանեալ արտաքոյ քաղաքին հատին զգլուխ նորա Մարտի ԻԸ: Եւ լոյս մեծ ծագեաց ի վերայ նորա: Եւ գաղտ բարձեալ զնա քրիստոնէիցն թաղեցին պատուով ի նշանաւոր տեղւոջ: Եւ բազում բժշկութիւնք լինին ի նշխարաց սրբոյն ի հիւանդս եւ յայլսն:

Յայսմ աւուր վկայութիւն Փերփետուայ եւ աղախնոյն

6. Երանելի կանայքն էին Պարսիկս քրիստոնեայք, յաւուրս Սաբուռիոսի հրապաշտ արքային: Սոքա քորք էին սրբոյն Շմաւոնի եպիսկոպոսին, որ յառաջ քան զայս մարտիրոսացաւ հանդերձ հազար խոստովանող վկայիւք ի Պարսիկս:

3. Vahan, whom the Arabs had renamed Wahab, was also released, so he went back to his district in Goghtn and took for himself a wife from the region of Siwnikʿ. He also openly professed Christ, whom the Arabs had forced him to deny since his youth, and he developed aspirations to die as a martyr. He then went out to the desert and began to live a life of asceticism.

4. In those days Umar, the ruler of the Arabs, died, and Hisham,[4] also known as Shehm, came to the throne. Vahan then went to him so that either [Hisham] might also give support to Christianity or that he himself might die as a martyr. When he went to the gate, no one dared to say anything about Christianity, so he himself wrote of his Christian faith and showed it at the palace. He was immediately summoned into the presence of Hisham, who asked him whether he was a Christian. [Vahan] then boldly proclaimed Christ as God and as Son of God. [Hisham] promised him gifts and honors if he would become obedient to him, but [Vahan] absolutely refused. [Hisham] then gave the command for him to be killed by the sword.

5. They then led [Vahan] outside the city and cut off his head on the twenty-eighth of March. And a great light shone above him. The Christians secretly took him up and buried him with honors in a distinguished place. Many healings occurred from the relics of this holy one for those who were ill as well as for others.

On this day is the martyrdom of Pherboutha and her sister

6. These blessed women were Christians from Persia who lived in the days of that fire-worshipping king Shapur. They were both sisters of the holy bishop Symeon,[5] who had recently been martyred along with a thousand confessor-martyrs in Persia.

---

4. Hisham ibn Abd al-Malik, the tenth Umayyad caliph, ruled from 724 to 743.
5. Bishop Symeon bar Sabbae was martyred on Good Friday around the year 339 in Karka d-Ledan. The relevant texts concerning his martyrdom are now edited with English translation in Smith, *Martyrdom and History of Blessed Simeon bar Sabba'e*.

7\. *Եւ եղեւ հիւանդանալ Պարսից թագուհւոյն եւ գչարէին հրապաշտքն զսրբուհեաց եթէ նոքա կախարդեցին զթագուհին: Եւ հրամայեաց թագաւորն Մաքտատեայ մոգպետին քննել զկանայսն վասն որոյ մատնեցանն: Եւ յորժամ կացին առաջի՝ տեսեալ մոգպետին զգեղեցկութիւն երեսացն Փերփութէի՝ ցանկացաւ նմա տռփութեամբ, եւ կայր ապշեալ ընդ երեսն անմռունչ եւ չրտուցեալ ոչ ինչ հարցանէր:*

8\. *Եւ գիտացին երանելի կանայքն զպատճառս կոչմանն առաջի մոգպետին, եւ ասեն. Մեք քրիստոնեայք եմք եւ ոչ աղանդ ինչ գիտեմք եւ ոչ կախարդութիւն: Եւ արգելին զնոսա ի տան մի, եւ ազդեցին արքային զպատասխանիս նոցա: Եւ մոգպետն առաքեաց կանայս յերանելին Փերփութեա. Եթէ կամիցիս ազատիլ ի մահուանէ ամուսնացիր ինձ: Եւ նորա լուեալ անարգանօք դարձոյց յետս զպատգամաւոր կանայսն առ մոգպետն:*

9\. *Եւ հրամայեաց թագաւորն. Եթէ ուրանան զՔրիստոս եւ պաշտեն զարեգակն եւ զհուր՝ ազատեա զնոսա, ապա թէ ոչ՝ հատ զգլուխս նոցա: Եւ յորժամ ոչ հաւանեցան անօրէն հրամանին՝ հանին զնոսա ի զենումն: Եւ ոմանք ի պիղծ աղանդաւորացն ասացին. Եթէ ոչ յերկուս հերձնուն զնոսա՝ որ անցանէ թագուհին ի վերայ՝ ոչ ողջանայ: Ապա կապեցին զնոսա զմեքենայից, եւ սղոցեցին յերկուս մասունս որպէս փայտ, եւ էանց ի վերայ նոցա թագուհին եւ ամենայն բանակն որ զկնի երթային, եւ յորժամ դարձաւ յապարանսն իւր՝ չար մահուամբ սատակեցաւ:*

10\. *Իսկ երանելի սուրբ կանայքն զանմահ կեանս ընկալան Մարտի ԻԸ, եւ պսակեցան ի Քրիստոսէ տուողէ նոցա այնչափ զօրութիւն եւ համբերութիւն, եւ են բարեխօս առ Քրիստոս վասն տօնողացս:*

7. Once, when the queen of the Persians fell ill, those fire worshippers brought accusations that these holy women had put a spell on the queen. The king then commanded the *magupatan*, the chief magi, to examine the women concerning why they had been delivered up. When they stood before him and the *magupatan* beheld the beauty of Pherboutha's face, he was overcome with a burning desire for her. He stood there dumbfounded and enraptured by her face; distracted in this manner, he asked no more questions.

8. When these blessed women learned the reason for their having been summoned before the chief magi, they said, "We are Christians, so we have no knowledge of any magic or sorcery." They then shut [the women] up in a house, while they informed the king of their response. Then the chief magi sent some women to the blessed Pherboutha [to say], "If you wish to be delivered from death, marry me." But when she heard this, she sent those female envoys back to the chief magi with insults.

9. Then the king gave the order, "If they renounce Christ and worship the sun and the fire, free them; but if they do not, cut off their heads." When they refused to consent to such an unjust command, they led them out to the place of execution. A few followers of that filthy religion then said, "If they do not cut them into two pieces that the queen can pass between, she will not be healed. So they bound [the women] to machines and they sawed them into two halves just like a log, and the queen passed between them, as did her entire entourage that followed after her. But when she returned to her palace, she perished by an awful death.

10. These blessed holy women thus received eternal life on the twenty-eighth of March, and they were crowned by Christ who had given them so much power and endurance. They also became intercessors before Christ for all those who celebrate their feast.

Արեգի ԻԱ

Մարտի ԻԹ

Վկայութիւն երեսուն եւ վեց մարտիրոսաց յորոց էին սուրբքն. Մակարիոս, Զենոն, Աղեքսանդրոս, Թէոդորոս եւ այլ երեսուն եւ երկու ընկերք

1. *Յամս Դեկոսի անօրէն արքային՝ կացուցին զսուրբսն առաջի դատաւորին Բուրտիանոսի, յԱփրեա քաղաքին, եւ ասէ. Ընդէ՞ր ոչ զոհէք աստուածոց մերոց: Եւ նոքա ասեն. Մեք քրիստոնեայք եմք, եւ ոչ զոհեմք պիղծ աստուածոց ձերոց:*
2. *Եւ բարկացեալ բռնաւորին՝ հրամայեաց եւ ձաղկեցին զսուրբսն դալար բրովք եւ արջառաջլօք: Եւ համբարձեալ զձեռս իւրեանց յերկինս աղաղակեցին բարձր ձայնիւ. Օգնեա մեզ Աստուած ծառայիցս քոց եւ փրկեա զմեզ ի հակառակողէս յայսմանէ:*
3. *Եւ զայն լուեալ դատաւորին մոլեգաւ, եւ հրամայեաց հարկանել զնոսա ուժգին մինչեւ խորտակեցան գաւազանքն եւ լուծան կապանքն, եւ փոխեցան այլ դահիճք, եւ այնչափ տանջեցին մինչեւ բացան ոսկերքն եւ պատառեցան որովայնքն եւ սիրտքն երեւէին, բայց երեսք իւրեանց էին պայծառք: Եւ յոյժ զարմացան ամենեքեան ընդ ժուժկալութիւն սրբոցն: Եւ ապա հրացեալ չանթիւք այրեցին զթիկունս նոցա, եւ խիստ քացախ աղացեալ աղիւ հեղին ի վերայ թիկանցն վիրաւորելոցն եւ խոշոր խորգով տրորէին զնոցսն, եւ սուրբքն սաղմոսէին առ Աստուած:*
4. *Եւ նոյնժամայն հրամայեաց՝ եւ հատին զերեսուն եւ վեց մարտիրոսացն զգլուխսն Մարտի ԻԹ: Եւ երթեալ քրիստոնէիցն թաղեցին մեծաւ պատուով զսուրբ եւ զպատուական մարմինս նոցա ի նշանաւոր տեղւոջ, յորում բժշկութիւնք լինին ի վերայ հիւանդաց եւ ախտաժետաց:*

March 29

Areg 21

The martyrdom of thirty-six martyrs, among whom were Macarius, Zenon, Alexander, Theodorus, and thirty-two other companions

1. In the days of the impious emperor Decius, these holy ones were brought before the judge Burtianus in the city of Apri,[1] who asked them, "Why do you not sacrifice to our gods?" And they replied, "We are Christians, and we do not sacrifice to your abominable gods."

2. That tyrant became enraged and gave the command to flog these holy ones with fresh green branches and bullwhips. They then raised up their hands to heaven and cried out in a loud voice, "Help us, O God, your servants, and deliver us from this opponent."

3. When the judge heard this, he became even more furious and commanded that they beat them violently until the switches broke and the binding came apart. Then other executioners took their places and tortured them until their bones became exposed, their bellies were ripped open, and even their hearts became visible. But their faces remained radiant. And everyone there marveled at the endurance of those holy ones. Then they heated up red hot irons and seared their hind parts, they mercilessly mixed vinegar and salt and poured it over the backs of those who were wounded, and they scraped their open wounds with coarse burlap; yet those holy ones continued to sing psalms to God.

4. Presently, on the twenty-ninth of March, [the judge] commanded that the heads of these martyrs be cut off. The Christians came and buried their holy and revered corpses with great honor in a distinguished place where healings took place on behalf of the sick and the infirm.

---

1. Formerly Theodosiopolis, near the Sea of Marmara.

Յայսմ աւուր յիշատակ սուրբ առաքելոյն Հերոդիոնոսի

5. *Աստուածային առաքեալն Հերոդիոնոս հետեւող սուրբ առաքելոցն գլխաւորաց, զի էր ի կարգէ եօթանասնիցն, եւ պաշտելով հաւատարմապէս եւ սպասաւորելով Պօղոսի եւ Պետրոսի, որ եւ հաւասար նոցա պայծառացաւ ի շնորհս, ի նշանս, ի վարդապետութիւնս, եւ ի համբերութիւն ազգի ազգի նեղութեանց եւ հալածանաց կրից որ ի հրէից եւ ի հեթանոսաց:*

6. *Զսա յիշէ Պօղոս ի թուղթս իւր եւ ողջունէ, որ եւ սքանչելապէս կատարեցաւ ի Քրիստոս, ի բազումս տարածեալ զաւետարանն: Հանգեաւ սուրբ եւ փառաւորեալ առաքեալն Քրիստոսի ի Ռողոնի ԻԹ Մարտի ամսոյ, ի փառս Քրիստոսի, որ է օրհնեալ յաւիտեանս, ամէն:*

Յայսմ աւուր յիշատակ երանելի Թագաւորին Երմունալդի զոր Երմինիգոս կոչեմք

7. *Զսա հայրն իւր սպան վասն Քրիստոսի հաւատոցն. զի հայրն էր արիոսեան աղանդով, իսկ Երմինիգոս որդի նորա սիրեաց զուղղափառութիւն: Վասն որոյ զրկեաց զնա հայր իւր ի թագաւորութենէ, եւ կապանօք էարկ զնա ի բանդ. եւ ապա ետ կտրատել զնա կացնով, եւ գլխատել անդէն ի բանդին:*

8. *Եւ եղեւ հրաշալի բարբառ զուարթնոց ի մէջ գիշերի ի բանդի անդ, եւ ծագեաց լոյս պայծառ ի վերայ մարմնոյ սրբոյն: Եւ բազմութիւն քաղաքին դիմեաց ի բանդն, եւ հայր նորա ամենայն տամբ իւրով դարձաւ յուղղափառութիւն, ընդ նմին եւ բազումք ի չարափառաց ընկալան զուղիղ հաւատն:*

9. *Զսա յիշէ Գրիգոր պապն ի քսան եւ ութ ճառ երկրորդ գրոց:*

On this day is the memorial of the holy apostle Herodion

5. The divine apostle Herodion was a follower of the chief apostles, for he was one of the seventy, and he faithfully served and ministered to Paul and Peter. He distinguished himself as equal to them in grace, in signs, in teaching, and by his patient endurance of various sorts of afflictions and severe persecutions from both Jews and pagans.

6. Paul remembered and greeted him in his letter.[2] Having spread the gospel throughout many lands, he died admirably in Christ. This holy and glorious apostle of Christ fell asleep in Rhodes on the twenty-ninth of the month of March, in the glory of Christ, who is blessed forever. Amen.

On this day is the memorial of the blessed king Hermigildus, whom we call Erminidos

7. This one was killed by his father for his faith in Christ, for his father was a member of the Arian heresy, while Erminidos was a lover of orthodoxy. For this reason his father dispossessed him of the kingship and threw him bound into prison, and then he had him chopped up by an axe and beheaded there in prison.

8. Then during the middle of the night there arose a marvelous sound of angels in that prison, and a radiant light shone upon the body of that holy one. A multitude from the city hastened to the prison, and his father along with his entire household converted to orthodoxy; along with him a number of other heterodox accepted the orthodox faith.

9. Pope Gregory makes note of him in the twenty-eighth homily of his second volume.[3]

---

2. Cf. Romans 16:11.

3. In the Latin version, the account of Hermigildus is found in Gregory's *Book of Dialogues* (see p. 81n7 above), III.xxxi.

Արեգի ԻԲ

Մարտի Լ

Վկայաբանութիւն Գուշնազաթայ պարսիկ ներքինւոյն

1. Յաւուրս Սաբուհոսի հրապաշտ արքային Պարսից՝ երանելի ներքինին Գուշղազաթ սնուցեալ էր զարքայն, եւ էր ծերունի եւ մեծաւ պատուով իշխան եւ թագադիր. լեալ էր երբեմն քրիստոնեայ, եւ վասն սիրոյ եւ երկեղի արքային երկիր եպագ արեգական եւ հրոյ:

2. Եւ ի միում աւուր նստէր աթոռով ի վերայ դրանն արքունի, եւ տեսանէ զսուրբն Շմաւոն եպիսկոպոսն, որ յետոյ մարտիրոսացաւ, յարեաւ յաթոռոյն գնաց ընդ առաջ երկիր եպագ եւ կամէր համբուրել. եւ եպիսկոպոսն դարձոյց զերեսս իւր ի նմանէ եւ անց: Իսկ Գուշղազաթ յոգւոց եհան զղջմամբ եւ ասէ. Եթէ Շմաւոն եպիսկոպոսն որ մարդ է իբրեւ զիս՝ դարձաւ յինէն, ապա Աստուած ո՞րչափ դարձուցանէ զերեսս իւր յինէն որ ուրացայ զնա: Գնաց ի տուն իւր եւ զգեցաւ հանդերձ սգոյ սեաւ եւ ողբաց զուրացութեան մեղս իւր:

3. Եւ լուեալ արքային կոչեաց զնա առաջի իւր, եհարց. Ընդէ՞ր զգեցար հանդերձ սեաւ սգոյ եւ ողբաս: Եւ նա ասէ. Վասն զի արարի զկամս քո եւ ուրացայ զԱստուածն իմ եւ երկիր պագի արեգական եւ հրոյ: Ասէ թագաւորն. Եթէ զայդ լաս եւ ողբաս, ով չար ծերունի, ես փութով դարձուցից զողբս քո ի գլուխ քո: Եւ յետ բազում խրատու եւ աղաչանաց՝ յորժամ ամենեւին ոչ հաւանեցաւ, բարկացաւ եւ հրամայեաց հատանել զգլուխ նորա:

March 30

Areg 22

The martyrdom of Gushdazat, the Persian eunuch

1. In the days of Shapur, the fire-worshipping king of the Persians, the blessed eunuch Gushdazat, who raised the king, was now an old man; he was a prince with great honor and held the position of crowning the king. He had once been a Christian, but due to his love for and fear of the king, he worshipped the sun and fire.

2. One day he was seated on a chair at the gate of the royal palace, and he saw the holy bishop Symeon, who would later be martyred.[1] He rose up from his chair, went up to him, prostrated himself before him, and even wanted to embrace him, but the bishop turned his face away from him and passed by. Gushdazat groaned in contrition and said, "If the bishop Symeon, who is a man like me, turns away from me, then how much more will God turn his face away from me who have renounced him?" He then returned to his house and put on black garments of mourning and bewailed his sins of renunciation.

3. When the king heard of this, he summoned him to his presence and asked him, "Why have you put on these black garments of mourning and are weeping?" [Gushdazat] replied, "Because I have done what you wished and have thus denied my God and have worshipped the sun and the fire." The king responded, "If this is the reason you are weeping and lamenting, O wicked old man, then I will quickly bring your laments down upon your head." After much exhortation and pleading, when [Gushdazat] was completely unswayed, [the king] became incensed and ordered that his head be cut off.

1. I.e., Bishop Symeon bar Sabbae; see p. 171n5 above.

4. *Ասէ Գուշգազատ. Գիտես Հաւաստեաւ զի ես գրկովք խմովք սնուցեալ եմ զքեզ, եւ միամտութեամբ ծառայեալ, այժմ կատարեա զխնդրուածս իմ, եւ առաքեա քարոզս ի մէջ քաղաքիս՝ որ մեծաւ ձայնիւ աղաղակեն յամբոխ քաղաքին եւ Հրապարակին եթէ Գուշգազատ ոչ վասն նենգութեան եւ ոչ վասն յայտնելոյ զխորՀուրդս արքային, եւ ոչ վասն այլ ինչ չար գործոց մեռանի սրով, այլ վասն Հաւատոցն Քրիստոսի: Եւ Հրամայեաց թագաւորն եւ արարին ըստ կամաց նորա:*

5. *Եւ զայս ետ առնել սուրբ վկայն Քրիստոսի Գուշգազատ՝ վասն զի յառաջ քրիստոնեայ էր եւ ուրացաւ զՔրիստոս եւ բազում քրիստոնեայս գայթակղեցոյց: Եւ յորժամ Հանին զնա արտաքոյ քաղաքին՝ առաջի ամենայն ժողովրդեան Հատին զգլուխ նորա յաւուր մեծի կիւրակէի սրբոյ Զատկին՝ յորում էր Արեգ ամսոյ ԻԲ եւ Մարտի Լ:*

Յայսմ աւուր վկայութիւն աշակերտացն Մաշտոցի որ յԱղուանս կատարեցան

6. *Արքայն Հիւսիսոյ զօրաժողով լեալ՝ եկն բազում բարբարոսօք եւ ել ընդ դուռն Դարբանդայ. եւ Հասեալ ի մեծ գետն որ կոչի Կուր եւ բանակեալ անդ՝ Հրաման տայր զօրացն ասպատակ սփռել յերիս աշխարՀսն՝ Հայոց, Վրաց եւ Աղուանից. եւ առեալ աւարս եւ գերիս բազումս ածին առ նա:*

4. Gushdazat responded, "You certainly know that I had raised you in my own arms and that I have served you with perfect loyalty. Now carry out my wishes and send messengers throughout the city to cry out in loud voices to the populace of the city and to the crowds that Gushdazat is to die by the sword not for any falsehood, nor for having revealed the plans of the king, nor for any other evil deed, but for his faith in Christ." And the king commanded that it be done according to his wishes.

5. The holy martyr of Christ, Gushdazat, had this done because he had previously been a Christian but then renounced Christ and so scandalized many Christians. After they had taken him outside the city, in the presence of all the people, they cut off his head on a Sunday, the great day of the holy paschal feast, which was the twenty-second of Areg, or the thirtieth day of March.

On this day is the martyrdom of the disciples of Mashtotsʿ who died in Astghblur

6. The king of the north[2] assembled his army, departed with many barbarians, and went out through the gates of Derbent. He arrived at the great river called the Kur and set up camp there. He sent out the command to his soldiers to begin their incursions into three countries: Armenia, Georgia, and Albania. And they took much plunder, and they brought numerous prisoners to him.

2. I.e., the king of the Khazars, a nomadic Turkic tribe.

7. *Մի ոմն յիշխանացն գնաց յերկիրն Խաչենոյ, եւ աւար Հարեալ զնա՝ ետես ի գերեալսն կին մի գեղեցիկ եւ մեծազգի, եւ Հրամայեաց ծառայից իւրոց պաՀել զնա նմա ի խառնակութիւն գիչերոյ։ Եւ իբրեւ երեկոյ եղեւ՝ բանակեցաւ ի տեղի մի տափարակ մօտ յԱկանայ քաղաք, եւ Հրամայեաց ածել զկինն. եւ նա ոչ չոգաւ. եւ ի քարշ տարան զնա առ նա։ Եւ կամեցեալ զօրագլխին բռնադատել զնա, եւ նա առնաբար մարտեաւ ընդ նմա՝ եւ պատառեաց զՀանդերձս նորա եւ ել ի նմանէ բռնութեամբ։ Եւ նա բարկացեալ յոյժ Հրամայեաց կապել զնա զագոյ ամեՀի ձիոյ եւ արձակել զնա ի դաշտն, եւ ձիոյն քարշեալ զնա ընդ մացառս եւ ընդ քարս, քանդեցաւ ամենայն մարմինն, եւ պատառ պատառ Հատեալ յերկիր անկաւ, եւ արիւնն ոռոգանէր զերեսս երկրին. եւ այնպէս կատարեցաւ նաՀատակութեամբ սուրբ տիկինն ԹագուՀի։ Եւ իբրեւ երեկոյ եղեւ լոյս սաստիկ ծագեաց ի վերայ սուրբ մարմնոյն եւ ի տեղիս կաթուածի արեանն, եւ տեսեալ իշխանին եւ զօրաց նորա զարՀուրեցան։*

8. *Եւ էր ընդ գերեալսն քաՀանայ մի Աթանաս անուն, որ եկեալ էր յԵրուսաղեմէ ընդ աշակերտսն Մաշտոցի. եւ ընկերսն նորա սպանեալ բարբարոսացն՝ եւ զքաՀանայն ունէին ի կապանս։ Եւ կոչեցեալ զնա զօրագլուխն՝ Հարցանէր եւ ասէր թէ. Զի՞նչ իցէ լոյսն այն։ Եւ նա ասաց. Որ վասն Աստուծոյ մեռանի սրբութեամբ՝ Աստուած նշանօք պատուէ զնա աստ եւ ի Հանդերձեալ կեանսն, որպէս կինն որ նաՀատակեալ ի ձէնջ կատարեցաւ։*

9. *Եւ զաՀի Հարեալ իշխանն ուսաւ ի նմանէ զամենայն կարգ եւ զկրօնս քրիստոնէութեան, եւ մկրտեցաւ որդւովք եւ ամենայն զօրօքն, եւ անուանեցաւ Թէոփիլոս, եւ որդիքն՝ Մովսէս եւ Երանողիս. եւ արձակեաց զամենայն քրիստոնեայսն որ գերեալն էին։ Եւ կատարեցին զտօն սուրբ Զատկին ուրախութեամբ ի տեղւոջն որ կոչի այժմ Աստղաբլուր վասն լուսոյ ծագմանն։*

7. One of the princes went into the land of Xachen and, after having plundered it, beheld a certain woman taken prisoner who was beautiful and from a noble family. He commanded his servants to keep her for him that he might sleep with her that night. When evening came, he set up camp on a flat place near the city of Akana and commanded that the woman be brought to him. But she would not go, so they dragged her to [the prince]. The head soldier wanted to rape her, but she fought against him like a man. She ripped his garments and by her force got away from him. Then he, now thoroughly enraged, commanded that she be bound to the tail of a wild horse and then let it go on the plain. The horse dragged her through thickets and over rocks, battering her entire body. Cut into shreds, she fell to the ground, and her blood flowed over the surface of the ground. In this way, this holy queen died in martyrdom. When evening came, a great light shone upon her holy body and on every place where her blood was spilled. When the prince and his troops saw this, they became terrified.

8. Among those who had been taken prisoner, there was a priest, Athanasius by name, who had come from Jerusalem along with the disciples of Mashtotsʿ.[3] The barbarians had killed all his companions, but they kept this priest alive and in chains. The troop commander summoned him and asked him, saying, "What is that light?" And [Athanasius] answered, "Whoever dies in holiness on behalf of God, God honors that one with signs both here and in the life to come, just like this woman who has died, having been martyred by you."

9. The prince, struck with fear, learned from [Athanasius] every institution and custom of Christianity, and he was baptized with his sons and with all his soldiers. He received the name Theophilos, and his sons were named Moses and Eranolis. He released all the Christians who had been taken prisoner, and they all celebrated the holy paschal feast with joy in that place that is now called Astghblur[4] because of that shining light.

---

3. Mashtotsʿ, the inventor of the Armenian, Georgian, and Albanian alphabets, had been in Albania just before the events recorded here.

4. Astghblur, or Astghablur, is Armenian for "hill of the star."

10. *Եւ լուեալ արքայն բարբարոսաց եԹէ քրիստոնեայք եղեն զօրագլուխքն եւ զօրքն, կոչեաց զնա եւ զայլ իշխանսն առ ինքն, եւ բազում ողոքանօք եւ սպառնալեօք ոչ կարաց խախտել զնոսա ի Հաւատոցն Քրիստոսի, եւ ապա Հրամայեաց սրոք սպանանել զսուրբն Թէոփիլոս եւ զիշխանսն որ ընդ նմա: Եւ լուեալ որդւոցն նորա Մովսէսի եւ Երանողայ՝ փախեան զօրօք իւրեանց ի մեծ լեառն որ կոչի Դիզափայտ:*

11. *Եւ առաքեաց բարբարոս արքայն բազում զօրս զկնի, եւ Հասեալ կոտորեցին զնոսա առ Հասարակ վասն Հաւատոցն Քրիստոսի, եւ կուտեալ ի վերայ միմեանց այրեցին ամենեսեան Հանդերձ միայնակեցօքն որ անդ էին: Եւ կոչեցաւ անուն լերինն Դիզափայտ մինչեւ ցայսօր: Եւ կատարի տօն սրբոցս Արեգի ԻԲ եւ Մարտի Լ ի փառս Քրիստոսի:*

10. When the king of the barbarians heard that the officers and the soldiers had become Christians, he summoned [Theophilos] and all the other princes to him, but even with much supplication and with many threats, he was unable to turn them back from their faith in Christ. So he then commanded that the holy Theophilos and all the princes with him be slain by the sword. When his sons Moses and Eranolis heard this, they fled with their own troops to the great mountain that is called Dizapayt.

11. The barbarian king sent numerous troops after them. When they caught up to them, they slaughtered them all together on account of their faith in Christ. They heaped up all their bodies on top of each other and burned them all, along with those who were living the solitary life there. The name of this mountain is called Dizapayt until this day.[5] The feast of these holy ones is celebrated to the glory of Christ on the twenty-second of Areg, or the thirtieth of March.

---

5. This massive annihilation is briefly recounted in Movsēs Dasxurantsʿi, *History of the Caucasian Albanians*, II.4–5.

Արեգի ԻԳ

Մարտի ԼԱ

Վկայաբանութիւն սրբոյն Դաւթի Դվնեցւոյն

1. *Սուրբ վկայն Քրիստոսի Դաւիթ պարսիկ էր ազգաւ, եւ եկեալ յաշխարհն Հայոց՝ յԱյրարատ գաւառ, հաւատաց ի Քրիստոս եւ մկրտեցաւ. եւ մեծ իշխանն Գրիգոր առ զնա յաւագանէն եւ զանուն հօր իւրոյ եդ նմա՝ Դաւիթ կոչելով զնա: Եւ կեայր առաքինի եւ սուրբ վարուք ամուսնացեալ ըստ աշխարհական կարգաց:*
2. *Եւ յետ ժամանակաց ամիրայ ոմն եկն ի Դվին քաղաք Հայոց Սրջահան անուն եւ լուեալ վասն Դաւթի եթէ յառաջ տաճիկ հաւատով էր եւ այժմ է քրիստոնեայ՝ կոչեաց զառաջեաւ եւ ստիպէր զնա ուրանալ զՔրիստոս եւ դառնալ յառաջին հաւատն իւր, եւ ընդունել ի նմանէ պատիւս եւ իշխանութիւնս: Եւ նա ոչ առ յանձն, այլ խոստովանէր զՔրիստոս համարձակ Աստուած եւ Որդի Աստուծոյ: Եւ հրամայեաց արգելուլ զնա ի բանդ, եւ չարչարէր զնա սովով եւ ծարաւով. եւ նա ոչ ձանձրացաւ՝ այլ օրհնէր զՔրիստոս զուարթութեամբ:*
3. *Ապա հրամայեաց խաչել զնա ի վերայ փայտի, եւ զերեսն առնել ի հարաւ, եւ շրջեցաւ փայտն ինքն առանց մարդոյ, եւ դարձոյց զերեսս նորա յարեւելս, եւ գեղարդեամբ խոցեցին զնա ընդ սիրտն, եւ այնպէս աւանդեաց զհոգին իւր առ Աստուած՝ Մարտի ԼԱ:*

March 31

Areg 23

The martyrdom of the holy David of Dvin

1. David, the holy martyr for Christ, was a Persian by race. But he came into the land of Armenia, to the region of Ararat, where he came to believe in Christ and was baptized. The great prince Grigor[1] received him from the baptismal font and gave him the name of his own father, calling him David. He lived a virtuous and holy life and was married according to the regulations for the nonreligious.

2. Some time afterwards a certain emir came to the Armenian city of Dvin, Srjahan by name, and he heard that David had once been a Muslim but was now a Christian. He summoned [David] to his presence and pressed him to renounce Christ and to return to his former faith, and he would receive from him honors and privileges. But he refused; he rather continued to boldly profess Christ as God and the Son of God. So [the emir] gave the command to shut up [David] in prison, and he had him tortured by hunger and thirst, but he did not weaken at all; he rather continued to joyfully praise Christ.

3. Then [the emir] gave the command to hang [David] from a tree and to direct his face to the south, but the tree turned back on its own without any human assistance and turned his face to the east. They then pierced him with a lance through his heart, and in this fashion he rendered up his soul to God on the thirty-first of March.

---

1. Grigor Mamikonean was the first Armenian prince (Arm. *ishkan*) appointed by an Arab caliph; he was appointed by Muʿawiyah ibn Abu-Sufyan Grigor and served as prince from approximately 662 to 685.

4. Եւ կաթողիկոսն Հայոց Անաստաս՝ բազում եպիսկոպոսօք եւ քահանայիւք իջուցին զմարմինն ի խաչէն՝ եւ թաղեցին պատուով ի նշանաւոր տեղւոջ, եւ տօն մեծ կարգեցին ամ ամէ: Եւ զխաչն տարան ի գեղաքաղաքն Զագ եւ կանգնեցին յեկեղեցւոջն, որ եւ բազում նշանս եւ սքանչելիս կատարէ զօրութեամբն Քրիստոսի, որք հաւատով ապաւինին ի բարեխօսութիւն սրբոյն Դաւթի:

Յայսմ աւուր վկայութիւն սրբոյն Յակոբայ քահանայի, եւ Ազա սարկաւագի եւ Դոմնայ եւ Մակեդոնի ընթերցողի

5. Այս Քրիստոսի վկայքս էին ի Պարսից. Յակոբ քահանայ եւ Ազա սարկաւագն կացին առաջի մոգպետին Արքասքարայ, եւ խոստովանեցան զՔրիստոս Աստուած՝ արարիչ արեգականն եւ լուսնի եւ աստեղաց եւ հրոյ եւ ջրոյ: Եւ արկին յոռնգունս նոցա մանանեխ քացախով տրորեալ, եւ կախեալ՝ յոյժ գանեցին զնոսա դալար բրովք: Եւ յաւուր ձմերայնի ի գիշերի՝ ընկեցին զնոսա ի ցուրտ սառնամանիս մերկ երկաթի շղթայիւք կապեալ, եւ բռնադատէին եւ նեղէին զնոսա ուրանալ զՔրիստոս եւ երկիր պագանել արեգական եւ լուսնի եւ աստեղաց եւ հրոյ եւ ջրոյ զոր պաշտէին Պարսիկքն: Եւ յորժամ ոչ հաւանեցան՝ արկին զնոսա ի բանդ:
6. Եւ քոյրն քահանային Յակոբայ ետես երազ եւ պատմեաց նոցա: Ասէ Յակոբ ցսարկաւագն իւր. Փութով կատարեմք զընթացս մեր առ Քրիստոս: Եւ ի վաղւին յերրորդ ժամու աւուրն հատին զգլուխս նոցա Մարտի ԼԱ: Եւ երթեալ դահճին լուաց զսուրն իւր, եւ յորժամ եհաս արիւնն ի ջուրն, առժամայն լիճն յարիւն դարձաւ՝ որ ոչ մարդ եւ ոչ անասուն կարէին ըմպել, եւ յետ երեսուն աւուր ցամաքեցաւ ամենայն լիճն:
7. Եւ ի տեղւոջն ուր կատարեցան սուրբքն՝ զերիս գիշերս հրեղէն սիւն երեւէր ի վերայ նշխարացն, եւ երթեալ քրիստոնէիցն թաղեցին զնոսա:
8. Եւ էր սուրբ քահանայն Յակոբոս ի գեղջէն Բիթնիրի, եւ Ազա սարկաւագն՝ ի գեղջէն Փառգաթայ:

4. Anastas, the Armenian catholicos,[2] along with many bishops and priests, took his body down from the cross and buried him with honor in a distinguished place. And they regulated that a great feast be celebrated every year. And they transported the cross to the small town of Tzage and erected it in the church. Here it worked many signs and miracles by the power of Christ on those who entrust themselves to the intercession of Saint David.

On this day is the martyrdom of the holy priest Hakob and the deacon Aza

5. These martyrs for Christ were from Persia. The priest Hakob and the deacon Aza stood in the presence of the chief magi Arkaskar and professed Christ as God, creator of the sun, the moon, the stars, fire, and water. The [Persians] then forced into their nostrils mustard dissolved in vinegar, hung them up and then struck them violently with fresh green branches. Then on a wintry night they threw them out naked onto the frozen ice and bound them in iron chains. They then pressed and coerced them to renounce Christ and to worship the sun, the moon, the stars, fire, and water that the Persians worship. When they refused, they threw them into prison.

6. The sister of the priest Hakob had a dream and recounted it to them. Hakob said to his deacon, "We are soon going to end our race for Christ." And at the third hour on the following day they cut off their heads on the thirty-first of March. The executioner went and washed off his sword, but when the blood got into the water the lake immediately turned into blood so that no person or animal could drink it. Thirty days later the entire lake dried up.

7. At the place where these holy ones were killed, a pillar of fire appeared over their remains for three nights. Christians then came and buried the[ir bodies].

8. The holy priest Hakob was from the village of Bithnir and the deacon Aza was from the village of Phargath.

2. Anastas of Akori was catholicos from 661 to 667.

Յայսմ աւուր վկայութիւն սրբոյն Ղուկիոսի

9. *Քրիստոսի վկայն Ղուկիոս էր ի Լիբիացւոց Կիւրենայ, նախարար եւ աթոռակից իշխանաց եւ դատաւորին, եւ էր կռապաշտ, եւ թզաւ մի երկայն քան զայլ մարդիկն եւ հաստ անձն։*

10. *Եւ յետ մարտիրոսանալոյն սրբոյն Թէոդորոսի Կիւրենոյ եպիսկոպոսին՝ հաւատաց ի Քրիստոս եւ մկրտեցաւ. հաւանեցոյց եւ զՏիգնիանոս դատաւորն եւ արար քրիստոնեայ եւ մկրտեաց։*

11. *Եւ նաւեցին ի միասին ի Կիւրենոյ ի Կիպրոս, եւ գտին անօրէն դատաւոր մի զի կոտորէր զքրիստոնեայս վասն ոչ ուրանալոյ զՔրիստոս եւ պաշտելոյ զկուռսն։ Գնաց Ղուկիոս գաղտ ի Տիգնիանոսէ ի տաճար կռոցն՝ եւ զարկ ոտիւքն զբագինսն եւ կործանեաց եւ խորտակեաց, եւ մտեալ ի ժողովուրդն աղաղակէր. Քրիստոնեայ եմ եւ Քրիստոս ճշմարիտ Աստուած է։ Եւ ի տեղւոջն յայնմիկ հատին զգլուխ նորա ի նմին ժամու։*

12. *Եւ գիտացեալ Տիգնիանոս՝ գնաց առ զմարմին սրբոյ վկային, եւ օծեալ անուշահոտ խնկօք պատեաց մաքուր կտաւովք եւ եդ պատուով ի տապանի։ Եւ յետ տարւոյ միոյ բացին զտապանն եւ գտին ի վերայ կրծիցն ծաղիկ վարդի, եւ յորժամ կամէին հաւատով առնուլ ի վարդէն՝ աներեւոյթ լինէին։ Եւ յաւուրս քրիստոնէութեան շինեցին վկայարան ի վերայ։ Կատարեցաւ սուրբն Ղուկիոս Մարտի ԼԱ։*

On this day is the martyrdom of the holy Loukios

9. Loukios, the martyr for Christ, was from Cyrene in Libya. He was a prefect and of equal dignity with the princes and the judge. He was also an idol worshipper. He was a palm taller than all other men and robust in stature.

10. After the martyrdom of Theodore, the bishop of Cyrene, he came to believe in Christ and was baptized. He also persuaded the judge Tignianos to accept the faith, made him a Christian, and baptized him.

11. They sailed together from Cyrene to Cyprus, where they found an unjust judge who was slaughtering Christians because they would not renounce Christ for the worship of idols. Loukios then went, without Tignianos's knowledge, to the temple of the idols. By stomping his feet, he overturned and smashed the altar. Then he went among the people and cried out, "I am a Christian, and Christ is the true God!" At that very moment they cut off his head in that place.

12. When Tignianos learned of this, he went and took the body of the holy martyr, anointed it with fragrant incenses, covered it with clean linens, and placed it with honor in a tomb. A year later, they opened the tomb, and they found upon his breast a bouquet of roses, but when they wished in good faith to take up the roses, they disappeared. In the days of Christianity they built a martyrium above [the tomb]. Saint Loukios is celebrated on the thirty-first of March.

Bibliography

Editions and Translations

Bayan, Gevorg, ed. *Le Synaxaire arménien de Tēr Israel*. Patrologia Orientalis 21:1 (101), pp. 107-40; 21:2 (102), pp. 145-229. Paris: Firmin-Didot, 1927, 1928.

The Great Synaxaristes of the Orthodox Church: March. Buena Vista, CO: Holy Apostles Convent Publications, 2005.

Mathews, Edward G., Jr., trans. and ed. *On This Day (Yaysmawurkʿ): The Armenian Church Synaxarion—January*. Eastern Christian Text Series 3. Provo, UT: Brigham Young University Press, 2014.

———. *On This Day (Yaysmawurkʿ): The Armenian Church Synaxarion—February*. Eastern Christian Text Series 4. Provo, UT: Brigham Young University Press, 2015.

Petrosyan, Yeznik, ed. *Yamabarbaṛ Yaysmawurkʿ G: Mart (naxatserentsʿyan 6 xmbagrutʿyunneri)/Synopsis Synaxarion III: March (6 pre Tserentsʿ versions)*. Etchmiadzin, Armenia: Holy See of St. Etchmiadzin, 2010.

Important Secondary Works

Artsruni, Tʿovma. *Thomas Artsruni, History of the House of the Artsrunikʿ*. Translated by Robert W. Thomson. Byzantine Texts in Translation. Detroit: Wayne State University Press, 1985.

Bedrosian, Garo. *Feasts of the Armenian Church and National Traditions*. Translated from Armenian by Arra S. Avakian. Los Angeles: Western Prelacy Press, 1990.

Benedict of Nursia. *Rule of Benedict*. Translated by Carolinne White. New York: Penguin Classics, 2008.

Cameron, Averil. "The History of the Image of Edessa: The Telling of a Story." In OKEANOS. Essays presented to Ihor Sevcenko = *Harvard Ukrainian Studies* 7 (1983), 80-94.

Cyril of Jerusalem. *Catechetical Lectures*. In *Cyril of Jerusalem and Nemesius of Emesa*. Translated by William Tefler. Library of Christian Classics, 4. London, 1955. Pp. 64-192.

Dasxurantsʿi, Movsēs. *The History of the Caucasian Albanians by Movsēs Dasxuranci.* Translated by C. J. C. Dowsett. London Oriental Series, volume 8. London: Oxford University Press, 1961.

Eghishē. *Elishe, History of Vardan and the Armenian War.* Translated by Robert W. Thomson. Harvard Armenian Texts and Studies, 5. Cambridge, MA: Harvard University Press, 1982.

Gregory the Great. *Saint Gregory the Great, Dialogues.* Translated by Otto Zimmermann. The Fathers of the Church, 39. Washington: Catholic University Press, 1959.

Issaverdens, Jacques. *The Uncanonical Writings of the Old Testament.* Venice: St. Ghazar Press, 1901.

Maksoudian, Krikor, Arten Ashjian, and George Terian, trans. *The Light of the World: Lives of Armenian Saints.* New York: Saint Vartan Press, 2000.

Mark the Monk. *Mark the Monk: Counsels on the Spiritual Life.* Volumes One and Two. Translated by Tim Vivian and Augustine Casiday. Popular Patristic Series, 37. Crestwood, NY: St. Vladimir's Seminary Press, 2009.

Pʿarpetsʿi, Ghazar. *The History of Lazar Pʿarpecʿi.* Translated by Robert W. Thomson. Occasional Papers and Proceedings, 4. Atlanta: Scholars Press, 1991.

Porphyry of Gaza. *The Life of Porphyry, Bishop of Gaza, by Mark the Deacon.* Translated by G. F. Hill. Oxford: Clarendon, 1913.

Symeon bar Sabba'e. *The Martyrdom and History of Blessed Simeon bar Sabba'e.* Translated by Kyle Smith. Persian Martyr Acts in Syriac: Text and Translation, 3. Piscataway, NJ: Gorgias Press, 2014.

Thomson, Robert W. *A Bibliography of Classical Armenian Literature to 1500 AD.* Corpus Christianorum. Turnhout: Brepols, 2005.

Index of Scripture Citations

Index of Names

About the Translator

Edward G. Mathews Jr. (PhD Columbia University) taught at The Catholic University of America, Our Lady of Lebanon Maronite Seminary, University of Scranton, Hebrew University in Jerusalem, the Armenian Evangelical Seminary in Yerevan, and St. Nersess Armenian Seminary. In addition to his translation of the Armenian Church *Synaxarion* for BYU Press, Dr. Mathews is currently translating *Jacob of Sarug's Homilies on the Hexaemeron* for Gorgias Press. Other recent books include *The Armenian Commentaries on Exodus-Deuteronomy attributed to Ephrem the Syrian* (Peeters), *The Armenian Prayers attributed to Ephrem the Syrian* (Gorgias), and *Jacob of Sarug's Homily on the Creation of Adam and the Resurrection of the Dead* (Gorgias).

About the Series

To understand Eastern Christianity one must study its literature, a rich and varied resource that is vital to many fields of religious and academic inquiry. Yet scholars and students are often deterred from its study by the lack of accessible and reliable texts and the remoteness of the source languages. EASTERN CHRISTIAN TEXTS provides specialists and nonspecialists with reliable English-language translations of seminal works paired with original-language texts. Each volume is produced to meet the highest academic and editorial standards and is elegantly designed to reflect the dignity of the tradition it represents.

EASTERN CHRISTIAN TEXTS is published by Brigham Young University Press and distributed by the University of Chicago Press.

http://meti.maxwellinstitute.byu.edu